THE
VEST
POCKET
Guide to GAAP

THE
VEST
POCKET
Guide to GAAP

 Steven M. Bragg

WILEY

John Wiley & Sons, Inc.

Published by John Wiley & Sons, Inc., Hoboken, New Jersey.

Published simultaneously in Canada.

For general information on our other products and services or for technical support, please contact our Customer Care Department within the United States at (800) 762-2974, outside the United States at (317) 572-3993, or fax (317) 572-4002.

Wiley also publishes its books in a variety of electronic formats. Some content that appears in print may not be available in electronic books. For more information about Wiley products, visit our Web site at www.wiley.com.

Library of Congress Cataloging-in-Publication Data:

ISBN 978-0-470-76782-5; 978-0-470-94630-5 (ebk); 978-0-470-94631-2 (ebk); 978-0-470-94632-6 (ebk)

Printed in the United States of America.

10 9 8 7 6 5 4 3 2 1

CONTENTS

About the Author   vii

What This Book Will
Do for You   ix

PART I   **THE FINANCIAL STATEMENTS**   **1**

One   Financial Statements Presentation   3

Two   Operating Segments   27

Three   Earnings per Share   37

Four   Interim Financial Reporting   49

Five   Related Party Disclosures   59

Six   Subsequent Events   63

PART II   **ASSETS, LIABILITIES,
AND EQUITY**   **67**

Seven   Receivables   69

Eight   Investments–Debt and Equity
Securities   79

Nine   Investments–Equity Method
and Cost Method   91

Ten   Inventory   99

Eleven   Other Assets and Deferred Costs   111

Twelve   Property, Plant, and Equipment   119

Thirteen   Intangible Assets   133

Fourteen   Asset Retirement and
Environmental Obligations   151

Fifteen	Contingencies	163
Sixteen	Debt	167
Seventeen	Equity	183

PART III REVENUE AND EXPENSES 193

Eighteen	Revenue Recognition	195
Nineteen	Employee Benefits and Benefit Plans	217
Twenty	Stock Compensation	235
Twenty-One	Other Expenses	257
Twenty-Two	Research and Development Expenses	265
Twenty-Three	Income Taxes	269

PART IV SPECIAL TRANSACTIONS 289

Twenty-Four	Accounting Changes and Error Corrections	291
Twenty-Five	Business Combinations	299
Twenty-Six	Derivatives	315
Twenty-Seven	Fair Value	329
Twenty-Eight	Foreign Currency Matters	341
Twenty-Nine	Interest	353
Thirty	Leases	363
Thirty-One	Nonmonetary Transactions	385
Thirty-Two	Not-for-Profit Entities	393
Index		411

ABOUT THE AUTHOR

*S*teven Bragg, CPA, has been the chief financial officer or controller of four companies, as well as a consulting manager at Ernst & Young. He received a master's degree in finance from Bentley College, an MBA from Babson College, and a Bachelor's degree in Economics from the University of Maine. He has been the two-time President of the Colorado Mountain Club, and is an avid alpine skier, mountain biker, and certified master diver. Mr. Bragg resides in Centennial, Colorado. He has written the following books:

Accounting and Finance for Your Small Business
Accounting Best Practices
Accounting Control Best Practices
Accounting Policies and Procedures Manual
Advanced Accounting Systems
Billing and Collections Best Practices
Business Ratios and Formulas
Controller's Guide to Costing
Controller's Guide to Planning and Controlling Operations
Controller's Guide: Roles and Responsibilities for the New Controller
Controllership
Cost Accounting
Cost Reduction Analysis
Essentials of Payroll
Fast Close
Financial Analysis
GAAP Guide
GAAP Policies and Procedures Manual
GAAS Guide
Inventory Accounting
Inventory Best Practices
Investor Relations
Just-in-Time Accounting
Management Accounting Best Practices
Managing Explosive Corporate Growth
Mergers and Acquisitions
Outsourcing
Payroll Accounting
Payroll Best Practices
Revenue Recognition

Run the Rockies
Running a Public Company
Sales and Operations for Your Small Business
The Controller's Function
The New CFO Financial Leadership Manual
The Ultimate Accountants' Reference
Throughput Accounting
Treasury Management
Vest Pocket Controller
Vest Pocket GAAP
Vest Pocket IFRS Guide

WHAT THIS BOOK WILL DO FOR YOU

*T*his is a handy pocket problem-solver for the accountant, controller, and chief financial officer. It provides broad coverage of generally accepted accounting principles (GAAP), using a question-and-answer format that provides concise explanations and hundreds of supporting examples for all GAAP topics. The layout is designed for quick comprehension of such questions as:

- Can I offset information in the balance sheet?
- What are the direct and indirect method layouts for the statement of cash flows?
- What are the thresholds for segment reporting?
- How do I calculate diluted earnings per share?
- Do I retrospectively adjust interim financial statements?
- What related party information should I disclose?
- How do I account for subsequent events after the reporting period?
- How do I measure losses from uncollectible receivables?
- How do I account for held-to-maturity investments?
- How do I use the equity method of accounting?
- What costs can I include in inventory?
- How do I account for preproduction costs?
- What depreciation method should I use?
- How do I assign goodwill to reporting units?
- How do I account for an asset retirement obligation?
- When do I recognize a loss contingency?
- What is the effective interest method?
- How do I account for treasury stock?
- When can I recognize revenue?
- How do I account for pension plans?
- How do I account for a share-based payment?
- What is a claims-made insurance contract?
- What is a research and development arrangement?
- How do I recognize a tax loss carryback?
- How do I disclose a change in accounting principle?
- How do I account for a business combination?
- What is hedging, and how do I account for it?

○ When can I record assets and liabilities at their fair values?
○ How do I determine an entity's functional currency, and how do I report transactions in that currency?
○ When should I capitalize interest cost?
○ How do I account for a capital lease?
○ How do I account for a non-monetary exchange?

Vest Pocket GAAP is divided into sections, where each deals with four main categories of GAAP: the financial statements, assets and liabilities, revenue and expenses, and special transactions.

Part I, The Financial Statements (Chapters 1-6) addresses GAAP for the construction of financial statements. Part I is divided into separate chapters to address the basic form of the financial statements, how to consolidate them, and how to report on special situations. These special situations include the reporting of operating segments, earnings per share, and interim reporting, all of which are required for publicly-held entities. Other chapters address special disclosures, including related-party disclosures and the reporting of subsequent events.

Part II, Assets and Liabilities (Chapters 7-17) addresses GAAP for accounting issues related to assets, liabilities, and equity. There are separate chapters covering the accounting for receivables, investments, inventory, deferred costs, fixed assets, and intangible assets, as well as for asset retirement obligations, contingencies, debt, and equity.

Part III, Revenue and Expenses (Chapters 18-23) delves into a variety of revenue and expense topics. These include revenue recognition, employee benefits, stock compensation, research and development expenses, and income taxes.

Part IV, Broad Transactions (Chapters 24-32) addresses a broad range of accounting transactions. These include accounting changes, business combinations, derivatives, fair value accounting, foreign currency matters, and the appropriate handling of interest cost, as well as leases, non-monetary transactions, and not-for-profit entities.

Throughout, *Vest Pocket GAAP* has been structured to provide concise answers to the GAAP questions that an accountant is most likely to encounter during a typical business day. Keep it handy for easy reference and daily use.

Free On-Line Resources by Steve Bragg

Steve issues a free accounting best practices podcast. You can sign up for it at www.accountingtools.com, or access it through iTunes. The www.accountingtools.com Web site also contains hundreds of articles about a broad range of accounting topics.

PART I

THE FINANCIAL STATEMENTS

CHAPTER 1

FINANCIAL STATEMENTS PRESENTATION

 What Is Profit or Loss?

Profit or loss is the total of an entity's revenues and expenses, not including any components of other comprehensive income (see the next question). It is also known as *net income*.

Total comprehensive income is the combination of profit or loss and other comprehensive income.

 What Is Other Comprehensive Income?

Other comprehensive income contains all changes including financial items that are not permitted in profit or loss. Items that you should insert in other comprehensive income include:

- ○ Available-for-sale securities fair value changes that were previously written down as impaired
- ○ Available-for-sale securities unrealized gains and losses
- ○ Cash flow hedge derivative instrument gains and losses
- ○ Debt security unrealized gains and losses arising from a transfer from the available-for-sale category to the held-to-maturity category
- ○ Foreign currency gains and losses on intra-entity currency transactions where settlement is not planned or anticipated in the foreseeable future
- ○ Foreign currency transaction gains and losses that are hedges of an investment in a foreign entity
- ○ Foreign currency translation adjustments
- ○ Pension or post-retirement benefit plan gains or losses
- ○ Pension or post-retirement benefit plan prior service costs or credits

○ Pension or post-retirement benefit plan transition assets or obligations that are not recognized as a component of the net periodic benefit or cost

It is acceptable to either report components of other comprehensive income net of related tax effects, or before related tax effects with a single aggregate income tax expense or benefit shown that relates to all of the other comprehensive income items.

An example of a possible format for reporting other comprehensive income in the income statement is:

EXAMPLE 1.1

GUTTERING CANDLE COMPANY STATEMENT OF INCOME AND COMPREHENSIVE INCOME FOR THE YEAR ENDED DECEMBER 31, 20X1

Revenues		$1,000,000
Expenses		800,000
Net income		200,000
Other comprehensive income, net of tax:		
Foreign currency translation adjustments		10,000
Unrealized gains on securities:		
Unrealized holding gains arising during the period	$12,000	
Less: reclassification of gains included in net income	(3,000)	
		9,000
Defined benefit pension plans:		
Net loss arising during the period	(2,000)	
Prior service cost arising during the period	(4,000)	
Less: amortization of prior service cost included in net periodic pension cost	1,000	
		(5,000)
Other comprehensive income		14,000
Comprehensive income		$ 214,000

You should list the total of other comprehensive income for each reporting period to a component of equity that is displayed separately from retained earnings and additional paid-in capital in the balance sheet, and call it *accumulated other comprehensive income*. An example showing the placement of this line item within the equity section of an entity's balance sheet follows:

EXAMPLE 1.2	
Equity:	
Common stock	$1,000,000
Paid-in capital	10,000
Retained earnings	450,000
Accumulated other comprehensive income	25,000
Total equity	$1,485,000

If an item listed in other comprehensive income becomes a realized gain or loss, you then shift it out of other comprehensive income and into net income or loss. This can happen, for example, when you sell an investment security for which you already recorded an unrealized gain in other comprehensive income. At the point of sale, this is now a realized gain, which shifts into net income. You can display this reclassification adjustment either on the face of the financial statements, or in the accompanying notes.

Total comprehensive income is the combination of profit or loss and other comprehensive income.

What Information Is Included in a Complete Set of Financial Statements?

All of the following financial reports should be included in a complete set of financial statements for a reporting period:

Statement	Description
Balance sheet (Statement of financial position)	Contains all asset, liability, and equity items
Statement of comprehensive income	Contains all income and expense items
Statement of changes in equity	Reconciles changes in equity for the presented periods
Statement of cash flows	Displays all cash inflows and outflows from operating, financing, and investing activities
Notes	Summarizes accounting policies and explanatory information

You should clearly identify these financial statements and distinguish them from other information presented in the same report, so that users will be more likely to understand which documents within the report adhere to specific accounting standards.

You should include in the financial statements a prominent display of the name of the reporting entity (and note any change in it from the preceding reporting period), whether the statements are for a single entity or group of entities, the period covered by the statements, and the level of rounding used to present amounts. This information is usually most easily presented in column and page headers.

 ## What Line Items Do I Include in the Balance Sheet?

There is no specific requirement for the line items to be included in the balance sheet. The following line items, at a minimum, are normally included in the balance sheet:

Assets

- Cash and cash equivalents
- Trade and other receivables
- Investments
- Inventories
- Property, plant, and equipment
- Intangible assets
- Assets held for sale

Liabilities

- Trade and other payables
- Accrued expenses
- Current tax liabilities
- Other financial liabilities
- Liabilities held for sale

Equity

- Capital stock
- Additional paid-in capital
- Retained earnings

You should add headings and subtotals to this minimum set of information if it will improve a user's understanding of the financial statements. You should add other line items when their size, nature, or function makes separate presentation relevant to the user.

EXAMPLE 1.3

Holystone Dental Corporation presents its balance sheet in the following format:

HOLYSTONE DENTAL CORP. STATEMENT OF FINANCIAL POSITION

(000s)	as of 12/31/x2	as of 12/31/x1
ASSETS		
Current assets		
Cash and cash equivalents	$ 270,000	$ 215,000
Trade receivables	147,000	139,000
Inventories	139,000	128,000
Other current assets	15,000	27,000
	571,000	509,000
Non-current assets		
Property, plant, and equipment	551,000	529,000
Goodwill	82,000	82,000
Other intangible assets	143,000	143,000
	776,000	754,000
Total assets	$1,347,000	$1,263,000
LIABILITIES AND EQUITY		
Current liabilities		
Trade and other payables	$ 217,000	$ 198,000
Short-term borrowings	133,000	202,000
Current portion of long-term borrowings	5,000	5,000
Current tax payable	26,000	23,000
Accrued expenses	9,000	13,000
Total current liabilities	390,000	441,000
Non-current liabilities		
Long-term debt	85,000	65,000
Deferred taxes	19,000	17,000
Total non-current liabilities	104,000	82,000
Total liabilities	494,000	523,000
Shareholders' Equity		
Capital	$ 100,000	$ 100,000
Additional paid-in capital	15,000	15,000
Retained earnings	738,000	625,000
Total equity	853,000	740,000
Total liabilities and equity	$1,347,000	$1,263,000

When Do I Present Information as Current or Non-Current?

You should classify all of the following as current assets:

- *Cash.* Cash that is available for current operations, and any short-term, highly liquid investments that are readily convertible to known amounts of cash and which are so near their maturities that they present an insignificant risk of value changes. Do not include cash whose withdrawal is restricted, to be used for other than current operations, or segregated for the liquidation of long-term debts.
- *Inventory.* Includes merchandise, raw materials, goods in process, finished goods, operating supplies, and maintenance parts.
- *Accounts receivable.* Includes trade accounts, notes, and acceptances that are receivable. Also include receivables from officers, employees, affiliates, and others, if they are collectible within a year. Do not include any receivable that you do not expect to collect within 12 months.
- *Marketable securities.* Includes those securities representing the investment of cash available for current operations, including trading securities.
- *Prepaid expenses.* Includes prepayments for insurance, interest, rent, taxes, unused royalties, advertising services, and operating supplies.

You should classify an asset as current when an entity expects to sell or consume it during its normal operating cycle or within 12 months after the reporting period. If the operating cycle is longer than twelve months, then use the longer period to judge whether an asset can be classified as current. You should classify all other assets as non-current.

You should classify all of the following as current liabilities:

- *Payables.* All accounts payable incurred in the acquisition of materials and supplies that are used to produce goods or services.
- *Prepayments.* Amounts collected in advance of the delivery of goods or services by the entity to the customer. Do not include a long-term prepayment in this category.
- *Accruals.* Accrued expenses for items directly related to the operating cycle, such as the accruals for compensation, rentals, royalties, and various taxes.
- *Short-term debts.* Debts maturing within the next 12 months.

You should classify a liability as current when the entity expects to settle it during its normal operating cycle or within 12 months after the reporting period, or if it is scheduled for settlement within 12 months. You should classify all other liabilities as non-current.

Current liabilities include accruals for amounts that can only be determined approximately, such as bonuses, and where the payee to whom payment will be made cannot initially be designated, such as a warranty accrual.

Can I Offset Information in the Balance Sheet?

Offsetting involves reporting only the net amount of an asset and a liability in the balance sheet. Generally, it is improper to do so unless there is a *right of setoff*. A right of setoff is a debtor's legal right to discharge all or some portion of the debt owed by another party by applying the debt against an amount that the other party owes to the debtor. If a right of setoff exists, generally accepted accounting principles (GAAP) generally allows offsetting in the balance sheet only if there are just two parties involved.

There is a right of setoff when each party owes the other party a determinable amount, the reporting party has the right to set off the amount owed with the amount owed by the other party, the reporting party intends to set off the amounts, and the reporting party's setoff right is legally enforceable.

What Line Items Do I Include in the Income Statement?

You should present all items of income and expense for the reporting period in a statement of comprehensive income. Alternatively, you can split this information into an income statement and a statement of comprehensive income.

There are no specific requirements for which line items are included in the income statement, but the following line items are typically used, based on general practice:

- ○ Revenue
- ○ Tax expense
- ○ Post-tax profit or loss for discontinued operations and for the disposal of these operations
- ○ Profit or loss
- ○ Extraordinary gains or losses
- ○ Other comprehensive income, subdivided into each component thereof
- ○ Total comprehensive income

A key additional item is to present an analysis of the expenses in profit or loss, using a classification based on their nature or functional area, maximizing the relevance and reliability of presented information. If you elect to present expenses by their nature, the format looks similar to the following:

Revenue		XXX
Expenses:		
Change in finished goods inventories	XXX	
Raw materials used	XXX	
~~Employee benefits~~ expense	XXX	
Depreciation expense	XXX	
Telephone expense	XXX	
Other expenses	XXX	
Total expenses		XXX
Profit before tax		XXX

Alternatively, if you present expenses by their functional area, the format looks similar to the following:

Revenue	XXX
Cost of sales	XXX
Gross profit	XXX
Administrative expenses	XXX
Distribution expenses	XXX
Research and development expenses	XXX
Other expenses	XXX
Total expenses	XXX
Profit before tax	XXX

Of the two methods, presenting expenses by their nature is easier, since it requires no allocation of expenses between functional areas. Conversely, the functional area presentation may be more relevant to users of the information, who can more easily see where resources are being consumed.

You should add additional headings, subtotals, and line items to the items noted above if doing so will increase a user's understanding of the entity's financial performance.

EXAMPLE 1.4

Plasma Storage Devices presents its statement of financial position in two statements by their nature, resulting in the following format, beginning with the income statement:

PLASMA STORAGE DEVICES INCOME STATEMENT FOR THE YEARS ENDED DECEMBER 31

(000s)	20x2	20x1
Revenue	$ 900,000	$ 850,000
Other income	25,000	20,000
Changes in finished goods inventories	(270,000)	(255,000)
Raw materials used	(90,000)	(85,000)
Employee benefits expense	(180,000)	(170,000)
Depreciation and amortization expense	(135,000)	(125,000)
Impairment of property, plant, and equipment	0	(50,000)
Other expenses	(75,000)	(72,000)
Finance costs	(29,000)	(23,000)
Profit before tax	146,000	90,000
Income tax expense	(58,000)	(32,000)
Profit for the year from continuing operations	88,000	58,000
Loss for the year from discontinued operations	(42,000)	0
Profit for the Year	$ 46,000	$ 58,000
Earnings per share:		
Basic	$ 0.13	$ 0.16
Diluted	0.09	0.10

Plasma Storage Devices then continues with the following statement of comprehensive income:

PLASMA STORAGE DEVICES STATEMENT OF COMPREHENSIVE INCOME

(000s)	20x2	20x1
Profit for the year	$ 46,000	$ 58,000
Other comprehensive income:		
Exchange differences on translating foreign operations	5,000	9,000
Available-for-sale financial assets	10,000	(2,000)
Actuarial losses on defined benefit pension plan	(2,000)	(2,000)
Other comprehensive income, net of tax	13,000	5,000
TOTAL COMPREHENSIVE INCOME	59,000	63,000

How Do I Account for Extraordinary Items?

An extraordinary item is an event or transaction that is distinguished by both its unusual nature and the infrequency of its occurrence. Something is considered to be unusual if it represents a high degree of abnormality and is unrelated to an entity's typical activities. Something occurs infrequently if you do not reasonably expect it to recur in the foreseeable future.

Examples of extraordinary items are:

○ A tornado destroys crops in an area where tornado damage is rare.
○ An earthquake destroys a building.
○ A hurricane destroys a business in an area where there is no record of hurricane damage.

Items that are *not* considered to be extraordinary are:

○ Adjustments to accruals on long-term contracts
○ Asset disposal gains or losses
○ Effects of a strike
○ Foreign currency transaction gains or losses (including currency devaluations and revaluations)
○ Remaining excess of the fair value of acquired net assets over cost
○ Write-downs of accounts receivable, inventory, deferred research and development costs, and other intangible assets

The following are examples of events that are not extraordinary:

○ A farmer's grapes are destroyed by frost in an area where frost damage is relatively common.
○ A company is unable to complete a public equity registration.
○ A company incurs costs to defend itself from a hostile takeover.

If you classify an item as extraordinary, then classify it separately in the income statement if it is material in relation to the income before extraordinary items, or to the trend of annual earnings before extraordinary items. You should make this decision for individual items, and not in aggregate for multiple items.

Extraordinary items should be segregated from the results of ordinary operations and shown separately in the income statement, using the following format:

Income before extraordinary items	$XXX,XXX
Extraordinary items (less applicable taxes of $___) (Note XX)	X,XXX
Net income	$XXX,XXX

In the accompanying notes to the financial statements, disclose the nature of the extraordinary event and the principal items entering into its determination as an extraordinary item, as well as the related amount of income taxes. Also, if earnings per share disclosure are required, then separately disclose the earnings per share for extraordinary items.

What Line Items Do I Include in the Statement of Changes in Equity?

You should include the following line items in the statement of changes in equity:

- ○ Total comprehensive income (with separate presentation of the amounts attributable to the owners of the parent entity and to non-controlling interests)
- ○ Effects of retrospective applications or restatements on each component of equity (which are usually adjustments to the opening balance of retained earnings)
- ○ Reconciliation of changes during the period for each component of equity resulting from profit or loss, each item of other comprehensive income, and transactions with owners (including contributions by and distributions to them)
- ○ Dividends recognized, and the related amount per share (this item can alternatively be presented in the associated notes)

What Are the Main Components of the Statement of Cash Flows?

The statement of cash flows contains information about activities that generate and use cash. The primary activities are:

- ○ *Operating activities.* These are an entity's primary revenue-producing activities. Examples of operating activities are cash receipts from the sale of goods, as

Example 1.5

Musical Heritage Company presents its statement of changes in its equity as follows to reflect changes in its equity over a two-year period:

	Share Capital	Retained Earnings	Total	Non-Controlling Interests	Total Equity
Balance at Jan. 01, 20x1	$350,000	$50,000	$400,000	$40,000	$440,000
Accounting policy change	–	(3,000)	(3,000)	–	(3,000)
Restated balance	350,000	47,000	397,000	40,000	437,000
Changes in equity for 20x1					
Dividends	–	(25,000)	(25,000)	–	(25,000)
Total comprehensive income	–	42,000	42,000	4,000	46,000
Balance at Dec. 31, 20x1	350,000	64,000	414,000	44,000	458,000
Changes in equity for 20x2					
Dividends		(18,000)	(18,000)	–	(18,000)
Issue of share capital	125,000	–	125,000	–	125,000
Total comprehensive income	–	37,000	37,000	4,000	41,000
Balance at Dec. 31, 20x2	$475,000	$83,000	$558,000	$48,000	$606,000

14

well as from royalties and commissions, amounts received or paid to settle lawsuits, fines, payments to employees and suppliers, cash payments to lenders for interest, contributions to charity, and the settlement of asset retirement obligations.

○ *Investing activities.* These involve the acquisition and disposal of long-term assets. Examples of investing activities are cash receipts from the sale of property, the sale of debt or equity instruments of other entities, and repayment of loans made to other entities. Examples of cash payments that are investment activities include the acquisition of property, plant, and equipment, and purchases of the debt or equity of other entities.

○ *Financing activities.* This refers to those activities resulting in alterations to the amount of contributed equity and the entity's borrowings. Examples of financing activities include cash receipts from the sale of the entity's own equity instruments or from issuing debt, proceeds received from derivative instruments, as well as cash payments to buy back shares, pay dividends, and to pay off outstanding debt.

The statement of cash flows also incorporates the concept of *cash and cash equivalents.* A cash equivalent is a short-term, very liquid investment that is easily convertible into a known amount of cash, and which is so near its maturity that it presents an insignificant risk of changes in value because of changes in interest rates.

What Are the Direct and Indirect Method Layouts for the Statement of Cash Flows?

You can use the *direct method* or the *indirect method* to present the statement of cash flows. The direct method presents the specific cash flows associated with items that affect cash flow. Items typically affecting cash flow include:

○ Cash collected from customers
○ Interest and dividends received
○ Cash paid to employees
○ Cash paid to suppliers
○ Interest paid
○ Income taxes paid

Under the indirect method, the presentation begins with net income or loss, with subsequent additions to or deductions from that amount for non-cash revenue and expense items, resulting in net cash provided by operating activities.

Examples of both methods are located in the answer to the next question.

What Line Items Should I Include in the Statement of Cash Flows?

The statement of cash flows reports cash activities during a reporting period, subdivided into operating, investing, and financing activities. The information you should include in these activities is as follows:

- *Operating activities.* Use either the direct method (disclosing major classes of gross cash receipts and payments) or the indirect method (adjusting profit or loss for changes in inventories, receivables, payables, and a variety of non-cash items).
- *Investing activities.* Separately report the major classes of gross cash receipts and payments caused by investing activities. You should separately report investing cash inflows and outflows; for example, a payment for property, plant, and equipment is reported separately from a receipt from the sale of property, plant, and equipment.
- *Financing activities.* Separately report the major classes of gross cash receipts and payments caused by financing activities.

Examples of the direct method and indirect method of presenting a statement of cash flow follow.

EXAMPLE 1.6

Ajax Machining Company constructs the following statement of cash flows using the direct method:

AJAX MACHINING COMPANY STATEMENT OF CASH FLOWS FOR THE YEAR ENDED 12/31/X1

Cash flows from operating activities	
Cash receipts from customers	$45,800,000
Cash paid to suppliers	(29,800,000)
Cash paid to employees	(11,200,000)
Cash generated from operations	4,800,000

Interest paid	(310,000)	
Income taxes paid	(1,700,000)	
Net cash from operating activities		$2,790,000
Cash flows from investing activities		
Purchase of property, plant, and equipment	(580,000)	
Proceeds from sale of equipment	110,000	
Net cash used in investing activities		(470,000)
Cash flows from financing activities		
Proceeds from issuance of common stock	1,000,000	
Proceeds from issuance of long-term debt	500,000	
Principal payments under capital lease obligation	(10,000)	
Dividends paid	(450,000)	
Net cash used in financing activities		1,040,000
Net increase in cash and cash equivalents		3,360,000
Cash and cash equivalents at beginning of period		1,640,000
Cash and cash equivalents at end of period		$5,000,000

Reconciliation of net income to net cash provided by operating activities:

Net income		**$2,665,000**
Adjustments to reconcile net income to net cash provided by operating activities:		
Depreciation and amortization	$125,000	
Provision for losses on accounts receivable	15,000	
Gain on sale of equipment	(155,000)	
Increase in interest and income taxes payable	32,000	
Increase in deferred taxes	90,000	
Increase in other liabilities	18,000	
Total adjustments		125,000
Net cash provided by operating activities		$2,790,000

EXAMPLE 1.7

Eagle Construction Company constructs the following statement of cash flows using the indirect method:

EAGLE CONSTRUCTION COMPANY STATEMENT OF CASH FLOWS FOR THE YEAR ENDED 12/31/X1

Cash flows from operating activities		
Net income		$3,000,000
Adjustments for:		
Depreciation and amortization	$125,000	
Provision for losses on accounts receivable	20,000	
Gain on sale of facility	(65,000)	
		80,000
Increase in trade receivables	(250,000)	
Decrease in inventories	325,000	
Decrease in trade payables	(50,000)	
		25,000
Cash generated from operations		3,105,000
Cash flows from investing activities		
Purchase of property, plant, and equipment	(500,000)	
Proceeds from sale of equipment	35,000	
Net cash used in investing activities		(465,000)
Cash flows from financing activities		
Proceeds from issue of common stock	150,000	
Proceeds from issuance of long-term debt	175,000	
Dividends paid	(45,000)	
Net cash used in financing activities		280,000
Net increase in cash and cash equivalents		2,920,000
Cash and cash equivalents at beginning of period		2,080,000
Cash and cash equivalents at end of period		$5,000,000

Cash paid during the year for:

Interest (net of amount capitalized)	$ 100,000
Income taxes	420,000

You should disclose the following items related to the statement of cash flows:

- ○ *Cash equivalents.* The policy for determining which items are treated as cash equivalents.
- ○ *Interest and taxes paid.* If you use the indirect method of reporting cash flows, then disclose the amounts of interest paid, net of any amounts capitalized, and income taxes paid during the period.
- ○ *Investing and financing activities.* The investing and financing activities affecting recognized assets or liabilities, but which do not result in cash receipts or payments during the period. Examples are the conversion of debt to equity, acquiring assets by assuming related liabilities, exchanging non-cash assets for other non-cash assets, and obtaining an asset by entering into a lease. This disclosure can be in the financial statements or in the accompanying notes.

When Should I Report Discontinued Operations?

You should separately report the results of the operations of a component of an entity if it has either been disposed of or is classified by the entity as held for sale. More specifically, a discontinued operation is one where the operations and cash flows of the operation either have been or will be eliminated from the ongoing operations of the entity, and the entity will not have any significant continuing involvement in its operations after the disposal is complete. An example of the presentation of a discontinued operation follows:

EXAMPLE 1.8		
Income from continuing operations before income taxes	$100,000	
Income taxes	(30,000)	
Income from continuing operations		$70,000
Discontinued operations		
Loss from operations of discontinued business component		(15,000)
Income tax benefit		5,000
Loss on discontinued operations		(10,000)
Net income		$60,000

If there is a recognized loss on the disposal of a discontinued operation, then disclose it either on the face of the income statement or in accompanying notes.

If you adjust an amount previously reported in discontinued operations, and that is directly related to the disposal of an entity component from a prior period, then classify it separately in the current period, within discontinued operations. Such a situation may arise when an entity resolves contingencies related to the terms of a disposal transaction.

You should also allocate to discontinued operations the interest on any debt to be assumed by the buyer, as well as any debt that is to be repaid as a result of the disposal transaction.

Do not allocate general corporate overhead to a discontinued operation.

 ## What Information Should I Disclose about Discontinued Operations?

If you have a component of an entity that is a discontinued operation (see the criteria for a discontinued operation in the answer to the last question), then present the assets and liabilities associated with the discontinued operation separately in the asset and liability sections of the statement of financial position. Do not offset and present them as a single line item. In addition, present the major classes of these assets and liabilities either on the face of the statement of financial position, or in the accompanying notes.

In addition to the above information, present the following items in the notes to the financial statements:

○ *Adjustments.* The nature and amount of adjustments made to amounts that were previously reported in discontinued operations.

○ *Cash flows.* If the segment generates continuing cash flows, then disclose the nature of the activities causing the cash flows, the time period over which cash flows are expected to continue, and the main factors used to decide that the expected cash flows are not direct cash flows of the disposal group.

○ *Facts and circumstances.* The facts and circumstances leading to the expected disposal, and the manner and timing of the disposal.

○ *Gain or loss.* The gain or loss recognized on the discontinuance.

○ *Segment.* The segment in which the disposal group is reported.
○ *Taxes.* The amounts of revenue and pretax profit or loss reported for the discontinued operation.

What Accounting Policies Should I Disclose with the Financial Statements?

You should disclose those accounting policies followed by the entity that materially affects the determination of its financial position, cash flows, or results of operations. The disclosure should include all situations where there are several alternative policies available, any unusual or innovative applications of GAAP, or methods peculiar to a specific industry in which the entity operates. Examples of policies typically disclosed are:

○ Amortization of intangibles
○ Basis of consolidation
○ Depreciation methods
○ Inventory pricing
○ Profit recognition on long-term construction contracts
○ Revenue recognition related to franchising and leasing operations

What Information About Risks and Uncertainties Should I Disclose in the Financial Statements?

You include the following information about risks and uncertainties in the notes accompanying the financial statements:

○ *Nature of operations.* Describe the entity's major products or services and the locations of the markets in which the entity conducts its sales. If the entity reports more than one business, then indicate the relative importance of its operations in terms of their assets, revenues, or earnings.
○ *Use of estimates.* Explain that management used some estimates to prepare financial statements in accordance with generally accepted accounting principles.
○ *Significant estimates.* Discuss those estimates and contingencies for which it is reasonably possible that the estimates will change in the near term, and the effect of the change will be material. If the estimate

involves a loss contingency, disclose an estimate of the possible loss or range of loss, or state that you cannot make this estimate. An example of an area in which estimates change frequently is when technological advances increase the rate of obsolescence of inventory and specialized equipment.

○ *Concentrations.* Disclose any vulnerability to which the entity is exposed, as a result of excessive concentrations of activity with certain business partners, products, supplies, or markets. This disclosure is necessary only if the concentration exists as of the date of the financial statements, the concentration risk can result in a severe impact to the entity, and it is at least reasonably possible that the severe impact could occur in the near term.

How Frequently Should I Issue Financial Statements?

An entity should issue a complete set of financial statements at least once a year. If it changes the end of its reporting period, so that the current year is less or longer than 12 months, you should disclose the reason for the altered period and state that the amounts included in the financial statements are not entirely comparable with those of previous years.

How Consistent Should the Financial Statement Presentation Be?

You should retain the presentation and classification of items shown in the financial statements across all presented periods. The exceptions are when GAAP requires a presentation alteration, or when a significant change in an entity's operations makes a different presentation more appropriate. If the latter is the reason, then you should only do so if the significant change is likely to continue into the future.

How Do I Aggregate Information in the Financial Statements?

You should separately present each material class of similar items. Conversely, do not aggregate items of a dissimilar nature, unless they are immaterial. If an item is not material enough to be separately presented in the financial statements, you may still consider separate presentation in the accompanying notes.

Is the Accrual Basis of Accounting Required?

Yes. Under the accrual method of accounting, record revenues and expenses when they are incurred, irrespective of when cash is exchanged.

Can I Offset Assets and Liabilities or Revenues and Expenses?

Not unless specifically authorized by GAAP, which is typically only for a very restricted application. In nearly all situations, you should separately report assets and liabilities, as well as revenues and expenses. If you engage in offsetting these accounts, it detracts from the ability of users to understand the underlying transactions and to assess the entity's future cash flows.

You are not offsetting when you measure assets' net of valuation allowances, which is a common and acceptable practice for accounts receivable and inventory.

What Are Consolidated Financial Statements?

Consolidated financial statements are the financial statements of a group of entities that are presented as being those of a single economic entity. A *group* is a parent entity and all of its subsidiaries. A *subsidiary* is an entity that is controlled by a parent entity. Consolidated financial statements are presumed to be more meaningful than separate financial statements.

When Must a Parent Include Another Entity in its Financial Statements?

Consolidated financial statements must include all of the subsidiaries of the parent entity. These subsidiaries are entities over which the parent entity has:

○ More than half of the outstanding voting shares of the entity (unless such ownership does not constitute control)
○ The power to control through a lesser percentage of ownership, such as through a contract, agreement with other stockholders, or court decree

A parent entity must include a subsidiary in its consolidated financial statements, even if the subsidiary's business activities are not similar to those of the other sub-sidiaries whose results are included in the consolidated financial statements.

What Is the Process for Consolidating Financial Statements?

The general process for consolidating the financial statements of a parent entity and its subsidiaries is to combine the statements line by line. More specifically, the following eight steps are to be applied:

1. Adjust the financial statements of any member of the group to conform to the accounting policies used by the parent for consolidating the financial statements.
2. Make adjustments for the effects of significant transactions or events occurring between the dates of the financial statements of the subsidiaries and the parent, if they differ.
3. Eliminate all intra-group balances, transactions, incomes, and expenses. This includes the elimination of profits and losses resulting from intra-group transactions.
4. Eliminate the carrying amount of the parent's investment in each subsidiary and the parent's portion of equity of each subsidiary.
5. Identify non-controlling interests in the profit or loss of consolidated subsidiaries.
6. Separately identify the non-controlling interests in the net assets of the consolidated subsidiaries. These non-controlling interests include the amount of non-controlling interests at the date of the original combination and the non-controlling interests' share of any changes in equity since the date of combination.
7. Present non-controlling interests in the consolidated statement of financial position within equity, separately from the equity of the parent entity's owners.
8. Attribute profit or loss and other comprehensive income to the parent entity and to non-controlling interests.

As of What Date Do I Include the Revenues and Expenses of an Acquired Subsidiary?

You should include the revenues and expenses of a newly-acquired subsidiary in the consolidated financial statements of the parent entity beginning on the acquisition date.

What if the Fiscal Year-End of a Parent Is Different from That of a Subsidiary?

If the subsidiary cannot prepare financial statements for consolidation purposes that correspond to those of the parent company, then it is acceptable to use the annual results of the subsidiary for a different fiscal year, as long as the difference is not more than three months. If there is such a difference, then you should disclose the effect of any intervening events that would materially affect the entity's financial position or results of operations.

What Happens to a Consolidation if You Lose Control of a Subsidiary?

If the parent entity loses control of a subsidiary, it should deconsolidate the subsidiary as of the date when the parent no longer has a controlling financial interest in the subsidiary.

What Information Should I Disclose about Consolidated Financial Statements?

The parent entity should disclose the following information in its consolidated financial statements:

- ○ *Consolidation policy.* The policy followed for consolidating financial statements.
- ○ *Less than wholly-owned subsidiary.* If the parent has a less than wholly-owned subsidiary, it should disclose the amounts of consolidated net income and consolidated comprehensive income and their attribution, as well as the amounts attributable to the parent for income from continuing operations, discontinued operations, and extraordinary items. Also, disclose a reconciliation of the equity changes attributable to the parent and the non-controlling interest.
- ○ *Loss of control.* The gain or loss recognized upon loss of control in a subsidiary, the portion of that amount attributable to recognizing investments retained in the subsidiary at its fair value, and the line item where the gain or loss is recognized in the income statement.

CHAPTER 2

OPERATING SEGMENTS

 What Is an Operating Segment?

An operating segment is a component of a publicly-held entity that engages in business activities from which it may earn revenue and incur expenses, has discrete financial information available, and whose results are regularly reviewed by the entity's chief operating decision maker for purposes of performance assessment and resource allocation. An operating segment generally has a segment manager who is accountable to the chief operating decision maker for the results of the segment.

An entity's corporate headquarters is not considered an operating segment, nor are an entity's post-employment benefit plans.

 What Type of Entity Must Report about Its Operating Segments?

An entity shall disclose information about its operating segments if its debt or equity trades in a public market, or it files its financial statements with the Securities and Exchange Commission, or it provides financial statements in order to issue any class of securities in a public market.

 When Can I Aggregate Operating Segments?

You can aggregate two or more operating segments into a single segment if the segments have similar products, services, production processes, customers, distribution methods, and regulatory environments.

What Are the Quantitative Thresholds for Segment Reporting?

You must disclose an operating segment if it meets any of these thresholds:

- ○ *Revenue.* Its external and inter-segment sales are at least 10% of the combined revenue of all segments.
- ○ *Profit.* Its absolute profit or loss is at least 10% of the greater of the combined profit of all segments not reporting a loss and the combined loss of all operating segments reporting a loss.
- ○ *Assets.* Its assets are at least 10% of the combined assets of all operating segments.

If the total external revenue reported by operating segments meeting these thresholds is less than 75% of the entity's revenue, then report on additional segments until you meet the 75% threshold, even if the extra segments are individually below the threshold criteria.

EXAMPLE 2.1

Mobile Shipping Corporation has six operating segments. The following table shows the operating results of the segments:

Segment Name	Revenue	Profit	Loss	Assets
A	$ 101,000	$ 5,000	$ –	$ 60,000
B	285,000	10,000	–	120,000
C	130,000	–	(35,000)	40,000
D	500,000	–	(80,000)	190,000
E	440,000	20,000	–	160,000
F	140,000	–	(5,000)	50,000
Totals	$1,596,000	$35,000	$(120,000)	$620,000

Because the total reported loss of $120,000 exceeds the total reported profit of $35,000, the $120,000 is used for the 10% profit test. The tests for these segments are itemized in the next table, where test thresholds are listed in the second row. For example, the total revenue of $1,596,000 shown in the preceding table is multiplied by 10% to arrive at the test threshold of $159,600 that is used in the second column. Segments B, D, and E all have revenue levels exceeding this threshold, so an "X" in the table indicates that their results must be separately reported. After conducting all three of the 10% tests, the table shows that segments B, C, D, and E must be reported, so their revenues are itemized in the last column. The last column shows that the total revenue of all reportable segments exceeds the $1,197,000 revenue level needed to pass the 75% test, so that no additional segments must be reported.

Segment Name	Revenue 10% Test	Profit 10% Test	Asset 10% Test	75% Revenue Test
Test Threshold	$159,600	$12,000	$62,000	$1,197,000
A				
B	X		X	$285,000
C		X		130,000
D	X	X	X	500,000
E	X	X	X	440,000
F				
			Total	$1,355,000

The decision tree in Exhibit 2.1 shows how to determine which segments must be separately reported, as well as which segments should be aggregated, and which ones can be summarized into the "all other" segments category.

If an operating segment that was reported separately in the immediately preceding period has now dropped below the threshold criteria, management can still separately report its results if it believes the information is significant.

If a segment meets the threshold criteria for the first time, then report its results for any prior periods presented in the financial statements, unless the needed information is not available and would be excessively expensive to develop.

It is allowable to aggregate the results of smaller segments to create a reportable segment, but only if they share similar economic characteristics and a majority of the previously-noted aggregation criteria.

Is There a Limit to the Number of Reportable Segments?

There is no precise limit to the number of reportable segments, but consider a reduction if the number exceeds ten segments.

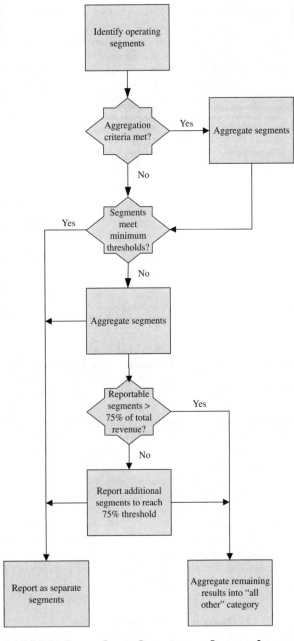

Exhibit 2-1 DECISION TREE FOR DETERMINATION OF REPORTABLE SEGMENTS

What Segment-Specific Information Do I Disclose?

In general, you disclose segment information that enables financial statement users to evaluate the entity's business activities and economic environment. In more detail, this requires the following disclosures:

○ *General information.* The factors used to identify reportable segments, and the types of products and services sold by each segment. Also note the basis of organization, which shows whether the organization is organized around products or services, geographic regions, regulatory environments, or some combination thereof.

EXAMPLE 2.2

Consolidated Green Products owns a number of subsidiaries that focus on reduced carbon emissions. It reports the results of its identifiable segments as follows:

(000s)	Electric Motors	Furnaces	LED Lighting	All Other	Totals
Revenues from external customers	$2,700	$4,500	$8,100	$900	$16,200
Inter-segment revenues		2,700	1,300		4,000
Interest revenue	400	650	230	50	1,330
Interest expense	100	120	90	10	320
Depreciation	180	80	40	20	320
Reportable segment profit	270	450	800	70	1,590
Reportable segment assets	1,800	3,200	3,700	800	9,500
Expenditures for reportable segment non-current assets	250	400	250	150	1,050
Reportable segment liabilities	900	1,600	2,000	400	4,900

- *Profit or loss information.* Revenues from external customers, inter-segment revenues, interest revenue, interest expense, depreciation and amortization, material expense items, equity method interests in other entities, income tax expense or income, extraordinary items, and other material non-cash items, as well as the resulting profit or loss.
- *Asset and liability information.* Equity method investments, and the amounts of additions to non-current assets (other than financial instruments, long-term customer relationships of a financial institution, mortgage and other servicing rights, deferred policy acquisition costs, and deferred tax assets).

These disclosures are only required if they are reported to the chief operating decision maker in order to make decisions about resource allocation and performance assessment.

What Additional Information Do I Disclose?

You must provide an explanation of the measurements used when deriving segment information, which includes:

- *Inter-segment accounting.* The basis of accounting for any inter-segment transactions.
- *Measurement differences.* The reasons for any differences between segment-level profits and losses, as well as assets and liabilities and the same information in aggregate for the entire entity.
- *Inter-period differences.* The reasons for any differences between the measurement of profits and losses, assets and liabilities, and the same information in prior periods.
- *Asymmetrical allocations.* The reasons for using different allocations to different segments, such as the allocation of depreciation expense to one segment, but not to another.

What Reconciling Information Do I Disclose?

You should disclose reconciling information alongside the segment reporting that includes the following:

- *Comparisons.* The total of the revenues, profit and loss, and assets for the reported segments, in comparison to the entity's totals for the same items.

○ *Other material items.* The total of any other significant amounts for the reported segments in comparison to the entity's totals for the same items. Separately identify and describe each material item.

When Do I Restate Segment Information?

If the entity changes its organizational structure sufficiently that it changes the composition of its reportable segments, then restate the corresponding information for earlier periods. This is not necessary if the required information is not available for the earlier periods and the cost of developing it would be excessive. However, the ability to create information for earlier periods is made at the line-item level, so you may provide information for some line items and not for others. If you restate information for earlier periods, then disclose this fact.

If it is not possible to restate information for prior periods to reflect a change in organizational structure, then disclose the year in which the organizational change occurs. Also, provide segment information for both the old and new organizational structures for the current period, unless this information is not available and would be excessively expensive to develop.

What Information Do I Disclose about Products and Services?

If you do not provide product and service information at the segment-reporting level, then do so for the entire entity. Do so for each product and service, or grouping thereof, unless this information is not available and would be excessively expensive to develop (in which case, disclose this fact).

EXAMPLE 2.3

The Company operates in the consumer products industry, in which the Company designs, manufactures, markets, and distributes footwear, apparel, and accessories. For the year ended December 31, 2010, the company sold $168 million of footwear, $19 million of apparel, and $11 million of accessories.

What Information Do I Disclose about Geographical Areas?

If you do not provide geographical information at the segment-reporting level, then do so for the entire entity. This involves the disclosure of:

- ○ *Revenues.* External revenues for the entity's country of domicile and the total for all other countries. If the revenues for an individual country are material, then disclose them separately. Also note the basis for attributing revenues to individual countries.
- ○ *Assets.* Non-current assets located in the entity's country of domicile and the total for all other countries. If the assets in an individual country are material, then disclose them separately. This disclosure does not include financial instruments, long-term customer relationships of a financial institution, mortgage and other servicing rights, deferred policy acquisition costs, and deferred tax assets.

EXAMPLE 2.4

The Company operates a single business segment that includes the installation and servicing of oil rigs for independent oil exploration and production (E&P) companies. The following table summarizes the Company's revenues and assets in different countries:

	2011	2010
Revenues:		
Iraq	$ 67,000,000	$61,000,000
Nigeria	31,000,000	26,000,000
Other foreign countries	11,000,000	9,000,000
Total	$109,000,000	$96,000,000
Assets:		
Iraq	$ 29,000,000	$28,000,000
Nigeria	17,000,000	13,000,000
Other foreign countries	4,000,000	4,000,000
Total	$ 50,000,000	$45,000,000

Do not disclose this information if it is not available and would be excessively expensive to develop (in which case, disclose this fact).

The entity may also provide subtotals of geographic information about groups of countries, at its option.

What Information Do I Disclose about Major Customers?

If you do not provide major customer information at the segment-reporting level, then do so for the entire entity. If revenues from a single customer are 10% or more of total entity revenues, then disclose that fact, as well as the total revenues for each such customer, and the identity of the segments reporting the revenues.

It is not necessary to disclose the identity of these major customers, nor the amount of revenues that each segment reports from them.

A group of customer entities under common control should be considered a single customer. Similarly, a government and entities controlled by that government are considered a single customer.

Example 2.5

The Company derives a significant portion of its net revenues from a limited number of customers. For the fiscal years ended December 31, 2011 and 2010, revenues from one client totaled approximately $15.7 million and $17.8 million, which represented 12% and 15% of total net revenues, respectively. For the fiscal year ended December 31, 2009, revenues from two clients totaled approximately $13.6 million and $10.9 million, which represented 16% and 12% of total net revenues respectively.

CHAPTER 3

EARNINGS PER SHARE

 ### What Is Common Stock?

Common stock is a stock that is subordinate to all other types of stock of the issuing entity. *Potential common stock* is a security or contract that may entitle its holder to obtain common stock.

 ### What Is a Contingent Issuance?

A contingent issuance is a possible issuance of shares of common stock that will not occur unless certain conditions are satisfied. *Contingently issuable shares* are shares that are issuable pursuant to a contingent stock agreement.

 ### What Is Preferred Stock?

Preferred stock is a security that has preferential rights when compared to the same entity's common stock.

 ### What Are Options and Warrants?

Options and warrants give their holders the right to purchase an entity's common shares. A *put option* gives its holder the right to sell common shares at a stated price for a stated period of time.

 ### Who Must Report Earnings per Share Information?

An entity must file earnings per share information if its common stock or potential common stock (e.g., options, warrants, convertible securities, and contingent stock agreements) is traded in a public market, or if it has made a filing or is in the process of filing with a regulatory agency in preparation for the sale of its securities in a public market.

 ## What Is Dilution and Anti-Dilution?

Dilution is the reduction in earnings per share or increase in loss per share that results when one assumes that convertible instruments are converted, that options and warrants are exercised, or that common shares are issued if specified conditions are satisfied. *Anti-dilution* is the increase in earnings per share or decrease in loss per share that results when one assumes the conversion of convertible instruments, the exercise of options and warrants, or that common shares are issued if specified conditions are satisfied.

 ## What Is Basic Earnings per Share?

Basic earnings per share is the amount of earnings for a reporting period that are available to each share of common stock outstanding during that reporting period. An entity whose capital structure only includes common stock should present only its basic earnings per share for income from continuing operations and for net income. This information should appear on the face of the income statement.

 ## How Do I Calculate Basic Earnings per Share?

You calculate basic earnings per share as follows:

$$\frac{\text{Profit or loss attributable to common equity holders of the parent entity}}{\text{Weighted average number of common shares outstanding during the period}}$$

This calculation is further split into the profit or loss from continuing operations attributable to the parent entity, and total profit or loss attributable to the parent entity. You should adjust both of these items for the effects of preferred stock.

Also incorporate the following adjustment into the numerator of the calculation of basic earnings per share:

○ *Dividends.* For the calculation of basic earnings per share, deduct from the profit or loss in the numerator the after-tax amount of any dividends declared on non-cumulative preferred stock as well as the after-tax amount of any dividends for preferred stock, even if the dividends have not been declared; this does not include the amount of such dividends paid or declared during the current period that relates to previous periods.

Also incorporate the following adjustments into the denominator of the calculation of basic earnings per share:

○ *Contingent stock.* If stock is contingently issuable, treat it as outstanding as of the date when there is no circumstance under which those shares would not be issued.

○ *Issuance date.* Include shares in the denominator as of the date when cash is receivable for sold shares, when dividends are reinvested, when interest ceases to accrue on convertible debt instruments for which shares are issued, when a liability is settled in exchange for shares, when an acquisition is recognized in exchange for shares, and as services are rendered in exchange for shares. If there is a mandatorily convertible instrument, then include the related shares in the denominator as of the contract date.

○ *Weighted average shares.* In order to calculate the weighted average number of shares outstanding during the period, adjust the number of shares outstanding at the beginning of the period for the number of common shares repurchased or issued during the reporting period, adjusted by the number of days that the shares are outstanding as a proportion of the total days in the period.

EXAMPLE 3.1

Ram-Jet International earns a profit of $10 million after tax in Year 1. In addition, Ram-Jet owes $250,000 in dividends to the holders of its cumulative preferred stock. Ram-Jet calculates the numerator of its basic earnings per share as:

$$\$10,000,000 \text{ profit} - \$250,000 \text{ dividends} = \$9,750,000$$

(*continued*)

Ram-Jet had 8 million common shares outstanding at the beginning of Year 1. In addition, it sold 500,000 shares on April 1 and 800,000 shares on October 1. It also issued 1,000,000 shares on July 1 as part of a share true-up transaction to the shareholders of a former acquisition. Finally, it bought back 100,000 shares on December 1. Ram-Jet calculates the weighted average number of shares outstanding as follows:

Date	Shares	Weighting (months)	Weighted Average
January 1	8,000,000	12/12	8,000,000
April 1	500,000	9/12	375,000
July 1	1,000,000	6/12	500,000
October 1	800,000	3/12	200,000
December 1	(100,000)	1/12	8,333
			9,083,333

Ram-Jet's basic earnings per share is $9,750,000 adjusted profits ÷ 9,083,333 weighted average shares, or $1.07 per share.

What Is Diluted Earnings per Share?

Diluted earnings per share is the amount of earnings for a reporting period that are available to each share of common stock outstanding during that reporting period, and to each share that would have been outstanding, assuming that common shares had been issued for all dilutive potential common stock outstanding during the period. An entity having more than common stock in its capital structure must present both basic and diluted earnings per share information for income from continuing operations and for net income. This information should appear on the face of the income statement.

How Do I Calculate Diluted Earnings per Share?

The calculation of diluted earnings per share goes beyond the calculation of basic earnings per share to also include the effects of all dilutive potential common shares. As a result, you increase the number of shares outstanding by the weighted average number of additional common shares that would have been outstanding if all dilutive potential common stock had been converted to common stock. This dilutive change may also impact the profit or loss in the numerator of the earnings per share calculation. You calculate diluted earnings per share as follows:

$$\frac{\text{Profit or loss attributable to common equity holders of the parent entity} + \text{Convertible preferred dividends} + \text{After-tax interest on convertible debt}}{\text{Weighted average number of common shares outstanding during the period, plus all dilutive potential common stock}}$$

This calculation is further split into the profit or loss from continuing operations attributable to the parent entity, and total profit or loss attributable to the parent entity.

The following two adjustments are key changes to the numerator of the calculation of diluted earnings per share:

○ *Dividends.* Adjust for the after-tax effect of dividends or other dilutive potential common shares.
○ *Interest expense.* Reverse any interest expense related to dilutive potential common stock, since these shares are assumed to have been converted to common stock, which eliminates the interest expense.

Also incorporate the following adjustments into the denominator of the calculation of diluted earnings per share; these adjustments are *in addition to* those already noted for basic earnings per share:

○ *Anti-dilutive shares.* Do not include in the calculation of diluted earnings per share any contingent stock issuances that would have an anti-dilutive effect on earnings per share. This situation arises when an entity has a loss, since the inclusion of dilutive shares in the earnings per share equation would then reduce the amount of the loss per share.
○ *Contingent shares, general.* Treat contingently issuable common stock as outstanding as of the beginning of the period, and therefore included in the calculation of diluted earnings per share, as long as the conditions required to issue the shares have been satisfied.
○ *Contingent shares.* If a contingent share issuance depends on the future market price of common shares, then include the shares in the diluted earnings per share calculation, based on the current market price

at the end of the period, if the effect is dilutive. If there is also a substantive non-market contingency feature, then do not include the shares in the diluted earnings per share calculation until the non-market contingency has been met.

If a share issuance is contingent upon satisfying certain conditions, and those conditions were satisfied by the end of the period, then include them in the diluted earnings per share calculation as of the beginning of the period. If the conditions were not satisfied by the end of the period, then include in the diluted earnings per share calculation, as of the beginning of the period, the number of shares (if any) that would be issuable if the end of the reporting period were the end of the contingency period, and if the result were dilutive.

If a contingent share payment is based on a specific amount of earnings and those earnings were attained in the period, then include the contingent shares in the diluted earnings per share calculation, if the result is dilutive.

- *Contracts settled in cash or shares.* If a contract can be settled in either common stock or cash, assume that it will be settled in common stock if the effect is dilutive.
- *Convertible instruments.* Include the dilutive effect of convertible instruments in diluted earnings per share when they are dilutive. Convertible preferred stock is anti-dilutive when the dividend on converted shares exceeds basic earnings per share. Convertible debt is anti-dilutive when the interest expense on its converted shares exceeds basic earnings per share. See Example 3.2 for Paulson Printing.
- *Dilutive shares.* Add to the denominator the weighted average number of common stock that the entity would issue if all dilutive potential common stock were converted. In the absence of other information, these additional shares are assumed to have been issued at the beginning of the reporting period.
- *Exercise price.* When calculating the number of potential shares, do so based on the most advantageous conversion rate from the perspective of the security holder.
- *Forward purchase contracts.* If a contract requires the entity to repurchase its own shares, and the settlement price is higher than the average market price during the period, and the effect is dilutive, then include them in the diluted earnings per share

calculation. For this calculation, assume that enough stock is issued at the beginning of the period to raise the proceeds to settle the contract, that the proceeds are used to buy back the required number of shares, and that the difference between these two amounts is included in the diluted earnings per share calculation.

○ *Multiple conversion rates.* If there are multiple bases of conversion of dilutive potential common shares, then use the most advantageous conversion rate from the perspective of the holder.

○ *Options and warrants.* Assume that all dilutive options and warrants are exercised at their exercise price, then convert the proceeds into the number of shares that would have been purchased at the average market price during the period. The incremental shares resulting from these transactions is the difference between the number of shares assumed to be issued and the number of shares assumed to be purchased. See Example 3.3 for Sonoma Silversmiths.

If dilutive options or warrants are issued or canceled during a reporting period, include them in the diluted earnings per share calculation for that period.

There is only a dilutive effect when the average market price is greater than the exercise price of the options or warrants.

○ *Purchased options.* Only include purchased put options in the diluted earnings per share calculation if the exercise price is higher than the average market price during the period, and only include the effects of a purchased call option if the exercise price is lower than the market price. All other scenarios with such options are anti-dilutive, and so should not be included.

○ *Share-based compensation.* If employees are awarded non-vested shares or share options as part of share-based compensation plans, treat them as options for the purpose of calculating diluted earnings per share. Consider these awards to be outstanding as of the grant date, even if they cannot be exercised until a later vesting date.

You should determine the number of dilutive potential common shares independently for each period presented. Also, do not alter the earnings per share reported for previous periods to reflect changes in the price of common shares that might otherwise alter the number of options or warrants exercised.

EXAMPLE 3.2

Paulson Printing earns a net profit of $1 million, and it has 10 million common shares outstanding. In addition, there is a $2 million convertible loan that has a 6% interest rate. The loan potentially converts to 3,000,000 of Paulson's common shares. Paulson's incremental tax rate is 35%.

Paulson's basic earnings per share is $1 million ÷ 10 million shares, or $0.10/share. The following calculation shows the compilation of its diluted earnings per share:

Net profit	$ 1,000,000
+ Interest saved on $2,000,000 debt at 6%	120,000
− Reduced tax savings on foregone interest expense	(42,000)
Adjusted net earnings	$ 1,078,000
Common shares outstanding	10,000,000
+ Potential converted shares	3,000,000
Adjusted shares outstanding	13,000,000
Diluted earnings per share ($1,078,000 ÷ 13,000,000)	**$0.08/share**

EXAMPLE 3.3

Sonoma Silversmiths earns a net profit of $1 million, and it has 10 million common shares outstanding that had an average fair value of $20 during the past year. In addition, there are three million share options outstanding that are convertible to common shares at $12 each.

Sonoma's basic earnings per share is $1 million ÷ 10 million common shares, or $0.10/share.

To determine Sonoma's diluted earnings per share, first calculate the number of shares that would have been issued at the average market rate. To do so, multiply the three million share options by their exercise price of $12, resulting in a total payment for the options of $36 million. Then divide this amount by the $20 average market price to arrive at 1,800,000 shares that could have been purchased with the option proceeds. Then subtract the 1,800,000 shares from the three million options originally exercised. Then add the difference of 1,200,000 shares to the 10 million common shares already outstanding to arrive at 11.2 million diluted shares.

Sonoma's diluted earnings per share is $1 million ÷ 11.2 million common shares, or $0.09/share.

EXAMPLE 3.4

Vintner Corporation has a net loss from continuing operations of $300,000, with 100,000 common shares outstanding, and 20,000 potential common shares. Vintner's basic earnings per share from continuing operations is $3.00. If Vintner were to include the potential common shares in the calculation of diluted earnings per share from continuing operations, the loss per share would be reduced to $2.50. Since this amount is less than the reported loss per share *without* the potential common shares, the potential common shares are antidilutive, and should be excluded from the calculation.

When Should I Make Retrospective Adjustments to Earnings per Share?

You should retrospectively adjust the calculation of basic and diluted earnings per share for all periods presented, if the number of shares outstanding changes due to a capitalization, share split, or reverse share split. Also, disclose the fact that the share calculations reflect these changes.

How Do I Disclose Earnings per Share Information for Discontinued Items and Extraordinary Items?

If you report a discontinued operation or an extraordinary item in a period, then you should present both basic and diluted earnings per share for these line items. The information can appear either on the income statement or in the accompanying notes.

How Do I Disclose Earnings per Share for Less-than-Wholly-Owned Subsidiaries?

If you have a less-than-wholly-owned subsidiary included in a consolidated group, then calculate both basic and diluted earnings per share without the income attributable to the non-controlling interest in that subsidiary.

How Do I Present Earnings per Share?

You should present basic and diluted earnings per share information in the statement of comprehensive income for every class of common shares that has a different right to share in the period's profits, and for every period for which you present a statement of comprehensive income. If you present diluted earnings per share for at least one period, then you must report it for all periods presented.

EXAMPLE 3.5			

Pelican Lawn Products presents its earnings per share information using the following layout:

Combined earnings per year	20x9	20x8	20x7
	$	$	$
From continuing operations			
Basic earnings per share	2.09	1.89	1.75
Diluted earnings per share	2.04	1.84	1.70
From discontinued operations			
Basic earnings per share	0.53	0.29	0.10
Diluted earnings per share	0.49	0.25	0.08
From total operations			
Basic earnings per share	2.62	2.18	1.85
Diluted earnings per share	2.53	2.09	1.78

 What Earnings per Share Information Should I Disclose?

You should disclose the following information regarding an entity's earnings per share:

- ○ *Anti-dilutive items.* The terms and conditions of any instruments not included in the diluted earnings per share calculation that could potentially dilute earnings per share in the future.
- ○ *Dividends.* The effect given to preferred dividends in arriving at income available to common shareholders in the computation of basic earnings per share.
- ○ *Reconciliation.* Reconcile the numerators and denominators of the basic and diluted earnings per share calculations for income from continuing operations.

○ *Subsequent transactions.* Any subsequent share-related transactions occurring after the reporting period that would have materially changed the number of common or potential common shares outstanding at the end of the period if they had occurred within the period. Examples are shares issued for cash, options issued, convertible instruments converted to shares, and conditions arising that would result in the triggering of convertible instruments. Do not adjust earnings per share calculations for these items.

CHAPTER 4

INTERIM FINANCIAL REPORTING

 **What Is an Interim Period?**

An interim period is a financial reporting period that is shorter than a full fiscal year.

 **Who Must Issue Interim Financial Reports?**

Interim financial reports are generally quarterly financial reports that are required for any publicly traded companies.

What Is Included in an Interim Financial Report?

An interim financial report includes, for the reporting period in question, the following:

- ○ Balance sheet
- ○ Income statement
- ○ Statement of cash flows

These reports can be in a condensed format.

What Information Should I Include with the Interim Financial Report?

The following information should be included in the interim report, at a minimum:

- ○ *Changes in accounting principles or estimates.*
- ○ *Contingent items.* Keep reporting a contingency in successive periods until it has been removed, resolved, or has become immaterial (as judged in comparison to full-year results).
- ○ *Cost of goods sold estimates.* If the cost of goods sold is estimated in an interim period, then disclose the

estimation method used and any significant adjustments resulting from a reconciliation with the annual physical inventory count.

○ *Defined benefit pension plans.* See the Retirement Benefit Plans chapter for more information.

○ *Disposals.* The disposal of a component of an entity, if the amount is material to the net income of the interim period.

○ *Earnings per share.* Basic and diluted earnings per share for each period presented.

○ *Extraordinary or unusual items.* Extraordinary, unusual, or infrequent items if the amount is material to the net income of the interim period.

○ *Fair value.* The use of fair value to measure assets and liabilities recognized in the balance sheet.

○ *Income statement items.* Sales, provisions for income taxes, extraordinary items, net income, and comprehensive income.

○ *Income taxes.* Significant changes in provisions for income taxes.

○ *Policies.* Describe any changes in accounting policy in the current interim period from those in the comparable interim period of the prior annual period, the preceding interim periods in the current annual period, and the prior annual report.

○ *Seasonal items.* The seasonal nature of revenue and expenses (if any).

○ *Segment information.* See the Operating Segments chapter for more information.

○ *Significant changes in financial position.*

It is acceptable to omit footnote disclosures that would substantially duplicate the disclosures contained in the most recent annual report or audited financial statements. This exclusion only applies if the details of the disclosure have not changed significantly in amount or composition since the end of the most recently completed fiscal year.

For Which Periods Must I Present Interim Financial Statements?

You must include interim financial statements for the following periods:

○ Balance sheet for the current interim period and the immediately preceding fiscal year.

○ Income statement for the current interim period and for the fiscal year-to-date, as well as for the current and year-to-date periods of the immediately preceding fiscal year.

○ Statement of cash flows for the current fiscal year-to-date, with a comparative statement for the year-to-date period of the immediately preceding fiscal year.

 ## How Do I Assess Materiality in Interim Periods?

When determining materiality for the purpose of reporting the correction of an error, relate amounts to the estimated income for the full fiscal year and to the effect on the earnings trend. If a change is material to the interim period but not material to the estimated income for the full fiscal year or the earnings trend, then disclose the item separately in the interim period.

EXAMPLE 4.1

The Chemical Detection Consortium has revenues of $12,000,000 in its first quarter, and will eventually generate revenues of $50,000,000 for its entire fiscal year. Chemical's controller traditionally has considered materiality to be 2% of revenues. In the first quarter, Chemical's Arabian Knights Security subsidiary, which is designated as discontinued, earns a profit of $360,000. This is 3% of Chemical's revenues in that quarter, and so is material enough to be segregated for reporting purposes within the third quarter. However, it is less than 1% of Chemical's full-year results, so there is no need to segregate this information in Chemical's annual financial report.

 ## How Consistently Should I Apply Accounting Policies to Interim Periods?

You should apply the same accounting policies from the annual financial statements to the interim financial statements. The exception is when you change an accounting policy after the last annual report, and expect to apply the new policy to the next annual report; in this case, apply the new accounting policy to the interim financial statements.

The consistency of accounting policies between interim periods means that the recognition of accounting transactions are made based on the expected results for the entire year, not just for a single interim period. This is known as the *integral view*. For example, an entity should recognize its income tax expense in an interim period based on its best estimate of the weighted average income tax rate that it expects to incur for the entire year. Also, you should accrue an expense provision within an interim period if an event has created a legal or constructive obligation where the entity has no realistic alternative other

---

EXAMPLE 4.2

Tidal Energy Company creates electrical generators that are triggered by wave action. Tidal incurs the following costs as part of its quarterly reporting:

○ It pays $15,000 in trade shows fees in the first quarter for a green technology trade show that will occur in the fourth quarter.

○ It pays $32,000 in the first quarter for a block of advertisements that will run throughout the year in *Energy Alternatives* magazine.

○ The board of directors approves a profit-sharing plan in the first quarter that will pay employees 20% of net annual profits. At the time of plan approval, full-year profits are estimated to be $100,000. By the end of the third quarter, this estimate has dropped to $80,000, and to $70,000 by the end of the fourth quarter.

Tidal uses the following calculations to record these scenarios:

	Quarter 1	Quarter 2	Quarter 3	Quarter 4	Full Year
Trade show[1]				$15,000	$15,000
Advertising[2]	$8,000	$8,000	$8,000	8,000	32,000
Profit sharing[3]	5,000	5,000	3,000	1,000	14,000

[1] The trade show expense is deferred until the show occurs in the fourth quarter.

[2] The advertising is proportionally recognized in all quarters as it is used.

[3] A profit-sharing accrual begins in the first quarter, when the plan is approved. At that time, ¹/₄ of the estimated full-year profit-sharing expense is recognized. In the third quarter, the total estimated profit-sharing expense has declined to $16,000, of which $10,000 has already been recognized. When the profit-sharing expense estimate declines again in the fourth quarter to $14,000, only $1,000 remains to be recognized.

than to make a payment. If there is only an intention or necessity to incur expenses later in the fiscal year, this is not sufficient grounds to accrue an expense in the current interim period.

This heightened level of accrual usage will likely result in numerous accrual corrections in subsequent interim periods to adjust for any earlier estimation errors.

If an asset no longer has any future economic benefits as of the end of an interim period, then charge it to expense at that time; do not wait for the end of the fiscal year to do so. Similarly, a recorded liability must still represent an existing obligation at the end of an interim period.

EXAMPLE 4.3

Boston Bakeries writes down the value of its white flour inventory by $40,000 during the second quarter of its fiscal year, and reports the change in its interim financial report for that period. During the third quarter, the market price of white flour increases somewhat, so Boston can justifiably reverse a portion of the original write-down; accordingly, it records a reversal of $28,000 in the third quarter, and reports the change in its interim report for that period.

 ### Do I Retrospectively Adjust Interim Financial Statements?

Generally, no. The adjustment of prior period interim financial statements is limited to changes in accounting policy (see the next question), the settlement of litigation claims, income taxes, renegotiation proceedings, or utility revenue under rate-making proceedings. These adjustments are allowable only if the affect of the adjustment is material for income from continuing operations for the entire fiscal year or the income trend, some portion of the adjustment can be identified with specific prior interim periods, and the adjustment amount could not have been estimated prior to the current interim period.

 ### How Do I Account for an Accounting Change in an Interim Period?

You should immediately report the accounting results of changes in accounting policy that occurred in an interim period. If there is a change in accounting estimate, then also report the change in the interim period in which it occurred.

You should restate the interim results of prior periods for a change in accounting policy, but not for a change in accounting estimate.

Whenever possible, adopt accounting changes in the first interim period of each year, so that they can be consistently applied across the remaining interim periods of the fiscal year.

 ### Should I Change Revenue Recognition Methodologies for an Interim Period?

No. You should recognize revenue from product and service sales on the same basis used for the full year. For example, revenue recognition under percentage-of-completion accounting for long-term construction contracts remains the same in interim periods.

 ### Can I Anticipate or Defer Seasonal or Cyclical Revenues?

No. It is not acceptable to accrue for revenues expected to arise in a later interim period, nor is it allowable to defer the recognition of revenues that have already occurred. Instead, recognize revenues as they occur. However, you should disclose the seasonal nature of activities, and can consider adding to interim reports additional information for 12-month periods ending at the interim date for both the current and preceding years.

 ### How Do I Recognize Expenses in Interim Periods?

If a cost is directly associated with revenue, as is typically the case with products sold, then charge them to expense in the period in which you recognize the related revenue. If a cost is not directly associated with revenue, then charge it to expense in interim periods on an allocated basis, using such factors as the amount of time expired, benefits received, or other activities associated with the interim periods. Here is general guidance on most types of costs not directly associated with revenue:

- Immediately charge to expense any costs clearly traceable to an interim period, such as salaries and wages.

○ Accrue expenses in every interim period for expenditures expected to be paid at a later date, such as vacation expense and property taxes. This guidance also applies to reserves for inventory shrinkage, uncollectible accounts, quantity discounts, and discretionary year-end bonuses.

○ Amortize expenditures already made that will affect more than one interim period, such as insurance premiums paid in advance. This guidance only applies if the benefits from the expenditure clearly extend beyond the interim period in which the expenditure is made.

○ If quantity discounts allowed to customers are based on annual sales volume, then accrue these discounts in each interim period based on estimated annual sales.

How Do I Recognize Extraordinary or Unusual Items in Interim Periods?

If there is an unusual, extraordinary, or infrequently occurring event, or a disposal transaction in an interim period that is material to that period but not to the fiscal year as a whole, then report it separately in the interim financial statements. Do not prorate these items over the remaining balance of the fiscal year.

What if I Liquidate a Last In First Out Layer in an Interim Period?

If you liquidate a layer of LIFO (last in first out) inventory in an interim period and expect to replace that layer by the end of the annual reporting period, then the inventory as of the interim reporting date does not give effect to the LIFO liquidation; the cost of sales for the interim period includes the expected cost of replacement of the liquidated LIFO base. This practice avoids the recognition of a cost layer that may potentially vary dramatically from current cost levels.

How Do I Record Inventory Losses from Market Declines?

If there is an inventory loss caused by a market decline, do not defer its recognition past the current interim period. If market prices subsequently increase, it is acceptable to record a recovery on these losses in later interim periods of the same fiscal year. Any recorded recovery cannot exceed the amount of any previously recognized losses.

If there is a reasonable expectation that a market decline will reverse itself later in the fiscal year, then it is not necessary to recognize the initial inventory loss.

How Do I Record Standard Cost Variances in an Interim Period?

If an entity uses a standard costing system and recognizes such variances as purchase price, wage rate, usage, and efficiency variances from standard costs, then it should do so at the end of each interim period. However, if you expect that the entity will absorb a variance by the end of the fiscal year, then defer recognition during interim

---

EXAMPLE 4.4

Spiffy Soap Company only conducts a physical inventory count of its thousands of bath products at the end of its fiscal year. For its quarterly interim reports, Spiffy instead uses the 62% gross margin percentage that it recorded in the preceding fiscal year. In the current year's third quarter, Spiffy's controller believes that a fraud situation has resulted in an exceptional amount of inventory loss, and mandates an extra physical inventory count. The result is a year-to-date actual gross margin of only 51%. Spiffy then conducts its normal physical count at the end of the fiscal year, resulting in an actual full-year gross margin of 56%. As shown in the following table, Spiffy recognizes the entire amount of the additional expense in the third quarter that was detected as a result of the extra physical count in that quarter.

	Quarter 1	Quarter 2	Quarter 3	Quarter 4	Full Year
Revenues	$18,000,000	$21,000,000	$23,000,000	$32,000,000	$94,000,000
Standard gross margin %	62%	62%			
Year-to-date actual gross margin			51%	56%	56%
Cost of goods sold	6,840,000	7,980,000	15,560,000	10,980,000	41,360,000
Gross margin	$11,160,000	$13,020,000	$7,440,000*	$21,020,000	$52,640,000

*($62,000,000 year-to-date revenues × 51% gross margin = $31,620,000) − $11,160,000 Quarter 1 gross margin − $13,020,000 Quarter 2 gross margin

periods. If there is an unexpected purchase price or volume variance, then report it immediately in the current interim period.

Is it Acceptable to Use More Estimates When Preparing Interim Financial Statements?

Yes. Some amount of estimation is required for both annual and interim financial reports, but you will likely need to rely on estimates to a greater degree when preparing interim financial information.

It is acceptable to estimate the cost of goods sold during an interim period, such as by using estimated gross profit rates, if there are no physical inventory counts during the interim period.

CHAPTER 5

RELATED PARTY DISCLOSURES

 What Is a Related Party?

A party is related to an entity if any of the following situations apply to it:

- ○ *Affiliate.* A party that controls, is controlled by, or is under common control with an entity.
- ○ *Equity method.* An entity for which an investing entity should record its investment using the equity method.
- ○ *Trusts.* A trust for the benefit of employees, such as a pension plan, which is administered by management.
- ○ *Owners.* The principal owners of an entity, as well as the members of their immediate families.
- ○ *Management.* Members of management and their immediate families.
- ○ *Significant influence.* Any party that can significantly influence an entity's management or operating policies to such an extent that the entity might be prevented from fully pursuing its own interests.

The determination of related party status depends on the substance of the relationship, not just its legal form.

 Who Is "Immediate Family"?

Immediate family are those family members who might control or influence a principal owner or manager, because of a family relationship.

 Who Is "Management"?

Management includes anyone who is responsible for achieving an entity's objectives, and who is authorized to establish policies and make decisions in order to pursue objectives. Management typically includes the board of directors, chief executive officer, chief operating officer, vice presidents in charge of primary functional areas, and those performing similar policy-making functions.

 ## Who Is a "Principal Owner"?

A principal owner is any owner of more than 10% of an entity's voting interests.

 ## What Is a Related Party Transaction?

A related party transaction is a transfer of obligations, resources, or services between related parties. Examples of general types of related party transactions are between:

○ Subsidiaries of a common parent
○ A parent entity and its subsidiaries
○ An employee pension plan administered by an entity's management
○ An entity and its management, members of management's families, or principal owners

Examples of possible related party transactions, depending upon the substance of the relationship, are:

○ Financing arrangements
○ Leases
○ Provision of guarantees or collateral
○ Purchase or sale of goods, assets (or property), or services
○ Risk-sharing in a defined benefit plan
○ Settlement of liabilities on behalf of another entity
○ Transfers of research and development, or under license agreements

---

EXAMPLE 5.1

Ajax Machining Company leases storage trailers from an entity owned by the chief executive officer's son. In addition, it is the beneficiary of a low-interest loan from one of its directors. Finally, it obtains half of its primary raw materials from the Strasbourg Steel Foundry; there is no ownership arrangement between Ajax and Strasbourg.

Ajax must disclose a related party relationship for the storage trailer lease, since it involves a family member. It must also disclose the low-interest loan, since it involves a member of key management. However, it does not have to disclose the supplier relationship, since there is no indication of a related party relationship.

What Related Party Information Should I Disclose?

Generally, you should disclose information about transactions with related parties that would make a difference in decision making. More specifically, disclose the following information about related parties in the notes accompanying an entity's financial statements:

○ The nature of the relationships
○ A description of the transactions
○ The dollar amounts of such transactions
○ Amounts due to or from related parties, and the terms and manner of settlement
○ Notes or accounts receivable from officers, employees, or affiliated entities
○ The nature of any control relationship where the reporting entity and other entities are under common control, and that control could yield operating results or a financial position that is significantly different from the situation if the entity were operating autonomously.

You may need to disclose the name of the related party, if it is necessary to an understanding of the relationship.

You should disclose transactions between related parties, even when the transactions are without charge and not recorded (such as for services provided between subsidiaries).

CHAPTER 6

SUBSEQUENT EVENTS

What Is a Subsequent Event?

A subsequent event is an event or transaction occurring after the balance sheet date, but before the financial statements are either issued or available to be issued. Subsequent events fall into two categories:

1. Events or transactions that provide additional evidence about conditions that existed as of the balance sheet date. In particular, they may lead to improved estimates that were incorporated into the financial statements.
2. Events that provide evidence about conditions that did *not* exist as of the balance sheet date; instead, they arose subsequent to that date.

When Are Financial Statements Available to be Issued?

Financial statements are available to be issued when they are complete in a form and format that complies with GAAP (generally accepted accounting principles). Also, you must have obtained issuance approval from all required parties, such as management and the board of directors.

How Do I Recognize Subsequent Events That Existed at the Balance Sheet Date?

If a subsequent event provides additional evidence about conditions that existed as of the balance sheet date, you should recognize those changes in the financial statements. You should make this evaluation through the date on which the financial statements are issued.

EXAMPLE 6.1

The Industrial Donut Company reaches a settlement with a government entity, regarding charges that it provided stale donuts for soldier's combat meals. The settlement confirms that Industrial had an obligation at the end of its reporting period of $250,000. Industrial had previously recognized a provision of $50,000, so it now increases the provision by $200,000.

Industrial Donut receives a report from an independent appraiser, stating that the carrying amount of its donut shrink-wrapping machine was impaired by $25,000 at the end of the reporting period. Accordingly, Industrial writes down the asset value within the reporting period.

Industrial Donut discovers that a major retail chain customer filed for bankruptcy two weeks after the end of the reporting period, which follows a long decline in the retailer's financial condition. Industrial has no reserve for bad debts, and so must write down the entire amount of the related $50,000 account receivable in the preceding reporting period.

Industrial Donut's internal audit staff discovers that the company's warehouse manager has been giving large quantities of donuts to the local police department in exchange for free security, and covered up the inventory shortfall at the end of the reporting period. The amount of the fraud is $10,000, which Industrial records within the reporting period.

In all of the above cases, Industrial Donut should only adjust the financial statements of the reporting period if the events occur prior to the financial statements being available for issuance or having been issued.

How Do I Recognize Subsequent Events That Did Not Exist at the Balance Sheet Date?

If a subsequent event provides additional evidence about conditions that did not exist as of the balance sheet date, but before the financial statements are issued, you should not recognize them in the financial statements.

EXAMPLE 6.2

Jolt Power Supply Company is impacted by all of the following events which occur on various dates following the most recent balance sheet date:

○ The market value of its investments decline precipitously. This decline in value does not relate to the marketability of the investments at the end of the reporting period.
○ Jolt acquires Live Wire Electric.
○ A tornado strikes a Jolt Warehouse in Oklahoma City.
○ A major customer suddenly goes bankrupt after a fire destroys its facility; Jolt's likely bad debt from this event is $25,000.

In all of the above cases, the events arose after the balance sheet date, and so should not alter Jolt's financial statements. However, Jolt should disclose these events in the notes accompanying its financial statements.

EXAMPLE 6.3

Following its year-end reporting period, Okeanos Shipping issues several press releases in which it announces the divestiture of its Indonesian subsidiary, the acquisition of a cruise line operating off the coast of Norway, the classification of a group of oil tankers as held for sale, the restructuring of its corporate headquarters staff, a reverse share split, and the issuance of a significant loan guarantee for its African subsidiary.

In all cases, these events did not exist at the balance sheet date. Therefore, Okeanos should not adjust its financial statements for the previous period, but it should disclose the events.

 Do I Include Subsequent Events in Reissued Financial Statements?

An entity may need to reissue its financial statements at a later date, as may happen in response to a request from the Securities and Exchange Commission. If so, you should not recognize events occurring between the time the financial statements were issued and the time they were reissued, unless an adjustment is required by GAAP or regulatory requirements.

How Do I Account for Dividends Declared after the Reporting Period?

If an entity declares dividends after the reporting period, either record them retroactively in the balance sheet with footnote disclosure, or include them in a pro forma balance sheet.

What Information about Subsequent Events Should I Disclose?

You should disclose the following information about subsequent events in the notes accompanying an entity's financial statements:

- The date through which you have evaluated subsequent events, and state whether that date is the date when the financial statements were issued, or the date when they were available to be issued.
- If the financial statements have been reissued, state the date through which subsequent events were evaluated in both the originally issued financial statements and the reissued statements.
- Any events that would be misleading if they were not disclosed. In such a case, estimate its financial effect, or state that an estimate cannot be made.

Also, you should consider including pro forma financial information as a supplement to the financial statements. This is particularly useful for showing the effect of an event as though it had occurred as of the balance sheet date.

PART II

ASSETS, LIABILITIES, AND EQUITY

CHAPTER 7

RECEIVABLES

What Types of Receivables Should I Classify as Current Assets?

A receivable is a current asset if you reasonably expect to realize it in cash or sell it during the normal operating cycle of the business. The types of receivables that are normally categorized within current assets (assuming they comply with the operating cycle restriction) include trade receivables, officer and employee receivables, and installment or deferred accounts, and notes receivable.

You should categorize accounts or notes receivable from officers, employees, or affiliated companies separately on the balance sheet.

EXAMPLE 7.1

Plucked Goose Company makes down-filled sleeping bags. Its ending receivable balance is $500,000. The following factors apply to Plucked Goose's receivables situation:

○ The allowance for uncollectible accounts receivable is $25,000, which reflects a historical bad debt rate of 5% of receivables.

○ A number of customers return Plucked Goose's sleeping bag products due to allergy problems, which averages a 12% return rate. Plucked Goose has recorded an allowance for returns of $60,000.

○ The company offers an early payment discount of 2%, which customers generally take. Plucked Goose has a $10,000 early payments allowance to record this arrangement.

○ One customer, Siberian Winters, is delinquent on a $50,000 invoice, so Plucked Goose's collections department has converted the invoice into a
(*Continued*)

short-term note receivable, payable over six months at an interest rate of 8%.

○ The company's owner, Marty Gannet, buys $5,000 of sleeping bags from the company for relatives.

Plucked Goose's controller, Antonio Anserini, reports this information on Plucked Goose's balance sheet with the following line items:

Accounts receivable, trade	445,000
Less: Allowance for doubtful accounts	(25,000)
Returns allowance	(60,000)
Early payment for discount allowance	(10,000)
	350,000
Receivables due from officers	5,000
Notes receivable due in current year	50,000

How Do I Measure Losses from Uncollectible Receivables?

You should recognize a loss on uncollectible receivables when it is probable that a receivable has been impaired as of the date of the financial statements, and that you can reasonably estimate the amount of the loss. This decision is based on the entity's historical experience, information about the ability of debtors to pay, and the current economic environment.

You may accrue a loss either on individual receivables or for groups of similar types of receivables (in which case it is not necessary to identify specific receivables).

EXAMPLE 7.2

Somnolent Sofas generates total credit sales of $10 million. It uses the percentage-of-sales method to determine a justifiable bad debt expense. Its bad debt ratio to credit sales in prior years averaged 1.5%. Therefore, in the current period, Somnolent calculates a bad debt expense of $150,000 ($10,000,000 credit sales X 1.5% bad debt ratio). Somnolent's controller records the following entry:

Bad debts expense	150,000	
Allowance for uncollectible accounts		150,000

EXAMPLE 7.3

The Appalachian Chocolate Company computes its bad debt allowance based on the age of its accounts receivable. It has historically found that 1% of its receivables aged under 30 days will become bad debts, while this percentage increases to 20% for receivables more than 90 days old. Anything between these two values experiences a 5% bad debt rate. The following table shows the calculation of the bad debt allowance for the current receivables situation:

| | Age of Receivables | | | |
	Under 30 days	30–90 days	Over 90 days	Total
Gross receivables	$2,000,000	$550,000	$120,000	
Bad debt %	1%	5%	20%	
Allowance required	$20,000	$27,500	$24,000	$71,500

Appalachian's controller should record the following entry:

Bad debts expense	71,500	
Allowance for uncollectible accounts		71,500

71

When Do I Record Receivable Prepayment Penalties?

Do not recognize a prepayment penalty until the associated loan or receivable has been prepaid.

When Do I Record Receivable Delinquency Fees?

You can recognize delinquency fees as soon as they are chargeable, if collectability is reasonably assured.

EXAMPLE 7.4

Portland Cement bills its customers a $25 late fee for making receivable payments that are more than 10 days overdue. However, it has considerable difficulty collecting the late fee, and so only records it upon receipt. In May, Portland billed customers $2,500 in late fees, and collected $225. Its controller records the following entry:

Cash	225	
Income – Delinquency fees		225

What Is a Factoring Arrangement?

A factoring arrangement is a method for selling accounts receivable to a transferee who assumes the full risk of collection, without recourse to the transferor if there is a loss. The transferor instructs its customers to send payments directly to the transferee. *Recourse* is the right of a transferee of a receivable to be paid by the transferor of the receivable for the failure by a debtor to pay the receivable when due.

EXAMPLE 7.5

Quaker Cabinets, an old-line manufacturer of fine mahogany furniture, enters into a factoring agreement with Generic Financial to sell a group of its receivables with a face value of $500,000 without recourse to Generic for $460,000. Quaker's controller records the following entry:

Cash	460,000	
Loss on sale of receivables	40,000	
Accounts receivable		500,000

As an alternative arrangement, Generic Financial enters into a separate arrangement with Quaker, whereby Quaker sells a different group of receivables to Generic, having a face value of $1,000,000. Under this arrangement, Generic charges a 4% fee, plus 24% interest, computed on the weighted-average time to maturity of the receivables of 40 days. The resulting journal entry is:

Cash	933,699	
Interest expense ($1,000,000 × 0.24 × 40/365)	26,301	
Factoring fee ($1,000,000 × 4%)	40,000	
Accounts receivable		1,000,000

How Do I Account for Credit Losses for Loans and Trade Receivables?

Deduct credit losses on loans and trade receivables from the bad debt allowance, and charge off the related loan or receivable balance at the same time. If you recover a loan or trade receivable, then record the reverse entry.

EXAMPLE 7.6

Tallahassee Trailers has built up a bad debt allowance of $450,000. It learns that a customer has gone bankrupt, and writes off $50,000 against the allowance with the following entry:

Allowance for uncollectible accounts	50,000	
Accounts receivable		50,000

After many months, the bankruptcy court approves the customer's plan to emerge from bankruptcy and pays Tallahassee $10,000, which fully resolves the amount owed. Tallahassee's controller makes the following entry to record the receipt:

Cash	10,000	
Allowance for uncollectible accounts		10,000

When Do I Record Interest Income on a Receivable?

If an entity has the contractual right to receive money on fixed or determinable dates that is linked to a receivable, then you must record interest income, even if there is no stated provision in the associated contract for the payment of interest.

EXAMPLE 7.7

Meridian and Baseline Company, maker of surveying instruments, has difficulty collecting a $24,000 receivable from the Texas Transit Company and agrees to convert it into a note, payable in $4,000 increments over six months. The note contains no stated interest rate. The market interest rate is 6%. Meridian uses the market interest rate to compile the following table, which breaks out the interest income it will earn:

Payment Number	Beginning Balance	Payment	6% Interest Paid	Principal Paid
1	$23,586	$ 4,000	118	3,882
2	19,704	4,000	99	3,901
3	15,802	4,000	79	3,921
4	11,881	4,000	59	3,941
5	7,941	4,000	40	3,960
6	3,981	4,000	20	3,980
	$ 0	$24,000	$414	$23,586

Since the discounted amount of the note payments is less than the $24,000 amount of the receivable, Meridian should write off the $414 difference at once, and then recognize interest income on the note over the course of the payments.

What Is the Recorded Value of a Note that I Exchange for Cash?

When an entity acquires a note in exchange solely for cash, and no other rights are exchanged, then the cash payment equals the present value of the note. If the entity also exchanges some rights along with the note, then you should give accounting recognition to the value of the rights transferred.

What Is the Recorded Value of a Note that I Exchange for Property?

When an entity acquires a note in exchange for property, goods, or services, then use the established exchange price for the property, goods, or services to value the note. However, if such notes are traded in an open market, then the market provides evidence of the note's present value.

What Is the Recorded Value of a Note Whose Terms Vary from the Market?

A note may not contain an interest rate, or its stated interest rate is unreasonable, or the face amount of the note materially differs from the current sales price for similar items. If so, record the note, sales price, and cost of goods at the fair value of the property, goods, or services sold, or at an amount reasonably approximating the market value of the note (whichever figure is more clearly determinable).

How Do I Measure a Loan Impairment?

You should consider the following factors when dealing with loan impairments:

- ○ *Recognition.* You should recognize a loan impairment when it is *probable* that you will be unable to collect all amounts due under the terms of the loan agreement, based on past events and conditions (including such environmental factors as industry, geographical, and political factors that are relevant to payment collection). *Probable* does not mean virtual certainty. You should recognize impairment by creating a valuation allowance with an offsetting charge to the bad debt expense account. If a loan payment is delayed or underpaid by an insignificant amount, this does not trigger a designation as a loan impairment. Loan impairment is also not triggered if there is a delayed payment where you expect to be paid accrued interest for the period of delayed payment. Do not recognize a loan loss before it is probable that the entity has incurred it, even if impairment is probable based on past experience with other losses.
- ○ *Loss calculation.* If some impaired loans have common risk characteristics, then you can aggregate them and use such historical metrics as the average

recovery period and average amount recovered to calculate impairment losses. The impairment loss calculation is based on the present value of future cash flows, discounted at the loan's effective interest rate. You can also measure impairment based on the fair value of a loan's collateral, less its estimated cost to sell. If foreclosure is probable, then measure impairment based on the fair value of the collateral.

○ *Deferral.* You should not defer the recognition of a loss to periods after the period in which the entity has incurred the loss.

○ *Loss allowance.* If you choose to create a loan loss allowance, then the allowance calculation must be well documented and applied consistently across reporting periods.

How Do I Subsequently Measure Loan Impairment?

If there is a significant change in the amount or timing of the expected future cash flows of an impaired loan, of its observable market price, or of the fair value of collateral, then recalculate the impairment and adjust the valuation allowance, either up or down.

The net carrying amount of the loan should never exceed the recorded investment in the loan.

How Do I Present a Loss Allowance on the Balance Sheet?

You should present a loss allowance for loans or receivables as a deduction from the assets to which the allowance relates.

What Information Should I Disclose about Loans and Trade Receivables?

You should disclose the following information about loans and trade receivables either on the face of the financial statements or in the accompanying notes:

○ *Allowances.* The amount of the various loss allowances related to loans and receivables.

○ *Categories.* The major categories of loans or trade receivables.

- ○ *Collateral.* The carrying amount of loans, trade receivables, standby letters of credit, securities and financial instruments that is collateral for borrowings.
- ○ *Impaired loans.* The total period-end investment in impaired loans, the average such investment during the period, the related interest income recognized during the period, and the policy for recognizing interest income on impaired loans.
- ○ *Loan credit losses.* The activity in the allowance for credit losses related to loans, showing beginning and ending balances and activity during the period.
- ○ *Policies.* The basis for accounting for the various types of receivables, as well as the methods for determining the value of loans and recognizing related interest income.

 ## How Do I Account for a Payment Under a Troubled Debt Restructuring?

A receivable that may be involved in a troubled debt restructuring can involve the sale of goods or services on credit, or the lending of cash. A troubled debt restructuring arises when the creditor grants a concession to the debtor in order to protect as much of its investment as possible.

A debtor may pay its creditor with assets (possibly including an equity interest in the debtor) to *partially* satisfy a receivable and to modify the terms of the remaining

---

EXAMPLE 7.8

Meridian Vacuum Company sells a group of compressors to Acme Machinery for $100,000, which is due for payment in 60 days. Acme subsequently suffers a considerable financial downturn, and is unable to pay the $100,000. Meridian agrees to accept $80,000 of Acme's stock, for which there is active trading on a national stock exchange, in payment for the full amount of the receivable. Meridian's controller records this transaction as follows:

Investments – available for sale	80,000	
Loss on sale of receivables	20,000	
Accounts receivable		100,000

receivable. If so, the creditor reduces its recorded investment in the receivable by the fair value of the assets received, less costs to sell (if any).

If a debtor pays its creditor with assets to *fully* satisfy a receivable, the creditor recognizes a loss that is calculated as the excess of its investment in the receivable, minus the fair value of assets received less their cost to sell.

When calculating the discounted expected future cash flows on a restructured loan, the creditor uses the original contractual rate specified in the original loan document, rather than the interest rate specified in the restructuring agreement.

In the event of a troubled debt restructuring, the creditor should charge all legal fees and other direct costs to expense as incurred.

 ## What Troubled Debt Restructuring Information Should I Disclose?

The creditor should disclose in its financial statements or accompanying notes the amount of any commitments to lend additional funds to debtors, who already owe the creditor receivables, whose terms have been modified under a troubled debt restructuring.

CHAPTER 8

INVESTMENTS–DEBT AND EQUITY SECURITIES

 What Is a Debt Security?

A debt security generally represents a creditor relationship with another entity. Examples of debt securities are municipal securities, corporate bonds, convertible debt, commercial paper, and collateralized mortgage obligations. A debt security is not an option contract, financial futures contract, forward contract, or lease.

 What Is an Equity Security?

An equity security is an ownership interest or the right to acquire or dispose of an ownership interest in an entity at a fixed or determinable price. Examples of equity securities are common stock, preferred stock, warrants, call options, and put options.

 How Do I Classify an Investment?

When you acquire a debt security or equity security, you must classify it as either a trading security, a held-to-maturity security, or an available-for-sale security, and document the reason for the classification. A *trading security* is a security that is bought and held primarily in order to sell it in the near term. A *held-to-maturity* security is one for which the entity has the intention and ability to hold it until its maturity date. An *available-for-sale* security is an investment not classified as either a trading security or as a held-to-maturity investment.

When Can I Use the Held-to-Maturity Investment Designation?

When assigning any of the preceding classifications, do not assign the held-to-maturity classification if there is uncertainty about the entity's intention to do so, or if it intends to hold the security only for an indefinite period. Also, do not use the held-to-maturity classification if the entity believes it will make a security available for sale if there are changes in market interest rates, a need for liquidity, changes in the yield on alternative investments, changes in funding sources and terms, or changes in foreign currency risk.

However, the held-to-maturity designation can be considered reasonable when an entity subsequently sells the security because there is evidence of a significant deterioration in the issuer's creditworthiness, or a tax law change that reduces the tax-exempt status of the interest on a debt security, or regulatory changes necessitating the sale or transfer of held-to-maturity positions. The designation is also reasonable if there is a business combination or disposition, and the entity is selling held-to-maturity securities in order to maintain its existing interest rate risk position or credit risk policy.

It is acceptable for an entity to use the held-to-maturity designation if it has sold debt securities when either the sale occurs near enough to its maturity date that the interest rate risk is substantially eliminated, or if the sale of the security occurs after the entity has already collected at least 85% of the principal outstanding on the debt as of the date when the entity acquired it. These conditions are considered equivalent to holding the security to maturity.

More generally, an entity's intent to use the held-to-maturity designate is not called into question if it sells such a security under *all* of the following conditions:

- The event is isolated.
- The event is nonrecurring.
- The event is unusual (for the entity).
- The event could not have been reasonably anticipated.

There should be very few situations where all four of these conditions would be met.

You should consider the entity's historical experience with held-to-maturity investments; if there is a pattern of selling securities that had been classified as held-to-maturity, this is an indicator that you should not do so again with new investments.

In short, you should consider classification of an investment as held-to-maturity to be an exception condition.

EXAMPLE 8.1

Barstow Water Sports, Inc. sells $5,000,000 of its held-to-maturity debt securities in order to fund its prospective acquisition of Charleston Canoe Company. The sale of these securities is *not* considered a reasonable exception to the rules for the designation of a held-to-maturity investment. The exception would only apply if the sales of securities were caused by Barstow's need to maintain its existing interest rate risk position or its credit risk policy as a result of the acquisition.

What Action Requires a Reclassification of Held-to-Maturity Investments?

When an entity engages in a sale or transfer of its held-to-maturity securities, and the transaction represents a material contradiction from the entity's stated intention to hold them to maturity, then you must reclassify *all* remaining held-to-maturity securities to the available-for-sale category. You should implement the reclassification in the reporting period in which the sale or transfer occurred.

How Frequently Should I Reassess Investment Classifications?

You should reassess the classifications of all debt and equity securities at each reporting date, and change their classifications as appropriate.

How Do I Account for an Investment Reclassification Between Categories?

If you transfer a security between categories of investments, you must do so at the investment's fair value. Thus, if an investment has an unrealized holding gain or loss at the date of the transfer to a new classification, you must account for it as follows:

Category	Action
All securities: From the trading classification	Any unrealized holding gain or loss will already have been recognized; do not reverse the recognized amount
All securities: Into the trading classification	Recognize in earnings the portion of the unrealized holding gain or loss at the date of the transfer
Debt security: From held-to-maturity to available-for-sale	Report the unrealized holding gain or loss at the date of transfer in other comprehensive income
Debt security: Into held-to-maturity from available-for-sale	Report the unrealized holding gain or loss in accumulated other comprehensive income, and amortize it over the remaining life of the security as a yield adjustment

When transferring any security from held-to-maturity to available-for-sale, carry over the security's amortized cost basis to the available-for-sale classification.

How Do I Measure Restricted Stock?

You should initially measure restricted stock based on the quoted price of an otherwise identical unrestricted security from the same issuer, adjusted for the effect of the restriction.

How Do I Measure an Equity Security Previously Recorded Under the Equity Method?

If an entity's ownership interest in another entity declines to the point where it can no longer account for the related equity security under the equity method, then the initial basis of the investment is the previous carrying amount of the investment.

How Do I Subsequently Account for Trading Securities?

If you have investments in debt and equity securities that are classified as trading securities, and also if the equity securities have readily determinable fair values, then subsequently record their fair values in the balance sheet and record any unrealized holding gains and losses in earnings.

EXAMPLE 8.2

The McGraw Rifle Company has the following experience with its trading portfolio of investments:

Security	Cost	Fair Value	Difference
Minnetonka bonds	$10,000	$ 9,000	$ (1,000)
New York bonds	25,000	27,000	2,000
Okeanos bonds	15,000	10,000	(5,000)
Parsippany bonds	20,000	14,000	(6,000)
	$70,000	$60,000	$(10,000)

McGraw records a $10,000 adjustment to recognize the decline in the fair value of its trading portfolio with the following entry:

Unrealized loss on trading securities	10,000	
Valuation allowance		10,000

In the following month, the trading portfolio's valuation increases by $3,000, which McGraw documents with this entry:

Valuation allowance	3,000	
Unrealized gain on trading securities		3,000

How Do I Subsequently Account for Available-for-Sale Securities?

If you have investments in debt and equity securities that are classified as available-for-sale securities, and also if the equity securities have readily determinable fair values, then subsequently record their fair values in the balance sheet. You should exclude any unrealized holding gains and losses from earnings, and instead report them in other comprehensive income until they have been realized (i.e., by selling the securities).

If an available-for-sale security is being hedged in a fair value hedge, then recognize the related holding gain or loss in earnings during the period of the hedge.

EXAMPLE 8.3

Plasma Storage Devices buys $10,000 of equity securities, which it classifies as available-for-sale. After one year, the quoted market price of the securities drops the total investment value to $8,000. In the following year, the quoted market price of the securities increases the total investment value to $11,000, and Plasma then sells the equity securities.

Plasma records the decline in value in the first year with the following entry:

Loss on available-for-sale securities (recorded in other comprehensive income)	2,000	
Investments – Available-for-sale		2,000

Plasma records the increase in value in the second year, as well as the sale of the investment, with the following entries:

Investments – Available-for-sale	3,000	
Gain on available-for-sale securities		1,000
Loss on available-for-sale securities (recorded in other comprehensive income)		2,000
Cash	11,000	
Investments – Available-for-sale		11,000

How Do I Subsequently Account for Held-to-Maturity Securities?

If you have investments in debt and equity securities that are classified as held-to-maturity, then subsequently record them at their amortized cost in the balance sheet.

How Do I Account for the Impairment of an Investment?

If an available-for-sale or held-to-maturity investment is impaired, take the following three steps:

1. *Determine whether an investment has been impaired.* An investment is impaired if the fair value of the investment is less than its cost. If it is not practicable to estimate the fair value of an investment, then

evaluate whether an event or change in circumstances has occurred in that period that may have had a significant adverse effect on the fair value of the investment. Impairment indicators include:

- A significant deterioration in the investee's financial condition.
- A significant adverse change in the investee's business environment or geographic area.
- A similar transaction or an offer to purchase the investment for an amount less than its cost.
- Investee going concern issues.

2. *Evaluate whether an impairment is other than temporary.* When the fair value of the investment is less than its cost as of the balance sheet date, you should classify the impairment as either "temporary" or "other than temporary." If the impairment is temporary, then do not recognize an impairment loss. If the impairment is other than temporary, then recognize an impairment loss. Here are factors to consider in determining whether an impairment is other than temporary:

- *Adverse conditions.* Non-beneficial changes in the investee's business environment or financial condition.
- *Collateral.* The value of any underlying collateral.
- *Duration and depth.* The length of time and extent to which the investment's fair value has declined below its amortized cost basis.
- *Payments.* The payment schedule of the security and the investee's ability to make payments in accordance with that schedule, including its historical ability to do so.
- *Rating.* Any changes in the security's credit rating.
- *Subsequent changes.* Any subsequent changes in the fair value of the investment following the balance sheet date.
- *Volatility.* The security's historical and implied fair value volatility.

Here are examples of when an impairment loss is likely to be other than temporary:

- The security will be disposed of before it matures, and the entity does not expect the fair value of the security to recover before the expected time of sale.
- The entity will be required to sell the security before it recovers its amortized cost basis.

- The entity does not expect to recover the entire amortized cost basis of the security, even if it does not intend to sell the security. You can reach this conclusion by comparing the present value of future cash flows expected from the investment to its amortized cost basis.

3. *Recognize an impairment loss.* If you determine that the investment impairment is other than temporary, then recognize an impairment loss equal to the difference between the cost and fair value of the investment at the balance sheet date. The resulting balance becomes the new cost basis of the investment. This measurement does not include partial recoveries after the balance sheet date.

EXAMPLE 8.4

The Shenandoah Golf Company buys $50,000 of the equity securities of Eagle Construction Company. In the first year, new regulations impacting the construction industry cause a downturn in Eagle's order backlog, so a credit rating agency issues a lower credit rating for it. During this time, the quoted price of Eagle's equity declines, resulting in a $15,000 reduction in the value of Shenandoah's investment. Shenandoah's management feels that the construction industry as a whole will rebound, and so it records the loss in other comprehensive income with the following entry:

Loss on available-for-sale securities (recorded in other comprehensive income)	15,000	
Investments – Available-for-sale		15,000

In the following year, the construction industry has not recovered, and Eagle's order backlog continues to decline. Shenandoah's management now feels that the price decline is other than temporary, and shifts the loss to net income.

How Do I Account for an Impairment Recovery?

If you write down an investment due to an impairment loss and the fair value of the investment subsequently rises, you do not adjust the new amortized cost basis to reflect the recovery in value.

How Do I Measure an Equity Security that Becomes Marketable?

If you have an investment that was previously not marketable, and it becomes marketable (such as through the elimination of a stock restriction), you should continue to record the equity at its cost. However, if the change in marketability provides evidence that an other-than-temporary impairment has occurred, then write down the investment by the amount of the impairment.

How Do I Account for the Sale of Trading Securities?

You should be recording changes in a trading security's fair value in earnings as the changes occur, so selling the investment may not result in the recognition of an additional gain or loss. A typical journal entry to record the transaction is:

Cash	XXX	
Investments – Trading securities		XXX

How Do I Account for the Sale of Available-for-Sale Securities?

The basic entry to record the sale of an available-for-sale security is noted below. In addition, if you already recorded a gain or loss on the investment in other comprehensive income, then you must reverse the entry to other comprehensive income and shift it into earnings.

Cash	XXX	
Investments – Available-for-sale securities		XXX

How Do I Account for Dividends and Interest Income from Investments?

You should include dividends and interest income from investments in current income. You should also record the periodic amortization of the premium or discount on an investment in current income.

How Do I Present Investment Information in the Financial Statements?

There are two methods for reporting an entity's investments in available-for-sale and trading securities on the balance sheet. One is to present the aggregate of their fair value and non-fair value amounts in the same line item, and then parenthetically disclose the amount of fair value included in the aggregate amount. The second alternative is to present two separate line items, one displaying those investments valued at their fair values, and another line displaying those investments not carried at their fair values.

How Do I Disclose Additional Information about Investments?

The disclosure requirements for investments vary depending on the type of investment, whether impairment is present, and whether sales or transfers have occurred. They are:

Disclosures for Available-for-Sale Securities

○ Amortized cost basis
○ Aggregate fair value
○ Total recognized other-than-temporary impairment
○ Total gains separately reported from total losses
○ Contractual maturities of the securities

Disclosures for Held-to-Maturity Securities

○ Amortized cost basis
○ Aggregate fair value
○ Total recognized other-than-temporary impairment
○ Gross unrecognized holding gains reported separately from gross unrecognized holding losses
○ Net carrying amount
○ Contractual maturities of the securities

Disclosures for Securities Transferred from the Held-to-Maturity Category

○ Net carrying amount of the sold or transferred security

○ Net gain or loss in accumulated other comprehensive income related to any derivative, hedging the forecasted acquisition of held-to-maturity securities
○ The related realized or unrealized gain or loss
○ The reasons for the decision to sell or transfer the security

Disclosures for Impairment of Securities

The following disclosures apply to all investments for which other than temporary impairments have not been recognized:

○ Aggregate fair value of investments with unrealized losses
○ Aggregate amount of unrealized losses
○ A description of the information considered by the entity to conclude that the impairments are *not* other than temporary (such as industry analyst reports, sector credit ratings, and current levels of subordination), as well as the nature of the investments, the causes of impairment, the number of unrealized loss positions, and the severity and duration of the impairments

If the entity has recognized a credit loss on a debt security, then use the following disclosures:

○ The methodology and significant inputs used to measure the credit loss. Examples of significant inputs are credit ratings, current levels of subordination, third-party guarantees, loan-to-collateral value ratios, and delinquency rates.
○ A tabular roll forward of the amount related to credit losses, showing the beginning balance of credit losses recognized in other comprehensive income, additions to and reductions from the credit loss amount, and the ending balance.

Sales, Transfers, and Related Matters

○ Proceeds from sales of available-for-sale securities, and the gross gains and gross losses realized from the sales
○ The cost basis used for the sold investments (for example, specific identification or average cost)
○ Gross gains and gross losses caused by transfers of securities from the available-for-sale category to the trading category

- ○ The net unrealized holding gain or loss on available-for-sale securities added to accumulated other comprehensive income, and the amount of gains and losses reclassified out of accumulated other comprehensive income
- ○ The portion of trading gains and losses related to trading securities still held at the balance sheet date

CHAPTER 9

INVESTMENTS–EQUITY METHOD AND COST METHOD

 ## What Is the Equity Method of Accounting?

The equity method of accounting is used to account for an entity's investment in another entity (the investee), when the investor has significant influence over the investee. Under this method, the investor recognizes its share of the profits and losses of the investee in the periods when these profits and losses are also reflected in the accounts of the investee. The equity method is only used when the investor can influence the operating or financial decisions of the investee.

A number of circumstances indicate an investor's ability to exercise significant influence over the operating and financial policies of an investee, including the following:

- Board of directors representation
- Policy-making participation
- Intra-entity transactions that are material
- Intra-entity management personnel interchange
- Technological dependence
- Proportion of ownership by the investor in comparison to that of other investors

If the investor has 20% or more of the voting stock of the investee, this creates a presumption that, in the absence of evidence to the contrary, the investor has the ability to exercise significant influence over the investee. Conversely, if the ownership percentage is less than 20%, there is a presumption that the investor does not have significant influence over the investee, unless it can otherwise demonstrate such ability. Substantial or even majority ownership of the investee by another party does not necessarily preclude the investor from also having significant influence with the investee.

If an investor owns 20% or more of an investee's voting stock, it may still not exercise significant influence over the investee (though predominant evidence to the contrary is needed to prove the point). The following is a non-inclusive list of indicators that an investor may be unable to exercise significant influence:

- The investee's opposition to the investor's influence, as evidenced by lawsuits or complaints to regulatory authorities.
- The investor signs an agreement to surrender significant rights as a shareholder.
- Another group of shareholders have majority ownership, and operate it without regard to the investor's views.
- The investor is unable to obtain sufficient information to apply the equity method.
- The investor is unable to obtain representation on the investee's board of directors.

How Frequently Should I Evaluate the Need for Equity Method Accounting?

You should reconsider the use of the equity method if there is a change in the contractual terms of the investment (such as converting debt to equity), there is a significant change in the capital structure of the investee, or when the investor increases or decreases its investment.

How Do I Initially Measure an Investment in an Investee's Equity?

If you invest in the common stock of an investee, you should initially measure it at cost.

How Do I Subsequently Measure an Investment under the Equity Method?

Under the equity method, the investor begins as a baseline with the cost of its original investment in the investee, and then in subsequent periods recognizes its share of the earnings or losses of the investee, both as adjustments to its original investment as noted on its balance sheet, and also in the investor's income statement.

The share of the investee's earnings that the investor recognizes is calculated based on the investor's ownership percentage of the investee's common stock. When calculating its share of the investee's earnings, the investor must also eliminate intra-entity profits and losses. Further, if the investee issues dividends to the investor, the investor should deduct the amount of these dividends from the carrying amount of its investment in the investee.

EXAMPLE 9.1

Glass Lamination International acquires 25% of the common stock of Periscope Designs for $500,000. Glass Lamination has significant control over Periscope's operating and financial policies, so it uses the equity method to account for its investment in Periscope. During the next year, Periscope has net income of $80,000. Glass Lamination records its 25% share of Periscope's net income with the following entry:

Investment in Periscope Designs	20,000	
Equity in Periscope Designs Income		20,000

Periscope then issues a cash dividend of $10,000, for which Periscope records its receipt of ¼ of the dividends with the following entry:

Cash	2,500	
Investment in Periscope Designs		2,500

Following these two entries, the carrying value of Glass Lamination's investment in Periscope Designs is now $517,500 ($500,000 + $20,000 − $2,500).

In the following year, Glass Lamination sells $50,000 of glass components to Periscope Designs. On the balance sheet date, Periscope holds in its inventory the full $50,000 of components sold to it by Glass Lamination, for which Glass Lamination has recorded a gross profit of $30,000. Glass Lamination should reduce its net income by $30,000 (not including income tax effects) to eliminate the intra-entity profit.

If the investee records adjustments in other comprehensive income, then the investor should record its share of these adjustments as changes to the investment account, with corresponding adjustments in equity. An investee's potential adjustments to other comprehensive income include these items:

○ Unrealized gains and losses on available-for-sale securities

○ Foreign currency items
○ Gains and losses, prior service costs or credits, and transition assets or obligations related to pension and other post-retirement benefits

If the investee is not timely in forwarding its financial results to the investor, then the investor can calculate its share of the investee's income from the most recent financial information it obtains. If there is a time lag in receiving this information, then the investor should use the same time lag in reporting investee results in the future, in order to be consistent.

How Do I Account for a Change *to* the Equity Method?

If an investor increases its share in or control over the investee to the point where it should start using the equity method, then it should adjust the investment, results of operations, and retained earnings retroactively to reflect the change.

How Do I Account for a Change *from* the Equity Method?

If the investor sells sufficient stock in the investee to lose its ability to influence investee policy, then the investor should stop using the equity method. The investor retains all changes that it previously made to the carrying amount of its investment in the investee, but does not continue recording its share of the investee's profits and losses.

If the investor receives any dividends from the investee in the future that exceed its share of the investee's earnings in those periods, then it should use them to reduce the carrying amount of its investment.

How Do I Account for the Investor's Share of an Investee's Losses under the Equity Method?

It is possible that the investor's share of an investee's losses may equal or exceed the carrying amount of the investor's investment in the investee. If so, the investor recognizes losses until they completely offset the carrying amount of its investment in the investee, plus the amount of any additional financial support it has made to the investee. Examples of additional financial support include investments in preferred stock, loans, investments in debt securities, and advances.

Once the investor's share of investee losses equals the carrying amount of its investment in the investee, the investor stops applying the equity method. However, there are two exceptions, where the investor should recognize additional losses, which are:

1. The investor has also guaranteed obligations of the investee or is obliged to provide additional financial support, in which case it must continue recognizing its share of investee losses.
2. If the investee appears to be assured of an imminent return to profitability, as would be the case when it records a one-time, non-recurring loss that is an exception from an ongoing pattern of profitability. If so, it should continue recognizing its share of investee losses.

If the investor has other investments in the investee and the investor is still recording its share of the investee's losses, then after eliminating the carrying amount of its investment in the investee, the investor should apply further losses against the other investments in order of their priority in liquidation. If the investee subsequently begins to earn profits, then the investor applies its share of the profits to the most senior securities first.

If the investor makes an additional investment in the investee for the purposes of funding prior losses, then the investor should recognize its share of previously suspended losses up to the amount of the additional investment.

If the investee once again begins to earn a profit, the investor does not resume its use of the equity method until such time as its share of that net income equals the share of former investee net losses that the investor did not recognize while the investor had suspended its use of the equity method.

EXAMPLE 9.2

Portland Cement acquires $1,000,000 of the common stock of Grout International, and uses the equity method to account for its investment. Portland's share of continuing losses by Grout has reduced the carrying amount of Portland's investment to zero. In addition, Portland has acquired some of Grout's preferred stock for $100,000, for which there is no quoted market price.

Grout records an additional loss in the following year, of which Portland's share is $120,000. Portland records the following entry:

(Continued)

Equity method loss	100,000	
Preferred stock investment		100,000

Since the amount of the preferred stock investment is now reduced to zero, Portland cannot record any additional share of Grout's losses, so it does not record its remaining $20,000 share of Grout's losses.

 ### How Do I Account for an Other than Temporary Decrease in Investment Value?

If the investee has a series of operating losses or other events indicating that an other than temporary decrease in value of the investment has occurred, the investor should recognize the decrease in value, even if it exceeds the loss amount that the investor would otherwise recognize under the equity method. An example of an event indicating an other than temporary decrease in value is the investee's inability to sustain an earnings pattern that justifies the carrying amount of the investment.

 ### How Do I Report the Results of an Equity Method Investment?

An equity method investment is a one-line consolidation on the investor's balance sheet. In addition, the investor records its share of the investee's profits or losses in its income statement as a single line item. However, if the investee records an extraordinary item, the investor should record its share of that extraordinary item as a separate line item on its income statement.

 ### What Information Should I Disclose about Equity Method Investments?

You should disclose the following information about an equity method investment:

○ The name of the investee
○ The percentage of the investor's ownership of the investee's common stock

○ The investor's accounting policy regarding its accounting for investments in common stock. Include the names of significant investee entities where the investor owns at least 20% of the common stock, but does not use the equity method, and state why such treatment is used. Also include the names of significant investee entities where the investor owns less than 20% of the common stock, but does use the equity method, and state why such treatment is used

○ Any difference between the carrying amount of an investment and the amount of the underlying equity in net assets, and discuss the entity's accounting for the difference

○ The material effects of possible conversions, exercises, or contingent issuances related to outstanding convertible securities, options, and warrants

○ If an investment is in the common stock of an entity for which a quoted market price is available, disclose the aggregate value of the investment, based on the market price

○ If the entity's investments accounted for under the equity method are, in aggregate, material, then consider providing summary information about the assets, liabilities, and results of operations of the investees

What Is the Cost Method of Accounting?

Under the cost method of accounting, you should record an investment at its original cost. If there is a nontemporary decline in the market value of an investment that is accounted for under the cost method, then the investor should write down the carrying amount of the investment to its market value as of the balance sheet date.

When using the cost method, any dividends paid to the investor by the investee that are distributed from the net accumulated earnings of the investee are recognized as income by the investor. However, any dividends received that are in excess of the investee's earnings subsequent to the date of investment are considered a return of investment, which constitutes a reduction of the cost of the investment.

You should use the cost method to account for an investment that is smaller than an investment that would be accounted for under the equity method. Thus, an investment in less than 20% of an investee's common stock is typically accounted for using the cost method.

EXAMPLE 9.3

Night Vision Optics Corporation invests $100,000 in the common stock of Eagle Eye Corporation. This amount is 15% of Eagle Eye's common stock, and so does not qualify for use of the equity method. In Year 1, Eagle Eye has $40,000 of net income and issues $30,000 of dividends; Night Vision's share of the dividends is 15%, or $4,500. Night Vision records the transaction with this entry:

Cash	4,500	
Dividend income		4,500

In Year 2, Eagle Eye has zero net income, but still issues $30,000 of dividends, of which Night Vision's share remains 15%, or $4,500. Since all of the dividend was in excess of Eagle Eye's earnings, Night Vision records it as follows, as a return of investment:

Cash	4,500	
Investment in Eagle Eye Corporation		4,500

What Information Should I Disclose about Cost Method Investments?

If you have cost method investments, then disclose the following information in the notes accompanying the financial statements:

○ The aggregate carrying amount of all such investments.

○ The aggregate carrying amount of such investments not evaluated for impairment.

○ That the fair value of such investments is not estimated if there are no identified events or changes in circumstances that would have a significant adverse effect on them, and either it is not practicable to estimate fair value, or the investor is exempt from estimating fair value.

CHAPTER 10

INVENTORY

 What Is the Definition of Inventory?

Inventory is an asset held for sale in the ordinary course of business, or which is in the process of being produced for sale, or the materials or supplies intended for consumption in the production process. This can include items purchased and held for resale. In the case of services, inventory can be the costs of a service for which related revenue has not yet been recognized.

Long-term assets subject to depreciation should not be categorized as inventory, neither should such assets that are held for sale.

 What Costs Can I Include in Inventory?

In general, you should include in the cost of inventory all expenditures and charges that an entity has either directly or indirectly incurred to bring an inventory item to its existing condition and location. Thus, the following costs can be included in the cost of inventory:

- Direct labor
- Freight
- Handling
- Import duties and related taxes
- Overhead for fixed and variable production costs
- Purchase price

Fixed production overhead costs include those costs that remain stable regardless of production volume, such as equipment and building maintenance, depreciation, and factory administration and management. The allocation of fixed overhead production costs is based on actual usage of production facilities in the period, divided by the normal capacity of those facilities. *Normal capacity* is the production that you expect a facility to achieve over a number of periods under normal circumstances, including a loss of capacity caused by planned maintenance.

When there are periods of abnormally high production, reduce the amount of fixed overhead allocated to each unit of production, so that you do not measure inventories above their cost. Conversely, do not increase the amount of fixed overhead allocated to each unit of production because of an abnormally low rate of production.

Variable production overhead costs include those costs that vary approximately with production volume, and are allocated based on actual usage of production facilities.

You should recognize any unallocated overhead as an expense in the period in which it occurs.

Do not include in inventory any of the following items:

- Abnormal waste related to materials, labor, or other production costs
- Administrative costs (unless clearly related to production)
- Selling costs

It is not acceptable to exclude all overhead costs from inventory costs.

 ## What Costs Can I Include in Service Inventory?

Any unbilled services can be charged to inventory at the cost of their production. Usually, these costs are comprised of the labor and related costs of those personnel engaged in providing a billable service. This can include the cost of supervisory personnel and overhead, as long as these costs are to eventually be billed. The cost of non-billable personnel must be charged to expense in the period incurred.

 ## What Methods Are Acceptable for Measuring Inventory?

The default cost assignment methodology is either the *first-in, first-out* (FIFO), or *last-in, first-out* (LIFO), or *weighted average* methods. The FIFO method assumes that those items purchased first are consumed first, thereby leaving the most recently purchased items still in stock at the end of the reporting period.

The weighted average method assigns costs based on the weighted average of the cost of similar items in stock at the beginning of or acquired during the reporting period.

EXAMPLE 10.1

Beartooth Industries produces fleece garments for sale to winter adventurers. Beartooth has incurred the following expenses, which are itemized in the table as being included in the cost of inventory or charged to expense in the current period:

Category	Amount Incurred	Include in Inventory	Charge to Expense
Accounting department costs	$ 58,000		$ 58,000
Dye purchases	229,000	$ 229,000	
Equipment maintenance	142,000	142,000	
Equipment depreciation	93,000	93,000	
Fleece purchases	1,580,000	1,580,000	
Freight on purchases	42,000	42,000	
Import broker commission	10,000	10,000	
Import duties	19,000	19,000	
Insurance on purchases	12,000	12,000	
Longshoreman handling fees	11,000	11,000	
Sales commission	28,000		28,000
Trade discounts on purchases	−30,000	−30,000	
Warranty costs	21,000		21,000
Totals	$2,215,000	$2,108,000	$107,000

EXAMPLE 10.2

Savannah Skirts, maker of stylish women's clothes, installs a FIFO inventory system. The following table (Exhibit 10.1) shows the FIFO cost calculations for a single inventory item, product number BK0043. The first row indicates the origination of the first layer of inventory, resulting in 50 units of inventory at a per-unit cost of $10.00. In the second row, the monthly inventory usage is 350 units. Under the FIFO system, Savannah uses the entire stock of 50 inventory units that were left over at the end of the preceding month, as well as 300 units that were purchased in the current

(*Continued*)

Exhibit 10.1 INVENTORY – FIFO

Column 1	Column 2	Column 3	Column 4	Column 5	Column 6	Column 7	Column 8
Date Purchased	Quantity Purchased	Cost per Unit	Monthly Usage	Net Inventory Remaining	Cost of 1st Inventory Layer	Cost of 2nd Inventory Layer	Extended Inventory Cost
05/03/10	500	$10.00	450	50	(50 × $10.00)	—	$ 500
06/04/10	1,000	$ 9.58	350	700	(700 × $9.58)	—	$6,706
07/11/10	250	$10.65	400	550	(300 × $9.58)	(250 × $10.65)	$5,537
08/01/10	475	$10.25	350	675	(200 × $10.65)	(475 × $10.25)	$6,999
08/30/10	375	$10.40	400	650	(275 × $10.25)	(375 × $10.40)	$6,719
09/09/10	850	$ 9.50	700	800	(800 × $9.50)	—	$7,600
12/12/10	700	$ 9.75	900	600	(600 × $9.75)	—	$5,850
05/07/11	200	$10.80	0	800	(600 × $9.75)	(200 × $10.80)	$8,010

month. This wipes out the first layer of inventory, leaving Savannah with a single new layer that is composed of 700 units at a cost of $9.58 per unit. In the third row, there are 400 units of usage, which again comes from the first inventory layer, shrinking it down to just 300 units. However, since extra stock was purchased in the same period, Savannah now has an extra inventory layer that comprises 250 units, at a cost of $10.65 per unit. The rest of the exhibit proceeds using the same FIFO layering assumptions.

Example 10.3

Savannah Skirts considers switching to a weighted average inventory system. Savannah's controller elects to model the results of the system using the same transactions just noted for its FIFO costing system. The results appear in the following table (Exhibit 10.2). The first row shows that Savannah had a remainder of 50 units in stock, at a cost of $10.00. Since there has only been one purchase so far, the controller can easily calculate that the total inventory valuation is $500 by multiplying the unit cost of $10.00 in column 3 by the number of units remaining in stock, as shown in column 6.

In the second row, Savannah has purchased another 1,000 units at a cost of $9.58 per unit. After monthly usage, there are 700 units in stock, of which 650 were added from the most recent purchase. To determine the new weighted average cost of the inventory, the controller first determines the extended cost of this newest inventory addition. As shown in column 7, he arrives at a cost of $6,227 by multiplying the value in column 3 by the value in column 6. The controller then adds this amount to the existing total inventory valuation ($6,227 + $500) to arrive at the new extended inventory cost of $6,727, as shown in column 8. Finally, the controller divides the new extended cost in column 8 by the total number of units now in stock, as shown in column 5, to arrive at the new per-unit cost of $9.61 The rest of the exhibit proceeds using the same weighted average calculations.

Exhibit 10.2 INVENTORY – WEIGHTED AVERAGE

Column 1	Column 2	Column 3	Column 4	Column 5	Column 6	Column 7	Column 8	Column 9
Date Purchased	Quantity Purchased	Cost per Unit	Monthly Usage	Net Inventory Remaining	Net Change in Inventory During Period	Extended Cost of New Inventory Layer	Extended Inventory Cost	Average Inventory Cost/Unit
05/03/10	500	$10.00	450	50	50	$ 500.00	$ 500.00	$10.00
06/04/10	1,000	$ 9.58	350	700	650	$6,227.00	$6,727.00	$ 9.61
07/11/10	250	$10.65	400	550	–150	$ -	$5,285.50	$ 9.61
08/01/10	475	$10.25	350	675	125	$1,281.25	$6,566.75	$ 9.73
08/30/10	375	$10.40	400	650	–25	$ -	$6,323.54	$ 9.73
09/09/10	850	$ 9.50	700	800	150	$1,425.00	$7,748.54	$ 9.69
12/12/10	700	$ 9.75	900	600	–200	$ -	$5,811.40	$ 9.69
05/07/11	200	$10.80	0	800	200	$2,160.00	$7,971.40	$ 9.96

The LIFO method assumes that those items purchased last are consumed first, thereby leaving the oldest purchased items still in stock at the end of the reporting period.

It is acceptable to use the *standard cost* method to measure the cost of inventory, as long as the results approximate actual cost. Under this method, a standard cost is assigned to each inventory item for costing purposes; the standard cost is compared to actual costs periodically, and adjusted to match the actual cost; it is a simplified way to track costs with reduced effort. The standard costs assigned to an inventory item should assume normal usage levels for materials, supplies, labor, and facility utilization.

It is also acceptable to use the *retail method*, which is used in the retail industry for measuring large volumes of items having similar margins. Under this approach, reduce the sales value of the inventory by a percentage gross margin that is based on actual results to arrive at the estimated inventory cost. If the gross margin varies substantially by retail department, it is allowable to conduct a separate calculation for each department, using the gross margin that pertains to each one.

The assignment of specific costs to individual inventory items is required when goods are produced for specific projects. However, *specific identification* of costs is not appropriate when there are many interchangeable inventory items.

 ## How Do I Write Down the Value of Inventory?

Always measure inventory at the *lower* of its cost or market. *Market* is the current replacement cost of inventory, provided that market does not exceed the net realizable value, and that market shall not be less than net realizable value as reduced by an allowance for normal profit margin. *Net realizable value* is the estimated selling price in the ordinary course of business, less reasonably predictable costs of completion and disposal.

You should always reduce the cost of inventory in the current period when its utility is less than its cost. This situation typically arises when the inventory has physically deteriorated, is obsolete, or there are reduced selling prices.

Do not write down the value of raw materials if the finished goods into which they are incorporated are expected to sell at or above cost. Further, if inventory is the hedged

EXAMPLE 10.4

Savannah Skirts also considers switching to a LIFO inventory system. Again, Savannah's controller models the results of the system using the same transactions noted in the preceding example. The results appear in the following table (Exhibit 10.3). The first row shows that Savannah had a remainder of 50 units in stock, at a cost of $10.00. The controller notes this first inventory layer in column 6, which becomes the first layer of inventory cost. The next row reveals that an additional inventory layer of 650 units has been created at a cost of $9.58 each, which is listed as the second inventory layer in column 7. In the third row, Savannah has reduced its inventory by 150 units, which it removes from the inventory layer in column 7. The earliest layer remains untouched, since it was the first layer of costs added and will not be used again until all other inventory layers have been eliminated. The rest of the exhibit proceeds using the same concepts, at one point increasing to four inventory layers.

Exhibit 10.3 INVENTORY – LIFO

Column 1	Column 2	Column 3	Column 4	Column 5	Column 6	Column 7	Column 8	Column 9	Column 10
Date Purchased	Quantity Purchased	Cost per Unit	Monthly Usage	Net Inventory Remaining	Cost of 1st Inventory Layer	Cost of 2nd Inventory Layer	Cost of 3rd Inventory Layer	Cost of 4th Inventory Layer	Extended Inventory Cost
05/03/10	500	$10.00	450	50	(50 × $10.00)	—	—	—	$ 500
06/04/10	1,000	$ 9.58	350	700	(50 × $10.00)	(650 × $9.58)	—	—	$6,727
07/11/10	250	$10.65	400	550	(50 × $10.00)	(500 × $9.58)	—	—	$5,290
08/01/10	475	$10.25	350	675	(50 × $10.00)	(500 × $9.58)	(125 × $10.25)	—	$6,571
08/30/10	375	$10.40	400	650	(50 × $10.00)	(500 × $9.58)	(100 × $10.25)	—	$6,315
09/09/10	850	$ 9.50	700	800	(50 × $10.00)	(500 × $9.58)	(100 × $10.25)	(150 × $9.50)	$7,740
12/12/10	700	$ 9.75	900	600	(50 × $10.00)	(500 × $9.58)	(50 × $10.25)	—	$5,803

item in a fair value hedge, then include the effects of the hedge in the inventory's cost basis (which may eliminate the need for a lower of cost or market adjustment).

The write down to net realizable value is normally on an individual item basis, but can also be applied to major inventory categories or to the total of all inventory.

Example 10.5

Grand Teton Designs is a Wyoming manufacturer of climbing equipment. It has five major product lines, which are noted in the following table. At its fiscal year-end, Grand Teton calculates the lower of its cost or net realizable value (NRV) in the following table:

Product Line	Quantity on Hand	Unit Cost	Inventory at Cost	Market per Unit	Lower of Cost or Market
Footwear	2,000	$190	$380,000	$230	$380,000
Ice tools	500	140	70,000	170	70,000
Outerwear	950	135	128,250	120	114,000
Ropes	1,250	180	225,000	140	175,000
Tents	780	270	210,600	350	210,600

Based on the table, the market value is lower than cost on the outerwear and rope product lines. Accordingly, Grand Teton should recognize a loss on the outerwear product line of $14,250 ($128,250 − $114,000) and a loss on the rope product line of $50,000 ($225,000 − $175,000).

You should write inventory down to the lower of cost or market unless there is substantial evidence that market prices will recover before the entity sells the inventory or, in the case of last-in, first-out (LIFO) inventory, there is substantial evidence that inventory amounts will be restored by year-end.

If there is a sales incentive that will result in a loss on the sale of a related product, this may be an indicator of impairment of the existing inventory for that item.

 ### Should I Write Down Losses on Purchase Commitments?

If an entity has a net loss on a firm purchase commitment for inventory, then recognize the loss in the period incurred. However, do not recognize a loss if the amounts to be realized from these inventory items are protected by firm sales contracts, or where other circumstances provide reasonable assurance of continuing sales without a price decline.

The calculation of the loss is the same as just noted for the lower of cost or market approach.

When Do I Write Down the Value of Inventory?

Conduct the assessment when circumstances arise that indicate that the market value has declined below the product cost, and charge any write-down to expense at that time. Continue to assess the situation in each subsequent period until circumstances causing the write-down have abated.

Can I Reverse an Inventory Write-Down?

No. Once you write down the cost of an inventory item, the newly-reduced cost becomes its cost for subsequent accounting purposes.

When Do I Charge Inventory Costs to Expense?

Charge inventory costs to expense when you recognize the revenue related to its sale.

When Can I State Inventories above Cost?

You can only state inventories above cost when an inventory item has immediate marketability at a quoted market price, with no substantial cost of marketing, and interchangeable units. These restrictions make it difficult to state any inventories above cost, other than for gold and silver, where there is a government-controlled market at a fixed monetary value.

When it is possible to state inventories above cost, state the inventory at its sale price, reduced by expenditures you expect to incur in the inventory's disposal.

What Inventory Information Do I Disclose?

Disclose the following information related to inventory:

- The basis for stating inventories, any changes in this basis, and the impact of such a change on net income
- Any goods that are stated above cost
- Any goods that are stated at their sales prices
- Significant estimates applicable to inventories

Also, if the amount of a loss from the application of the lower of cost or market rule is substantial, consider disclosing it as a separate line item in the income statement. You should also separately disclose the amount of any losses on firm purchase commitments in the income statement.

CHAPTER 11

OTHER ASSETS AND DEFERRED COSTS

 What Is a Prepaid Expense?

A prepaid expense is an asset that is normally used up or expires within an entity's operating cycle. It is typically paid in advance of its consumption. Examples of prepaid expenses are insurance, interest, rent, taxes, and prepaid advertising.

A prepaid expense is typically charged to expense when a specific future event occurs, or in increments over a predetermined time period.

EXAMPLE 11.1
Hostetler Corporation pays three months of rent in advance on its new corporate headquarters, in the amount of $90,000. It charges this prepayment to expense over three months, at the rate of $30,000 per month.

 What Is a Preproduction Cost?

A preproduction cost arises when a manufacturer incurs costs in advance of products they will supply to a customer under the terms of long-term supply arrangements. An example is the design and development costs for a new product, or for molds or dies to be used in its production. Depending on the supply arrangement, the supplier may be guaranteed reimbursement for these costs, either with a specific payment, or through increased product pricing.

 How Do I Account for Preproduction Costs?

If an entity incurs preproduction costs for products to be sold under long-term supply arrangements, you should expense them as incurred. The treatment of costs associated with the design and development of supplier-owned molds, dies, and other tools to be used in long-term supply arrangements has the following five alternative treatments:

1. Capitalize these expenses and amortize them over the usage period. Also, periodically assess them for impairment.
2. If these expenses relate to new technology, then charge them to expense as incurred.
3. If the supplier will not own the molds, dies, and other tools, and the arrangement gives the supplier the non-cancelable right to use the items during the term of the arrangement, then capitalize the expenses and amortize them over the usage period.
4. If the supplier will not own the molds, dies, and other tools, and the arrangement does not give the supplier the non-cancelable right to use the items during the term of the arrangement, then charge them to expense as incurred.
5. If there is a contractual guarantee to reimburse the supplier for these costs, then the supplier should recognize them as an asset and charge them to expense when it invoices the customer for these items. If there is a cap on the amount of reimbursement, then the supplier should recognize costs as an asset until it reaches the cap, and subsequently charge all additional costs to expense.

EXAMPLE 11.2

Hostetler Industries enters into a long-term arrangement with Pittsburgh Iron Works, under which Hostetler agrees to pay Pittsburgh $40 per part for the first 100,000 parts produced, and $35 for every part thereafter. There is no mention in the supply contract concerning reimbursement of Pittsburgh's mold design and development costs if fewer than 100,000 parts are produced under the contract.

Since Pittsburgh cannot objectively measure the amount of reimbursement it will receive for its design and development costs, it must charge the preproduction design and development costs to expense as incurred.

If the contract had instead stated that Hostetler would reimburse Pittsburgh $500,000 for its mold design and development costs, to be reduced by $5 per

> part produced under the contract, then Pittsburgh could objectively measure forthcoming compensation of $500,000, and therefore recognize a maximum of $500,000 of design and development costs as assets.

What Is Direct-Response Advertising?

Direct-response advertising involves activities where the audience can be shown to have responded specifically to an advertising campaign.

When Can I Capitalize Advertising Expenses?

You can capitalize advertising expenses when there is a reliable and demonstrated relationship between total costs and future benefits resulting directly from the incurrence of those costs. For example, an entity has reliable evidence that, if it sends out 100,000 pieces of direct-mail advertising, it will receive 2,500 responses. Thus, the cost of obtaining 2,500 responses is the cost incurred to send out the 100,000 mailings. With such information, an entity can use historical information to make reliable predictions about the relationship between current expenditures required to obtain future revenue.

If such historical information is available, then you can accrue advertising costs and charge them to expense when you recognize the related revenue.

If the advertising expenditures are for direct-response advertising, you can capitalize the expenditures *only* if the situation meets *both* of the following criteria:

1. The primary purpose of the advertising is to generate sales from customers who can be shown to have responded specifically to the advertising. You must be able to document customer responses, specifying the name of the customer and the advertising that elicited the response (such as a coded order form or response card).
2. The advertising activity results in probable future revenues that exceed future costs incurred to realize the revenues, which can be proven with verifiable historical patterns of results for the entity. If there is no operating history for a new product or service, an entity can use as proof, statistics for other products and services for which statistics can be highly

correlated. Industry statistics are not considered sufficiently objective evidence.

EXAMPLE 11.3

Manly Corporation is introducing its new Snort Soap for Men. It releases the product in a test market, where results support the view that the results of advertising Snort will likely be highly correlated with its older product, Horsepower Soap for Men. Based on the correlation report, Manly elects to capitalize the expenditures on a forthcoming advertising campaign to roll out Snort Soap nationwide.

Each significant advertising effort is treated as a separate standalone cost pool, where each pool must meet the preceding criteria before it can be capitalized.

Which Direct-Response Advertising Costs Can I Capitalize?

If a direct-response advertising campaign meets the criteria noted in the preceding answer, then you can capitalize the following costs, which may be billed by third party suppliers and/or incurred as in-house costs:

- ○ Idea development
- ○ Writing advertising copy
- ○ Artwork
- ○ Printing and mailing
- ○ Magazine space

Only capitalize payroll costs related to these items for that portion of employee time spent specifically on those activities.

How Do I Amortize Capitalized Advertising Costs?

You should amortize capitalized advertising expenses using the ratio of current period revenues related to the advertising costs, to the total of current and estimated future period revenue related to the advertising costs. It may be necessary to periodically adjust the estimated amounts of future revenues, which then requires a recalculation of the ratio.

You should amortize costs separately for each pool of advertising costs (which are typically segregated for each advertising campaign).

EXAMPLE 11.4

Hostetler Corporation incurs $60,000 in costs for a direct-response marketing campaign, which it capitalizes. Hostetler projects future net revenues arising from the campaign to be $40,000, $30,000, $20,000, and $10,000 over the next four months, for a total of $100,000. Based on this information, the planned amortization schedule follows:

	Month 1	Month 2	Month 3	Month 4
Projected future net revenues	$40,000	$30,000	$20,000	$10,000
Proportion of costs recognized	40%	30%	20%	10%
Expected cost recognition	$24,000	$18,000	$12,000	$6,000

At the end of Month 3, Hostetler's marketing manager concludes that no further revenues can be expected from the marketing campaign, so the controller accelerates recognition of the final $6,000 of capitalized cost into Month 3.

You should also evaluate the realizability of the amounts of advertising assets at each balance sheet date, by comparing the carrying amount in each cost pool to the probable remaining future net revenue expected to result from the advertising. *Future net revenues* are gross revenues minus all probable future costs necessary to earn those revenues (including cost of goods sold). If the carrying amount of the advertising exceeds the remaining future net revenues, then report the excess carrying amount as an advertising expense in the current period.

If estimates of future net revenues subsequently increase, do not adjust the reduced carrying amounts of advertising costs upward.

Over What Period Should I Amortize Advertising Costs?

There is no limit to the period over which you can amortize advertising costs. However, since the reliability of accounting estimates decreases over time, the amortization period is typically no more than one year or one operating cycle. The duration of amortization is driven by the type of advertising; many campaigns only last for a few months, while the impact of a mail order catalogue may be substantially longer.

Can I Change the Accounting if There Is Subsequent Evidence of Advertising Benefits?

No. If you did not initially capitalize direct-response advertising costs because you could not demonstrate that the advertising would result in future benefits, you cannot do so retroactively if subsequent evidence proves that the advertising did result in future benefits.

How Do I Account for Tangible Assets Used in Multiple Advertising Campaigns?

If you have tangible assets that are re-used for multiple advertising campaigns, such as company-owned billboards, then capitalize and depreciate them over their useful lives.

What Information Should I Disclose About Advertising Assets?

You should disclose the following information about an entity's advertising:

○ The accounting policy for advertising, stating whether costs are expensed as incurred or the first time the advertising takes place
○ Description of any direct-response advertising reported as an asset, the accounting policy for it, and its amortization period
○ The amount charged to advertising expense, with a separate disclosure of any write-down to net realizable value
○ Total amount of advertising reported as assets in the balance sheet

EXAMPLE 11.5

Hostetler Corporation expenses the production costs of advertising as incurred, except for direct-response advertising, which it capitalizes and amortizes over the expected period of future benefits.

Direct-response advertising consists primarily of direct mailings of coupons for the Company's products. The capitalized cost of the advertising is amortized over the two-month period following issuance of each mailing.

At December 31, 20X1, $250,000 of advertising was reported as an asset. Advertising expense was $1,250,000 in 20X1, including $200,000 for amounts written down to net realizable value.

CHAPTER 12

PROPERTY, PLANT, AND EQUIPMENT

  What Is Property, Plant, and Equipment?

Property, plant, and equipment (PP&E) is tangible items that are expected to be used in more than one period, and which are used in production, for rental, or for administration. This can include items acquired for safety or environmental reasons, since they may be necessary for deriving future economic benefits from other assets.

  What Is an Asset Group?

An asset group is a unit of accounting, which represents the lowest level for which identifiable cash flows from one or more assets are mostly independent of the cash flows of other asset groups.

EXAMPLE 12.1

Electro Tram operates an articulated tram system in New Orleans. It does so under a contract with the city government to provide a minimum amount of system-wide service. It is possible to identify cash flows by tramline, and one of the tramlines clearly operates at a loss. The service contract is for the entire city area, and Electro Tram is not allowed to modify or terminate any tramline. Consequently, the lowest level of identifiable cash flows is for the entire tram network.

EXAMPLE 12.2

Lakehurst Airship operates a semi-rigid blimp for use in advertising at arena sporting events. The blimp is comprised of two primary assets–the gas bag and the control car. The cash flow specifically traceable to
(Continued)

either the gas bag or the control car is essentially zero. Instead, the two assets must be grouped together into a cash-generating unit to evaluate their combined cash flows as an operating vehicle.

Can I Accrue for Planned Major Maintenance Activities?

No. You are not allowed to accrue in advance for planned major maintenance activities. This prohibition applies to both interim and annual financial reporting periods.

What Costs Do I Include in PP&E?

In general, the costs to include in PP&E are an item's purchase cost and any costs incurred to bring the asset to the location and condition needed for it to operate in the manner intended by management. More specifically, include the following costs in PP&E:

- ○ Purchase price of the item and related taxes
- ○ Construction cost of the item, which can include labor and employee benefits
- ○ Import duties
- ○ Inbound freight and handling
- ○ Interest costs incurred during the period required to bring an asset to the condition and location necessary for its intended use
- ○ Site preparation
- ○ Installation and assembly
- ○ Asset startup testing
- ○ Professional fees

Also, include in PP&E the cost of major periodic replacements. For example, an aircraft requires new engines and a building requires a new roof after a certain usage interval or time period. Upon replacement, the new items are recorded in PP&E, and the carrying amounts of any replaced items are derecognized.

EXAMPLE 12.3

Pelham Peanuts is building a new peanut processing facility in Pelham, Georgia. The following table shows the costs it incurs for the Pelham facility, and whether they can be capitalized or charged to expense as incurred:

Cost Type	Expenditure	Capitalized	Expensed
Accounting charges	$ 65,000		$ 65,000
Architect's fees	280,000	$ 280,000	
Borrowing costs	185,000	185,000	
Construction cost	4,095,000	4,095,000	
Operating losses	150,000		150,000
Shipping and handling	410,000	410,000	
Site preparation	500,000	500,000	
Startup testing	100,000	100,000	
Totals	$5,785,000	$5,570,000	$215,000

EXAMPLE 12.4

Alaskan Ballistics Corporation (ABC), operator of the Kodiak Launch Complex in Alaska, uses a $175,000 tractor to haul sounding rockets to its launch towers. Seven years after it purchased the tractor, the tractor engine fails and must be replaced. A new engine costs $75,000. A new engine provides economic benefits and its cost can be measured, so ABC should recognize it as an asset.

The original invoice for the tractor did not separately specify the cost of the engine, so ABC can use the cost of the replacement engine as the basis for determining the cost of the original engine. To do so, it uses its 6% cost of capital to discount the $75,000 engine for seven years, yielding a discounted cost of $49,880 ($75,000 × 0.66506).

ABC then eliminates the $49,880 cost of the original engine from the asset record, and adds the new engine, resulting in a total new tractor cost of $200,120 ($175,000 − $49,880 + $75,000).

How Do I Calculate Borrowing Costs to Include in PP&E?

Generally, borrowing costs attributable to a PP&E item are those that would otherwise have been avoided if the asset had not been acquired. There are two ways to determine the borrowing cost to include in PP&E:

○ *Directly attributable borrowing costs.* If borrowings specifically occurred to obtain the asset, then the borrowing cost to capitalize is the actual borrowing cost incurred, minus any investment income earned from the interim investment of those borrowings.

○ *Borrowing costs from a general fund.* Borrowings may be handled centrally for general corporate needs, and may be obtained through a variety of debt instruments. In this case, derive an interest rate from the weighted average of the entity's borrowing costs during the period applicable to the asset. The amount of allowable borrowing costs using this method are capped at the entity's total borrowing costs during the applicable period.

EXAMPLE 12.5

The Arabian Knights security company is building a new world headquarters in Rockville, Maryland. Arabian made payments of $25,000,000 on January 1 and $40,000,000 on July 1; the building was completed on December 31.

For the construction period, Arabian can capitalize the full $25,000,000 of the first payment and half of the second payment, as noted in the following table:

Date	Payment	Capitalization Period [1*]	Average Payment
1/1	$25,000,000	12/12	$25,000,000
7/1	40,000,000	6/12	20,000,000
			$45,000,000

[1*]The number of months between the payment date and the date when interest capitalization ends.

During this time, Arabian has a loan outstanding on which it pays 7.5% interest. The amount of interest cost it can capitalize as part of the construction project is $3,375,000 ($45,000,000 × 7.5% interest).

Capitalization of borrowing costs terminates when the entity has substantially completed all activities needed to prepare the asset for its intended use. Substantial completion is assumed to have occurred when physical construction is complete; work on minor modifications will not extend the capitalization period. If the entity is constructing multiple parts of a project and it can use some parts while construction continues on other parts, then it should stop capitalization of borrowing costs on those parts that it completes.

EXAMPLE 12.6

Yarmouth Energy is constructing a wind farm off the coast of Cape Cod, Massachusetts. It can begin using each of the wind turbines as they are completed, so it stops capitalizing the borrowing costs related to each one as soon as it becomes usable.

Calculate the borrowing costs in any period by multiplying the interest rate by the average carrying amount of the asset during the period.

 ## What Costs Do I *Not* Include in PP&E?

Do *not* include the following costs in PP&E:

- ○ Administration and general overhead costs
- ○ Costs incurred after an asset is ready for use, but has not yet been used or is not yet operating at full capacity
- ○ Costs incurred that are not necessary to bring the asset to the location and condition necessary for it to operate
- ○ Initial operating losses
- ○ New customer acquisition costs
- ○ New facility opening costs
- ○ New product or service introduction costs
- ○ Relocation or reorganization costs

Do not recognize in PP&E the ongoing costs of servicing a PP&E item, which typically includes maintenance labor, consumables, and minor maintenance parts; these costs should instead be charged to expense as incurred.

 ## When Do I Stop Accumulating Costs in PP&E?

Only recognize costs in the carrying amount of PP&E until the item is in the location and condition for it to be *capable of* operating in the manner intended by management. Thus, no further costs should be added to PP&E once the asset achieves this status, even if it is not yet actually used in the manner intended by management.

Over What Time Periods Do I Allocate Depreciation Expense?

Begin depreciating an asset when it is available for use, even if it is not actually in use at that time. Spread the depreciation on a systematic basis over the asset's useful life. Consider the following factors when determining an asset's useful life:

o *Expected usage.* Refers to the expected volume of production output.
o *Expected wear.* Can be impacted by such factors as the level of maintenance and the number of shifts over which the asset is used.
o *Legal limits.* Caused by government-mandated usage levels or lease expiration dates, for example.
o *Obsolescence.* Can be caused by changes in technology or market demand, for example.

EXAMPLE 12.7

Rollo's Brewery builds a brewery. Part of its brewing equipment is a large mash tun (for mashing), which has an original cost of $250,000. At the time of acquisition, management estimated that the mash tun would have a useful life of ten years, with a residual value of $50,000. Thus, the depreciable asset value was $200,000 ($250,000 − $50,000).

At the end of year seven, management reviews both the useful life and residual value of the mash tun; it concludes that the useful life can be extended to 13 years, due to its use of a spray ball for periodic deep cleaning. Given the longer useful life and greater usage, however, the mash tun's residual value will likely decline to $25,000.

At the end of year seven, Rollo's had accumulated $140,000 of depreciation on the mash tun. The original depreciable asset value of $200,000 has declined to $60,000 because of the ongoing depreciation, but is now increased by the $25,000 reduction in the mash tun's residual value, for a remaining depreciable asset value of $85,000. With the change in useful life, the mash tun can now be depreciated for six more years. Consequently, the future annual depreciation rate should be $14,167 ($85,000 ÷ 6 years).

Stop depreciating the asset at the earlier of the date when it is classified as being held for sale, the date when it is derecognized, or when it is fully depreciated. Thus, do not stop depreciating an asset simply because it is currently idle or retired from active use. However, if the asset is being depreciated based on some method of asset usage, then there may be no depreciation while the asset is not being used.

 ## What Amount of an Asset Do I Depreciate?

The depreciable portion of an asset is its entire cost, less any *residual value*. An asset's residual value is the estimated amount that the owner would currently obtain by disposing of the asset, less any disposal cost, assuming that the asset is at the age and condition to be expected at the end of its useful life. In most cases, the residual value is so small as to be immaterial to the depreciation calculation.

Continue charging depreciation expense until such time as the asset's residual value matches its carrying value, and then stop.

 ## What Depreciation Method Should I Use?

Select a depreciation method that reflects the pattern in which the entity expects to consume the asset's future economic benefits.

Review the depreciation method applied to an asset periodically, and revise the method if there has been a significant change in the pattern of consumption.

The following are some of the acceptable depreciation methods:

○ *Diminishing balance method.* Charges depreciation at a decreasing rate over the useful life of the asset.
○ *Straight-line method.* Charges depreciation at a constant rate over the useful life of the asset.
○ *Units of production method.* Charges depreciation based on expected usage.

EXAMPLE 12.8

Latham Lumber Company harvests timber in western Oregon, and maintains a sawmill on the outskirts of Cottage Grove, Oregon.

(Continued)

Straight-line method. Latham separately depreciates the building that houses its sawmill equipment. This structure cost $3,000,000 to construct, and should be usable for 30 years, with no residual value. Given the steady usage pattern likely to occur, Latham uses the straight-line depreciation method to depreciate it. The annual depreciation is $100,000 ($3,000,000 cost ÷ 30 years).

Diminishing balance method. Latham finds that the band saws it uses in the sawmill wear out fast, and so uses double-declining balance depreciation to reflect their rapid decline in value. Each band saw costs $40,000 and should be fully depreciated, with no residual value, after four years. The diminishing balance method requires use of twice the straight-line rate, multiplied by the book value at the beginning of the year. Any remaining asset value is fully depreciated in the final year. The calculation appears in the following table:

Beginning Balance	Straight Line Rate	Rate Doubler	Annual Depreciation	Remaining Balance
$40,000	× 25%	× 2	= $20,000	$20,000
$20,000	× 25%	× 2	= $10,000	$10,000
$10,000	× 25%	× 2	= $ 5,000	$ 5,000
$ 5,000	× Remaining value		= $ 5,000	$ 0

Units of production method. Latham owns a grapple-skidder to collect downed timber. Its wear pattern is closely tied to the number of trees that it collects, so the units of production method is the most appropriate form of production. The grapple-skidder cost $120,000 and has an estimated residual value of $20,000. Management estimates it can lift 200,000 trees during its estimated useful life, which results in per-unit depreciation of $0.50 ($100,000 depreciable value ÷ 200,000 units of production). In June, the grapple-skidder lifts 2,500 trees, so depreciation during that month is $1,250 (2,500 trees × $0.50/unit).

 ## Which Assets Are Not Depreciated?

Land is not depreciated, since it has an unlimited useful life. If land has a limited useful life, as is the case with a quarry, then it is acceptable to depreciate it over its useful life. If the cost of land includes any costs incurred for site dismantlement and/or restoration, then depreciate these costs over the period over which any resulting benefits are obtained.

If an entity acquires a parcel of land which includes a building, then separate the two assets and depreciate the building.

When Is an Asset Classified as Held for Sale?

You should classify an asset as held for sale when an entity wishes to dispose of or liquidate it. You should classify an asset as held for sale when all of the following criteria are met:

- ○ Management commits to a plan to sell or dispose of the asset
- ○ The asset is available for immediate sale in its current condition
- ○ There is an active program to locate a buyer
- ○ The sale is probable, and should be complete within one year
- ○ The sale price of the asset is reasonable in relation to its fair value
- ○ It is unlikely that the plan to sell will be altered or withdrawn

How Do I Present Assets Classified as Held for Sale?

You should present assets classified as held for sale in a separate line item in the balance sheet.

When Do I Recognize an Impairment Loss on a Fixed Asset?

You should only recognize an impairment loss on an item of property, plant, and equipment if the carrying amount of the asset is not *recoverable* and exceeds its fair value. You should conduct this analysis at the asset group level.

The carrying amount is not recoverable if it exceeds the sum of the undiscounted cash flows you expect to result from the use and disposition of the asset. These cash flow estimates should incorporate assumptions that are reasonable in relation to the assumptions the entity uses for its budgets, forecasts, and so forth. If there are a range of possible cash flow outcomes, then consider using a probability-weighted cash flow analysis. If there are multiple assets in the asset group being tested, then use as the remaining useful life of the group the remaining useful life of the primary asset in the group (which cannot be land or an intangible asset that is not being amortized).

EXAMPLE 12.9

Mother Load Mining operates the Turquoise Ridge gold mine in Nevada. The mine is gradually expanding to follow the deposits, which requires the expansion of sub-surface conveyor belts and other mining equipment. In testing the recoverability of the mine, Mother Load should include in its estimates of future cash flows the future expenditures needed to extend mining operations.

The amount of the impairment loss should be the amount by which the asset's carrying amount exceeds its fair value. An expected present value technique can be used to estimate fair value.

You should test for recoverability whenever circumstances indicate that an asset's carrying amount may not be recoverable. Examples of such instances are:

- ○ Significant decrease in the asset's market price
- ○ Significant adverse change in the asset's manner of use, or in its physical condition
- ○ Significant adverse change in legal factors or the business climate that could affect the asset's value
- ○ Excessive costs incurred to acquire or construct the asset
- ○ Historical and projected operating or cash flow losses associated with the asset
- ○ The asset is more than 50% likely to be sold or otherwise disposed of significantly before the end of its previously estimated useful life

EXAMPLE 12.10

Yarmouth Energy owns a wind farm off the coast of Cape Cod, Massachusetts. The gross cost of the facility is $80,000,000, less $15,000,000 of accumulated depreciation. The company has received a signed letter of intent to buy the facility for $68,000,000; the offer includes a requirement that Yarmouth complete $1,000,000 worth of maintenance prior to the sale. Is the wind farm's value impaired?

No. The carrying amount of the facility (gross cost less depreciation) is $65,000,000, and the fair value less costs to sell is $67,000,000, so its fair value exceeds its carrying amount.

If you recognize an impairment loss, the new carrying amount of the asset is its former carrying amount, less the impairment loss. This means that you should alter the depreciation of that asset to factor in its now-reduced carrying amount.

You cannot reverse a previously-recognized impairment loss.

 ## How Do I Allocate an Impairment Loss to an Asset Group?

If you recognize an impairment loss for an asset group, you should allocate the loss to the assets within the group on a pro rata basis, using the relative carrying amounts of those assets. The only exception is when such an allocation reduces the carrying amount of an asset below its fair value. In this case, you can only allocate that amount of the loss that will bring the asset's carrying amount down to its fair value.

EXAMPLE 12.11

Yarmouth Energy tests an asset group for impairment, and finds that the asset group's carrying amount is not recoverable and exceeds its fair value by $300,000. It allocates the $300,000 impairment to the individual assets within the group in accordance with the following table:

Individual Asset	Carrying Amount	Allocation %	Impairment Allocation	Adjusted Carrying Amount
Asset A	$1,421,000	52%	$(156,000)	$1,265,000
Asset B	993,000	36%	(108,000)	885,000
Asset C	263,000	10%	(30,000)	233,000
Asset D	49,000	2%	(6,000)	43,000
Totals	$2,726,000	100%	$(300,000)	$2,426,000

How Do I Account for Fixed Assets Held for Sale?

If you classify an asset or asset group as held for sale, then you should recognize any write-down to its fair value, less the cost to sell. You can recognize a gain for any subsequent increase in fair value less cost to sell, but only to the extent of cumulative losses that were previously recognized.

Do not depreciate an item of property, plant, or equipment as long as it is classified as held for sale.

If the entity decides not to sell an asset that it had previously classified as held for sale, then reclassify the asset as held and used. On the reclassification date, measure the asset at the lower of its fair value or its carrying amount before it was classified as held for sale, adjusted for any depreciation that would have occurred while it was classified as held for sale. The net effect is likely to be a "catch up" charge to expense for the depreciation that did not occur while the asset was held for sale.

How Do I Account for Fixed Assets that Are to be Abandoned?

If you plan to abandon an asset or asset group, you should consider it abandoned as soon as the entity ceases to use it. When you cease to use the asset or asset group, its carrying amount should equal its salvage value (if any).

If the entity plans to abandon an asset before the end of its previously-estimated useful life, then you should revise depreciation estimates to incorporate the shortened useful life.

If an asset or asset group is temporarily idled, do not classify it as abandoned.

When Do I Derecognize an Asset?

An asset is derecognized upon its disposal, or when no future economic benefits can be expected from its use or disposal. Derecognition can arise from a variety of events, such as an asset's sale, scrapping, or donation.

You can recognize a gain or loss from an asset's derecognition, though a gain on derecognition cannot be recorded as revenue. The gain or loss on derecognition is calculated as the net disposal proceeds, minus the asset's carrying value.

What Information Do I Disclose about Property, Plant, and Equipment?

You should disclose the following information about property, plant, and equipment in the financial statements or the accompanying notes:

○ Depreciation expense
○ Totals for the major classes of depreciable assets
○ Accumulated depreciation
○ Description of the methods used to compute depreciation

 What Information Do I Disclose about Fixed Asset Impairment?

You should disclose the following information about the impairment of property, plant, and equipment in the financial statements or the accompanying notes:

○ Describe the impaired asset or asset group, and the circumstances leading to the impairment
○ The amount of the impairment loss
○ The method used to determine fair value
○ If a public company, then note the segment in which the impaired asset is reported

CHAPTER 13

INTANGIBLE ASSETS

 What Is Goodwill?

Goodwill is the excess of the cost of an acquired entity over the net of all amounts assigned to assets acquired and liabilities assumed.

 What Is a Reporting Unit?

A reporting unit is an operating segment or one level below an operating segment. A component of an operating segment is a reporting unit if the component constitutes a separate business for which the entity compiles financial information, and management reviews the results of that component.

If two components of an operating segment have similar characteristics, then aggregate them into a single reporting unit. If all components of all operating segments are similar, it is possible that the entire entity may be a single reporting unit.

 How Do I Assign Goodwill to Reporting Units?

You should assign all goodwill acquired in a business combination to the entity's reporting units; do so to every reporting unit that is expected to benefit from the synergies of the combination. The methodology you use to do so should be reasonable and supportable, and consistently applied. This application is solely for goodwill impairment testing purposes–you do not have to record assigned goodwill in the reporting segment in which a reporting unit is located (see the Operating Segments chapter).

If you are assigning goodwill to a reporting unit that has not been assigned any of the assets acquired or liabilities assumed in the acquisition, then you can calculate the amount of goodwill to assign to that unit by determining the difference between the fair value of the reporting unit before the acquisition and its fair value afterwards; this difference in fair value represents the amount of goodwill to assign to the reporting unit.

EXAMPLE 13.1

Hoboken Highlanders, makers of Scottish clothing for New Jersey residents, attempts to expand out of its small niche by acquiring California Creations. Hoboken pays $4,000,000 for the acquisition. It assigns the payment to a variety of California assets and liabilities, as noted in the following table:

Purchase price	$4,000,000
− Accounts receivable	(380,000)
− Inventory	(450,000)
− Manufacturing equipment	(2,000,000)
− Acquired customer list	(600,000)
= Goodwill	$570,000

How Frequently Should I Test for Goodwill Impairment?

You should test the goodwill of a reporting unit for impairment on an annual basis, which you can perform at the same time of each succeeding year. It is not necessary to test all reporting units at the same time.

You should also test the goodwill of a reporting unit for impairment between the normal annual tests if there is a change that would more likely than not reduce its fair value below its carrying amount. Examples of such changes are:

○ Adverse action by a regulator
○ Loss of key personnel
○ Significant adverse change in legal factors
○ The reporting unit is more likely than not to be sold or disposed of

○ There was a goodwill impairment loss for a subsidiary of the reporting unit
○ Unanticipated competition

How Do I Determine Goodwill Impairment?

Impairment occurs when the carrying amount of goodwill
exceeds its implied fair value. To measure it, follow this
two-step process:

1. Compare the fair value of a reporting unit with its
carrying amount (including goodwill). If the fair
value exceeds the carrying amount, then there is no
goodwill impairment, and you do not need to continue to the next step. If the carrying amount exceeds
the fair value, then proceed to the next step. The best
source of information for the fair value of a reporting unit is from a quoted market price in an active
market, followed by a valuation technique based on
multiples of earnings or revenue.
2. This step involves measuring the amount of the impairment loss. Compare the implied fair value of the
reporting unit's goodwill with its carrying amount.
To calculate implied fair value, allocate the fair value
of a reporting unit to all of its assets and liabilities,
including any unrecognized intangible assets, as
though you were accounting for a business acquisition and the fair value was the price paid to acquire
it. The implied fair value of goodwill is the excess of
the fair value of the reporting unit over the amounts
assigned to its assets and liabilities.

If the carrying amount of the goodwill exceeds its implied fair value, then recognize an impairment amount
equal to the excess. You cannot recognize an impairment
loss greater than the goodwill carrying amount.

Should I Test Goodwill Impairment at the Subsidiary Level?

Yes. You should test goodwill at the subsidiary level,
using the subsidiary's reporting units. If you recognize a
goodwill impairment loss at the subsidiary level, and the
event causing the subsidiary's impairment is more likely
than not to reduce the fair value of the reporting unit for
which the subsidiary is a part, then you must also conduct
a goodwill impairment test for that reporting unit.

Can I Roll Forward a Fair Value Determination to the Next Year?

Yes. If you have constructed a detailed determination of the fair value of a reporting unit, it is acceptable to carry forward the analysis from one year to the next if the situation meets all of these criteria:

○ The assets and liabilities in the reporting unit have not changed significantly since the most recent fair value analysis.

○ The result of the last fair value determination was that the reporting unit's fair value exceeded its carrying amount by a substantial margin.

○ The likelihood of the current fair value being less than the reporting unit's carrying amount is remote.

Can I Reverse a Goodwill Impairment Loss?

No. Once you recognize an impairment loss, you cannot subsequently reverse it.

How Do I Account for Goodwill in a Reporting Unit Disposal?

When you dispose of a reporting unit, include the associated amount of goodwill in the reporting unit's carrying amount in order to determine gain or loss on disposal. If the disposal is part of a reporting unit, then assign goodwill based on the relative fair values of the business to be disposed of and that portion being retained.

EXAMPLE 13.2

The Long Walk Shoe Company is disposing of a portion of its Steppin' Out sneaker reporting unit. The entire Steppin' Out reporting unit has a fair value of $5,000,000, and Long Walk has received an offer of $2,000,000 for a portion of that unit. Accordingly, Long Walk should assign 40% ($2,000,000 ÷ $5,000,000) of the goodwill already assigned to the Steppin' Out division to the portion being sold.

What Goodwill Information Should I Disclose?

You should disclose the following information about goodwill in an entity's financial statements or accompanying notes:

○ Aggregate amount of goodwill, as a separate line item in the balance sheet
○ Aggregate amount of goodwill impairment losses, as a separate line item in the income statement
○ Goodwill impairment associated with a discontinued operation
○ Changes in the carrying amount of goodwill during the period
○ The amount of any unallocated goodwill and the reasons for not allocating it
○ For each goodwill impairment loss, describe the facts and circumstances leading to the impairment, the amount of the impairment, and the method used to determine the fair value of the associated reporting unit

EXAMPLE 13.3

Elbrus Investments records the following changes in the carrying amount of its goodwill:

(000s)	Gold Mining Segment	Iron Foundry Segment	Total
Balance as of January 1, 20X1	$2,400	$3,800	$6,200
Goodwill acquired during the year	300	100	400
Impairment losses	(400)	–	(400)
Goodwill written off related to business unit sale	–	(500)	(500)
Balance as of December 31, 20X1	$2,300	$3,400	$5,700

What Is an Intangible Item?

An intangible asset is an asset other than a financial asset that lacks physical substance. You can only acquire an intangible asset, either individually or as part of a group. All of the following are examples of intangible items:

Copyrights	Franchises	Mortgage servicing rights
Customer lists	Import quotas	Motion pictures
Customer loyalty	Market share	Patents
Customer relationships	Marketing rights	Software

What Is a Class of Intangible Assets?

A class of intangible assets is a group of assets having a similar nature and use in an entity's operations. Examples of intangible asset classes are brand names, copyrights, franchises, licenses, models, patents, and recipes.

What Is a Defensive Intangible Asset?

A defensive intangible asset is an intangible asset acquired by an entity which does not intend to actively use the asset, but instead intends to hold the asset to prevent others from using it.

You should account for a defensive intangible asset as a separate unit of accounting, and assign it a useful life that reflects expected consumption of the asset's benefits. The benefit of preventing other entities from using an intangible asset is the direct and indirect cash flows related to their not being able to use it.

A defensive asset rarely has an indefinite life, because its effect diminishes over time due to various competitive factors.

How Do I Account for Internally Developed Intangible Assets?

If an entity incurs costs to internally develop, maintain, or restore intangible assets that are not specifically identifiable, have indeterminate lives, or are inherent in the business, then you should recognize them as expenses when they are incurred.

How Do I Initially Measure an Intangible Asset?

You should initially measure an intangible asset that is acquired either alone or with a group of assets at its fair value. You can measure fair value at the more reliably measurable of either the fair value of the consideration paid or the fair value of the net assets acquired.

You should determine the fair value based on the assumptions that market participants would use to price the asset. If the entity does not intend to use the asset at its highest and best use, you should still measure it at its fair value.

How Do I Subsequently Measure an Intangible Asset?

If an intangible asset has a finite useful life, then you should amortize it over that period, less any residual value. The correct amortization period is the interval over which the asset is expected to contribute either directly or indirectly to the entity's future cash flows. The amortization method should reflect the pattern of economic benefits that you expect from the intangible asset; if there is no way to reliably determine the benefits pattern, then amortize using the straight-line method.

EXAMPLE 13.4

Hostetler Corporation acquires a patent that will expire in eight years. Hostetler actively markets a product that is protected by the patent, from which Hostetler expects to receive significant cash flows for at least eight years. Hostetler has accepted a firm offer from a competitor to sell the patent in five years.

Hostetler should amortize the patent asset over its five-year useful life.

You can estimate the asset's useful life based on a review of all of the following factors:

○ The asset's expected use
○ The expected useful life of a related asset
○ Any legal, regulatory, or contractual provisions that may limit its useful life, or enable its renewal or extension
○ The effects of obsolescence, demand, competition, and other economic factors on the asset
○ The amount of maintenance expenditures needed to obtain the expected amount of future cash flows from the asset

---

EXAMPLE 13.5

The Better Back Chair Company acquires the mailing
list of the Chiropractor Today magazine, with the intent of sending direct mail pieces to everyone on the
list. Better Back's marketing manager believes the
mailing list will have a useful life of between six and
18 months, and so adopts a useful life of 12 months
for the purpose of amortizing the acquisition cost of
the mailing list.

You should periodically evaluate the asset's remaining
useful life to determine whether it is necessary to revise the
remaining amortization period. If you do change the amortization period, then amortize the asset's remaining carrying value over the remainder of the revised useful life.

If there are no legal, regulatory, contractual, competitive, economic, or other factors limiting the life of an intangible asset, then it has an indefinite useful life, and you
should not amortize it. If conditions change and there are
no longer any limiting factors on the life of an intangible
asset that was previously amortized, you can stop amortizing the remaining carrying amount of the asset.

EXAMPLE 13.6

Harlequin Taxi owns a taxi operator's license, which
it acquired for $30,000. The license term is five years,
after which the city government routinely allows the
existing license holder to renew for a nominal fee. Under this scenario, Harlequin assigns the asset an indefinite useful life.

After two years, the city government announces
that it will auction all taxi licenses to the highest bid-
der at the end of their five-year terms. There is now a
three-year term left on Harlequin's license, so it amortizes the license at the rate of $10,000 per year in each
of the remaining three years.

 ## What Is the Residual Value of an Intangible Asset?

An intangible asset may have a residual value if you
expect it to have a useful life for another entity following

its use by the current entity, and both of the following conditions apply:

- ○ There is a commitment from a third party to acquire the intangible asset at the end of its useful life.
- ○ You can determine the residual value by referring to an exchange transaction in an existing market, and you expect that market to still exist at the end of the asset's useful life.

If the residual value increases to an amount equal to or greater than the asset's carrying amount, then there is no further amortization charge until such time as the residual value declines below the asset's carrying value.

EXAMPLE 13.7

Ralph's Brewery acquires the rights to a hops separation process patent for $150,000, which it believes it can use to increase the efficiency of its brewing operation. Ralph's believes it can achieve net cash inflows from the patent for at least the next ten years. Ralph's also has a signed commitment letter from Great Wall Breweries to buy the patent in three years for $100,000.

Based on this information, Ralph's amortizes the patent asset over a three-year period before it intends to sell the patent to Great Wall. The residual value of the patent is the present value of the $100,000 price at which Great Wall intends to buy it in three years.

The residual value of an intangible asset with an indefinite life is zero.

How Do I Test Intangible Assets for Impairment?

You should recognize an impairment loss on an intangible asset if its carrying amount is not recoverable and its carrying amount exceeds its fair value. Once you reduce such an asset's carrying amount with an impairment adjustment, you cannot subsequently reverse the impairment amount. Conduct impairment testing annually, or more frequently if circumstances indicate that the asset may be impaired.

EXAMPLE 13.8

Discharge Fire Candy acquires the Red Hot Chili Balls candy line from a competitor, along with the trademark for the Red Hot Chili Balls name. Discharge initially considered the Red Hot Chili Balls name to have an indefinite useful life, along with continuing cash flows at the current level. However, management estimates that recent competition from the Atomic Jalapenos candy line will reduce future cash inflows by 25%.

Based on this information, there is no need for Discharge to assign a useful life to the Red Hot Chili Balls trademark, but it should determine if the fair value is now less than its carrying amount. If so, Discharge should record an impairment charge to reduce the carrying amount to the fair value.

You should combine two or more intangible assets with indefinite lives into a single unit of accounting for impairment testing purposes under circumstances where some portion of the following indicators are in evidence:

○ The assets have been used together, and are complementary.
○ If the assets had been acquired in the same acquisition, they would have been recorded together as one asset.
○ The assets would yield the highest price if they were sold as a group.

Conversely, do not combine multiple intangible assets into a single unit of accounting if some portion of the following indicators is in evidence:

○ Each asset independently generates cash flows.
○ If sold, each asset would probably be sold separately.
○ The entity is considering selling one or more of these assets separately.
○ The assets are used exclusively by different asset groups.
○ Limitations on the economic life of one asset may not impact the other assets.

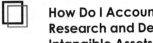

How Do I Account for Acquired Research and Development Intangible Assets?

If an entity acquires intangible assets in a business combination that are used in research and development activities, you should assign them indefinite useful lives until the associated activities have been completed or abandoned.

Once the entity has completed or abandoned the related research and development activities, you should determine the useful life of these assets and begin amortizing them over that period.

How Do I Present Intangibles Information in the Financial Statements?

You should aggregate all intangible assets and present them as a separate line item in the balance sheet, though you may also present more detailed information as separate line items. As appropriate, you may also present amortization expense and impairment losses for intangible assets in separate income statement line items.

What Information Should I Disclose about Intangible Assets?

You should disclose the following information about intangible assets in the notes accompanying the financial statements, and only in the period of asset acquisition:

○ For those intangible assets subject to amortization, report both in total and by major asset group the total amount of intangible assets acquired, significant residual values, and the weighted-average amortization period.

○ For those intangible assets not subject to amortization, report both in total and by major asset group the total amount of intangible assets acquired.

○ The amount of research and development assets acquired in the period, written off in the period, and the income statement line item in which the write-offs are aggregated.

In addition, on an ongoing basis, report the following:

○ For those intangible assets subject to amortization, the gross carrying amount, accumulated amortization, amortization expense for the period, and the estimated amortization expense for each of the next five years.

○ For those intangible assets not subject to amortization, the total carrying amount.

○ The policy on treating costs incurred to renew or extend the terms of intangible assets.
○ For those intangible assets not renewed or extended in the period, the costs incurred in the period to renew or extend the assets.
○ For intangible assets having renewal or extension terms, the weighted-average period before the next renewal or extension, broken down by major asset class.

EXAMPLE 13.9   NOTE XX: ACQUIRED INTANGIBLE ASSETS

(000s)	As of December 31, 20X1	
	Gross Carrying Amount	Accumulated Amortization
Amortized intangible assets		
Copyrights	$250	$ (50)
Patents	1,500	(375)
Trademarks	500	(100)
Total	$2,250	(525)
Unamortized intangible assets		
Broadcast license	$100	
Other	50	
Total	$ 150	

Aggregate Amortization Expense:

For year ended 12/31/20X1	$180

Estimated Amortization Expense:

For year ended 12/31/20X2	$180
For year ended 12/31/20X3	162
For year ended 12/31/20X4	140
For year ended 12/31/20X5	80
For year ended 12/31/20X6	67

If there are impairment losses, then also disclose the following information:

○ Describe the impaired asset and the facts and circumstances of the impairment.
○ The amount of the impairment loss.

- ○ The method for determining fair value.
- ○ The location of the impairment loss in the income statement.
- ○ If the entity is publicly held, the segment in which the impaired asset is reported.

 ## What Is Internal-Use Software?

Internal-use software is used solely to meet an entity's internal needs; it can be used by the entity in the production of products or services. During its development or modification, the entity has no substantive plan to market the software externally. Internal-use software is not part of or included in a product or service.

EXAMPLE 13.10

Hostetler Corporation develops its own treasury workstation software, as well as software for payroll direct deposit, employee alterations of work schedules, bad debt collections, on-line contract searches, and a staff purchasing catalogue. It does not intend to market any of these software packages. Hostetler can account for all of them as internal-use software.

 ## What Is a Preliminary Project Stage?

Software development is in a preliminary project stage when the entity is still making decisions to allocate resources between alternative projects, determining performance requirements, initiating vendor demonstrations, exploring performance requirements, determining the existence of required technologies, selecting a vendor, and/or selecting development or installation consultants.

 ## How Do I Initially Account for Software Developed or Obtained for Internal Use?

Costs associated with internal-use software development are either charged to expense as incurred or capitalized, as described further in these bullet points:

- ○ *Preliminary project stage.* Expense all related costs as incurred.

○ *Application development stage* (involves software coding, hardware installation, and testing). Capitalize development costs. These costs include the acquisition or development of software to access or convert old data by new systems. All other data conversion costs should be expensed. Further, you should charge all costs associated with training to expense in the period incurred.

○ *Post-implementation and operation stage* (involves training and maintenance). Expense all internal and external training as well as maintenance costs as incurred.

○ *Upgrades and enhancements.* Only capitalize these costs if it is probable that they will result in additional functionality. Thus, if an upgrade is essentially maintenance, charge it to expense.

You should not capitalize any costs associated with an internal-use software project until the preliminary project stage has been completed, management authorizes project funding, it is probable that the project will be completed, *and* the software will be used for the intended function.

You should stop capitalizing costs as soon as the software development project is substantially complete and ready for its intended use.

The only costs that you are allowed to capitalize for internal-use software are external direct costs of materials and services, payroll and related costs for those directly associated with the project, and interest costs incurred during development. You cannot capitalize any general and administrative or overhead costs.

Example 13.11

The Charleston Cracker Company is developing an automated control system for its baking operations. It pays $350,000 to a consulting firm for programming services, $100,000 to buy various software modules from other suppliers, $620,000 in payroll-related costs for software coding and testing, $10,000 for related employee travel, and $140,000 of related general and administrative costs.

Charleston can capitalize all of these costs except for the $140,000 of general and administrative costs, which it must charge to expense as incurred.

If it is probable that software will not be completed (as evidenced by programming difficulties, significant cost overruns, or technology obsolescence), then report it at the lower of its carrying amount or fair value less costs to sell. It is presumed that the value of the software at this point is zero, barring evidence to the contrary.

How Do I Amortize Capitalized Internal-Use Software Costs?

The default amortization method you should use is the straight-line method, unless there is another method more representative of the pattern of software use.

You should consider technological obsolescence and competition when determining the estimated useful life over which to amortize capitalized software costs. Given the speed of technological change, the useful life of software may be short.

If different components of a software project are ready for their intended use at different times, then begin amortizing each component as soon as it is ready for its intended use, even if the software has not yet been placed in service. You should consider software to be ready for its intended use when all substantial testing has been completed. However, if the functionality of a component is entirely dependent upon the completion of other modules, then delay amortization until the other modules are also ready for their intended use.

Do I Test Capitalized Internal-Use Software for Impairment?

Yes, you should test internal-use software for impairment. Events that may trigger an impairment test are a significant change in the software's use, a significant change to the program, or development costs significantly exceeding expectations.

What if I Subsequently Sell Internal-Use Software?

Once internal-use software development is complete, an entity may decide to market the software. If so, you should apply the proceeds from any sales (net of incremental costs) against the carrying amount of the software. You cannot recognize a profit until the carrying amount of the software has declined to zero. After that time, you may record additional sales as revenue.

How Do I Account for Software That is Being Replaced?

When you initiate new software development, review the remaining useful life of the software being replaced; this may call for an acceleration of any remaining amortization. Also, once new software is ready for its intended use, you should charge any remaining unamortized cost related to the software being replaced to expense.

How Do I Account for Website Development Costs?

You can capitalize some website development costs. The treatment of these costs is as follows:

- ○ *Planning stage.* Planning stage activities include project planning, hardware identification, technology analysis, vendor demonstrations, vendor selection, legal considerations, and software tools identification. Charge all planning stage costs to expense.
- ○ *Application and development stage.* Application and development stage activities include the acquisition of software tools, buying an Internet domain name, developing code, purchasing various types of hardware, installing applications on web servers, and testing applications. Capitalize these costs.
- ○ *Graphics development stage.* Graphics development stage activities include web page design, color, images, and the general look and feel of the site. Capitalize these costs.
- ○ *Content development stage.* Content development stage activities include text and various types of graphical information, which may be acquired or developed internally. Charge content input costs and data conversion costs to expense.
- ○ *Operating stage.* Operating stage activities include training, administration, backup, usage analysis, security reviews, and other types of maintenance. Charge these costs to expense as incurred. However, if a cost relates to providing additional functions or features, then capitalize it.
- ○ *Website hosting.* Charge hosting fees to expense over the period of benefit.

- *Domain procurement.* Capitalize the costs to obtain and register an Internet domain.
- *Search engine registration.* Charge these costs to expense as incurred.

You cannot capitalize website development costs, irrespective of the preceding discussion, if you plan to market the software externally.

The following table shows the proper accounting treatment of the various expenditures incurred to develop a web site:

Expenditure Type	Charged to Expense	Capitalized
Feasibility study	√	
Define specifications	√	
Evaluate alternatives	√	
Final system selection	√	
Domain name procurement		√
Computer hardware		√
Software development		√
Application installation		√
Web page design		√
Stress testing		√
Overhead allocations	√	
System backups	√	
System maintenance	√	
General and administrative	√	

The best estimate of a web site's useful life is generally short, so the amortization of its carrying amount will be compressed.

CHAPTER 14

ASSET RETIREMENT AND ENVIRONMENTAL OBLIGATIONS

 What Is an Asset Retirement?

An asset retirement is the other-than-temporary removal of a long-lived asset from service. Removal from service includes the sale, abandonment, recycling, or some other form of disposal. It does *not* include the temporary idling of an asset.

 What Is an Asset Retirement Obligation?

An asset retirement obligation is an obligation associated with the retirement of a long-lived asset. The existence of an asset retirement obligation is only based on a current law, statute, or contract, not on a forecasted change in the law or forecasted changes in the interpretation of a law.

 How Do I Initially Account for an Asset Retirement Obligation?

You should recognize the fair value of a liability for an asset retirement obligation in the period incurred, if you can make a reasonable estimate of its fair value. You should be able to make such an estimate if any of these conditions exist:

○ The fair value of the obligation is clearly included in the acquisition price of an asset.
○ There is an active market for transferring the obligation.
○ There is sufficient information available to apply an expected present value method.

If you cannot make such an estimate, then recognize the liability as soon thereafter as you can make such an estimate.

If an entity acquires a tangible asset having an existing asset retirement obligation, you should recognize the liability at the asset acquisition date.

When you initially recognize a liability for an asset retirement obligation, you should also capitalize its cost as an increase in the carrying amount of the related asset.

The only allowable method for determining the fair value of an asset retirement obligation is the expected present value technique, using a discount rate that is based on a credit-adjusted risk-free rate. You can infer the appropriate rate of interest from the observable rate of interest of some other liability having cash flow characteristics similar to those of the liability being measured.

How Do I Subsequently Account for an Asset Retirement Obligation?

If an entity incurs an additional asset retirement obligation (ARO) in a subsequent period, then account for it as an additional layer of the original liability. Measure each ARO layer at its fair value, and use it to alter the carrying amount of the asset. If you make an upward adjustment in the amount of undiscounted estimated cash flows, then discount these changes at the current risk-adjusted risk-free rate. If you make a downward adjustment in the amount of undiscounted estimated cash flows, then discount these changes using the credit-adjusted risk-free rate existing when you originally recognized the ARO.

Example 14.1
Through the first ten years of its existence, the nuclear power plant in Cooper, Nebraska accumulates an ARO of $212 million. Over the next ten-year period, the Cooper facility accumulates additional contamination, for which the fair value of the associated ARO is $72 million. The two layers of ARO combine for a total ARO of $284 million.

You should use a systematic method for allocating the ARO to expense over the useful life of the associated asset by applying an interest method of allocation to the amount of the liability, using the interest rate you originally used when you initially measured the ARO. In each period, recognize this expense as "accretion expense." Accretion expense is *not* considered to be interest expense.

In addition, in each succeeding period, you should recognize period-to-period changes in the ARO liability resulting from revisions to the timing or amount of the original estimate of undiscounted cash flows.

EXAMPLE 14.2

The Gillette Coal Company operates an open-pit coal mine in the Powder River Basin area of Wyoming. It is legally required to complete landscape remediation in six years, when it expects to complete mining operations. Gillette uses the following assumptions in determining its asset retirement obligation:

○ The current cost to remediate the property is $14,000,000, to be performed by an outside contractor.
○ The risk-free interest rate is 4%.
○ Gillette adds 3% to the risk-free rate to reflect the effect of its credit standing.
○ The assumed rate of inflation over the six-year period is 3%.

Given an average inflation rate of 3% per year for the next six years, the current remediation cost of $14,000,000 increases to $16,717,000 by the end of the sixth year. The expected present value of the $16,717,000 payout, using a credit-adjusted risk-free rate of 7%, is $11,139,206 ($16,717,000 × 0.66634 discount rate).

Gillette then uses the 7% credit-adjusted risk-free rate to calculate the amount of annual accretion, as shown in the following table:

Year	Beginning Liability Balance (January 1)	Accretion	Ending Liability Balance (December 31)
1	$11,139,206	$779,751	$11,918,957
2	11,918,957	834,334	12,753,291
3	12,753,291	892,738	13,646,029
4	13,646,029	955,230	14,601,259
5	14,601,259	1,022,097	15,623,356
6	15,623,356	1,093,644	16,717,000

The accretion expense and depreciation expense for the six years are outlined in the following table. The depreciation is based on straight-line depreciation

(Continued)

for six years of the expected present value of the asset retirement obligation ($11,139,206 ÷ 6 years).

Year	Accretion Expense	Depreciation Expense	Total Expense
1	$779,751	$1,856,534	$2,636,285
2	834,334	1,856,534	2,690,868
3	892,738	1,856,534	2,749,272
4	955,230	1,856,534	2,811,764
5	1,022,097	1,856,534	2,878,631
6	1,093,644	1,856,534	2,950,178
			$16,717,000 *

*Rounded up slightly

When Gillette completes the remediation work, the actual cost of remediation is $16,890,000.

Key journal entries associated with the asset retirement obligation are:

DATE: JANUARY 1, YEAR 1

Mine remediation asset	11,139,206	
Asset retirement obligation liability		11,139,206

Records the initial fair value of the asset retirement obligation liability

DATE: DECEMBER 31, YEARS 1-6

Depreciation expense	1,856,534	
Accumulated depreciation		1,856,534

Records straight-line depreciation on the asset retirement cost

Accretion expense	As scheduled	
Asset retirement obligation liability		As scheduled

Records accretion expense on the asset retirement obligation liability

DATE: DECEMBER 31, YEAR 6

Asset retirement obligation liability	16,717,000	
Loss on settlement of asset retirement obligation	173,000	
Accounts payable (outside contractor)		16,890,000

If, over time, it becomes apparent that no retirement activities will be required, then you should reduce both the liability and the remaining unamortized ARO to zero.

 ## How Do I Account for a Conditional Asset Retirement Obligation?

There may be an obligation to perform an asset retirement activity, but there is uncertainty about the timing or method of settlement. If so, this is a conditional asset retirement obligation, and you should recognize a liability for its fair value, if it is possible to reasonably estimate such a liability. You may need to factor any uncertainties into an expected present value technique by assigning probabilities to cash flows, and use the result as an estimate of the fair value of the conditional asset retirement obligation.

It should be possible to create an estimated present value technique if one of the following three conditions exists:

1. Other parties have specified the settlement date and method of settlement for the obligation. The only remaining uncertainty is whether the obligation will be enforced.
2. There is available information from which you can reasonably estimate the range of possible settlement dates and potential methods of settlement.
3. There are probabilities associated with potential settlement dates and methods of settlement.

There are multiple sources of information that may provide a basis for estimating potential settlement dates and settlement methods, including the entity's past practices, industry practices, management's intentions, or the estimated life of the asset.

The narrower the range of time over which an entity can settle an obligation and the fewer the potential methods of settlement, the more likely it will be for an entity to reasonably estimate the fair value of an asset retirement obligation.

If there is a low likelihood of being required to perform under an asset retirement obligation, you must still recognize a liability. You should factor this uncertainty level into your measurement of the fair value of the liability, but it does not impact the decision of whether or not to recognize a liability at all.

When Do I Account for the Settlement of an Asset Retirement Obligation?

You normally settle an ARO when the associated asset is retired, though there may be cases where a partial settlement of the ARO is required before the associated asset has been fully retired.

What Information Do I Disclose about Asset Retirement Obligations?

You should classify accretion expense as an operating item in the income statement. In addition, you should disclose the following information in the notes accompanying the financial statements:

- General description of the asset retirement obligations and related assets.
- The fair values of those assets legally restricted for settlement of the asset retirement obligations.
- Reconciliation of the beginning and ending asset retirement obligations, showing changes in liabilities incurred, liabilities settled, accretion expense, and revisions in estimated cash flows.
- If you cannot reasonably estimate the fair value of an asset retirement obligation, then discuss the reasons for it.

What Is a Hazardous Substance?

A hazardous substance is any element, compound, mixture, solution, or substance that may present substantial danger to the public health or the environment. It also includes specifically designated substances under the Federal Water Pollution Control Act, Resource Conservation and Recovery Act, Clean Air Act, and the Toxic Substances Control Act. This definition excludes petroleum, natural gas, or synthetic gas useable for fuel.

When Should I Accrue a Liability for an Environmental Remediation Obligation?

You should accrue a liability for an environmental remediation obligation when it is *probable* that an entity has incurred a liability, and you can *reasonably estimate* the amount of the liability (which initially may be a range of possible losses).

An environmental remediation obligation is *probable* if both of the following elements are present:

- ○ It has been asserted that the entity is responsible for remediation.
- ○ It is probable that the entity will be held responsible; this is likely the case if litigation has commenced, and the entity has either arranged for the disposal of hazardous substances at a site, or transported such substances to the site, or is the current or previous owner or operator of the site.

Reasonable estimates of the amount of an environmental remediation obligation tend to require significant modification over time, as you collect more information about the extent and types of hazardous substances at a site, the types of technology required for remediation, evolving standards of what is considered acceptable remediation, and both the number and financial condition of other potentially responsible parties.

It may not be possible to determine some components of a liability for an environmental remediation obligation, especially in the early stages of a remediation process. If so, recognize a liability for those components of the liability that can be reasonably estimated.

EXAMPLE 14.3

Acme Chemicals has sent waste to a Superfund site, and appears to be the sole potentially responsible party. Acme agrees to perform a remedial investigation and feasibility study. While Acme does not yet know the costs it will incur to fulfill its obligations, it does have a relatively tight range of cost estimates for the study. Thus, Acme should accrue its best estimate for the cost of the study, and then accrue additional costs at a later date, when it obtains estimates for the actual remediation work.

Are There Benchmarks When I Should Evaluate Environmental Remediation Obligation Liabilities?

Some federal statutes indicate benchmarks at which you should review and recognize remediation liabilities. The following six benchmarks are defined by the Resources

Conservation and Recovery Act for a Superfund remediation liability:

1. *Identification as a potentially responsible party.* If an entity receives notification that it may be a responsible party, or becomes aware that such may be the case, then it should review its records to determine if it has been associated with the site. If the entity can reasonably estimate some portion of the liability, it should recognize that amount.

2. *Receipt of unilateral administrative order.* If an entity receives an order to take action or risk penalties, it should accrue a liability for the indicated remediation.

3. *Participation in a remedial investigation-feasibility study.* If an entity agrees to pay the cost of a study, then accrue a liability for its share of the cost of the study, and any other liabilities that it can reasonably estimate.

4. *Completed feasibility study.* A feasibility study should include the calculation of a minimum remediation liability; if so, accrue a liability for the indicated amount.

5. *Issued record of decision.* The Environmental Protection Agency specifies a preferred remedy, which further refines the amount of the potential liability. This will likely call for an adjustment to the accrued liability.

6. *Remedial design through operation and maintenance.* This phase includes actual site remediation, and so involves the most precise cost estimates, which an entity uses to further refine its accrued liability adjustments. This phase continues through post-remediation monitoring.

How Do I Initially Account for Environmental Remediation Obligations?

You should record an environmental remediation liability based on your estimate of an entity's allocable share of a remediation liability. To do so, follow these five steps:

1. *Other parties.* Identify those parties potentially responsible for the site.

2. *Likelihood of payment.* Assess the likelihood that the other parties will pay their share of the liability. This is based on a review of their financial condition.

3. *Percentage allocation.* Determine the percentage of the total liability to allocate to the entity. This percentage should be based on the percentages agreed to by the various parties, or assigned by a consultant, or determined by the Environmental Protection Agency (EPA). If you use a different source for the percentage, then you must justify it with such information as experience with comparable situations or internal data refuting the EPA's determination.

4. *Derive costs.* Compile all direct costs of the remediation effort, and the costs of those employees spending significant time on remediation activities. These costs include pre-cleanup activities, remedial actions, activities related to government oversight, and post-remediation monitoring.

5. *Recovery costs.* If there are litigation costs related to potential recoveries, charge them to expense as incurred until it is probable that the entity will realize its claim. From that point forward, you can include remaining legal costs in the compilation of remediation costs.

When estimating remediation costs, you should estimate the amounts as of the dates when you expect them to be performed, which may be some time in the future. If

EXAMPLE 14.4

Acme Chemicals is named as a potentially responsible party in an environmental remediation situation. The various potentially responsible parties use outside arbitration to allocate fair share costs among the participating parties. The arbitrator computes the following allocations:

	% Allocation
Acme Chemicals	25%
Botulism Bionics Corp.	30%
Chemical Depot, Inc.	20%
Subtotal	75%
Orphan share (no potentially responsible party can be identified)	10%
Recalcitrant share (nonparticipating, potentially responsible parties)	15%
Total	100%

(Continued)

> The total remediation cost is estimated to be $2 million. Of that amount, Acme's direct share is $500,000 ($2,000,000 × 25% share), plus Acme's share of amounts allocable to those other parties not expected to pay their shares, which is $166,667 (25%/75% × the 25% orphan and recalcitrant share × $2 million).

so, you should include such factors as an inflation index and the effect of productivity improvements on the work force from gaining experience from other remediation activities.

 ## Should I Charge all Environmental Contamination Treatment Costs to Expense?

In most cases, you should charge environmental contamination treatment costs to expense. However, you may instead capitalize these costs in the following situations:

- ○ The costs incurred extend the life, increase the capacity, or improve the safety or efficiency of the property. The property must be owned by the entity.
- ○ The costs mitigate or prevent environmental contamination that has not yet occurred, and improve the property compared to its condition when built or acquired.
- ○ The costs were incurred to prepare for sale of the property.

If you capitalize treatment costs, then you should depreciate them over their remaining useful lives.

EXAMPLE 14.5

Acme Chemicals applies a rust prevention coating to a chemical storage tank. Acme spends $50,000 to apply the coating. By doing so, Acme improves the tank's condition compared to when it was built, and also mitigates the possibility that future rust will cause tank leaks. Acme can capitalize the $50,000 cost of the rust prevention coating, and should depreciate it over the remaining useful life of the storage tank.

How Should I Subsequently Account for Environmental Remediation Obligations?

There are likely to be ongoing changes in the estimated amount of a remediation liability, not only because of changes in the remediation cost, but also because of changes in the cost allocation amongst the various responsible parties, and changes in the laws governing the remediation.

If you have a change in a remediation liability, such as a revision to an entity's estimate of its share of the liability, then account for it as a change in estimate. As a change in estimate, there is no retroactive alteration in the remediation liability–the change only applies to the current and future periods.

How Do I Account for Recoveries?

An entity may claim a cost recovery from such other parties as insurers, potentially responsible parties, governments, and third-party funds. You should only recognize an asset relating to a recovery when it is probable that the entity will realize a recovery claim. If the recovery claim is currently under litigation, then you should assume that the claim cannot be realized.

You should measure a potential claim at its fair value.

How Should I Disclose Environmental Remediation Obligations?

You should not classify environmental remediation costs as extraordinary. Instead, include these costs as a component of operating income. If there is a recovery of environmental losses from a third party, then you should include it in the same line item as the remediation costs in the income statement.

If there are remediation expenses related to discontinued operations, then classify them as part of discontinued operations.

In addition, you should disclose whether the accrual for environmental remediation liabilities is measured on a discounted basis.

You should consider including the following disclosures in the notes accompanying the financial statements–disclosure is encouraged, but not required:

- The circumstances that trigger recognition of loss contingencies
- The policy for recognizing recoveries
- Environmental remediation loss contingencies
- The estimated time frame for disbursements
- The estimated time frame for realization of recognized probable recoveries
- Why you cannot estimate a loss or range of losses
- For individual sites, the cost accrued, the nature of the loss contingency, the entity's share of the obligation, the status of regulatory proceedings, and the resolution time frame

---

EXAMPLE 14.6 DISCLOSURE NOTE XX

Nevada Nuclear has been notified by the Environmental Protection Agency that it is a potentially responsible party with respect to environmental impacts identified at our nuclear waste containment facility in Tonopah, Nevada. Although a loss is probable, it is not possible at this time to reasonably estimate the amount of any obligation for remediation of the Tonopah site that would be material to Nevada Nuclear's financial statements, because the allocation among potentially responsible parties and remediation alternatives have not yet advanced to the stage where a reasonable estimate of any loss that would be material can be made. We expect that a reasonable estimate of a material obligation, if any, will be possible in 20X1.

CHAPTER 15

CONTINGENCIES

What Is a Contingency?

A contingency is a condition or situation involving uncertainty regarding a possible gain or loss that will be resolved when a future event either occurs or fails to occur. For example, loss contingencies are put in place for possible injuries caused by an entity's products, property damage, asset expropriation, litigation, and claims or assessments.

A contingency is *probable* if an event is likely to occur. A contingency is *reasonably possible* if the chance of an event is more than remote but less than likely. A contingency is *remote* if an event has a slight chance of occurring.

When Do I Recognize a Loss Contingency?

You should recognize a loss contingency when you can reasonably estimate the amount of the loss *and* it is probable that an asset has been impaired or a liability has been incurred at the date of the financial statements.

Do not delay accruing a loss until there is complete certainty regarding its amount. Instead, you should accrue some amount as soon as the loss can be estimated within a range.

If there is a reasonable possibility that a contingency event has arisen after the date of an entity's financial statements, but before the statements are available to be issued, do not accrue a loss contingency, on the grounds that the event did not exist as of the date of the financial statements.

If a loss contingency relates to a specific period, but it is not yet possible to estimate the amount of the loss, then accrue the contingency as soon as such information becomes available–do not record the accrual as a prior period adjustment.

What Amount Should I Accrue for a Loss Contingency?

If there is a range of potential losses associated with a loss contingency, accrue that amount that appears to be a better estimate than any other amount within the range. If no amount within the range appears better than another, accrue the minimum amount in the range.

EXAMPLE 15.1

Advanced Turbines has sold a wind turbine to Yarmouth Energy for its wind farm off the coast of Cape Cod in Massachusetts. Yarmouth calls in Advanced to fix a turbine that is malfunctioning. Advanced is liable for any repairs during the first year of operation. Advanced believes the most likely problem is worn bearings, which is a simple replacement costing $500. However, all other potential problems with the turbine are more expensive to repair, costing anywhere from $10,000 to $80,000. Advanced should accrue a loss contingency for the $500 amount, since that outcome is the most likely.

EXAMPLE 15.2

Lullaby Swing Company makes the Baby Care Swing product, for which it provides a one-year full warranty for all manufacturing defects. Lullaby sells 100,000 Baby Care Swings in the current year. Several consumers report a broken bolt that can lead to failure of the device. It appears likely that Lullaby should conduct a recall of all 100,000 swings. Initial indications are that the cost of the recall will range from $10,000,000 to $32,000,000, with no number in this range being more probable than another. Lullaby accrues a loss contingency for the $10,000,000 low-end estimate in the range, but plans to continually review cost estimates and revise its accrual as it obtains better cost information.

Should I Record a Loss Contingency for Uninsured Risks?

Every entity has some uninsured risks. It may have elected not to insure a risk because it is very unlikely to occur, or there may be a deductible clause in an insurance contract. It is likely that these events are not probable, and so do not meet the likelihood criterion for recording a loss contingency.

 ## Should I Record a Gain Contingency?

No. You should not record a contingency that may result in a gain; if you were to do so, this may constitute revenue recognition before its realization, which is prohibited.

If you intend to disclose information about a gain contingency, avoid misleading implications regarding the likelihood of realizing the gain.

 ## When Should I Record a Loss Contingency for Expropriation?

You should record a loss contingency for expropriation when expropriation appears to be imminent, and the compensation the entity will receive will be less than the carrying amount of the assets that will be expropriated. If there is a declaration by a government regarding an upcoming expropriation, then expropriation can be considered an imminent event.

 ## When Should I Record a Loss Contingency for Litigation?

There is not a clearly defined point at which you should record a loss contingency. You should consider the following factors when determining whether to record a loss contingency or at least disclose the underlying situation:

- The period in which the cause of the litigation occurred
- The degree of probability that the outcome of the litigation will be unfavorable. You should consider the following factors when assessing this probability:
  - The nature of the litigation
  - The progress of the case
  - The views of legal counsel
  - The entity's experience in similar cases
  - The experience of other entities in similar cases
  - Management decisions regarding how to respond to the suit (such as an out-of-court settlement)
- The ability to make a reasonable estimate of the amount of the prospective loss

You should disclose the existence of the litigation if it is reasonably possible, but not probable, that there will be an unfavorable outcome, or if you cannot determine the amount of the loss.

EXAMPLE 15.3

Littleton Petrochemicals is involved in litigation at the end of its fiscal year, and, following a trial, the judge hands down an unfavorable verdict. There is not yet any resolution of the amount of damages that Littleton will have to pay. Littleton estimates that the judgment will be for not less than $2 million or more than $5 million. No amount within that range appears to be more likely than any other amount. Littleton should record a loss contingency for the minimum amount in the range of estimates, which is $2 million.

What Information Should I Disclose for a Loss Contingency?

You should disclose the following information about loss contingencies in the notes accompanying the financial statements:

- ○ The nature and amount of the accrual.
- ○ Indicate if it is at least reasonably possible that a change in the estimate of probable liability could occur in the near term.
- ○ The existence of a contingency if there is a reasonable possibility of a loss. If so, note the nature of the contingency and estimate the possible loss or range of losses (or state that an estimate cannot be made).

It may be necessary to disclose loss contingencies that arise after the date of an entity's financial statements but before they are issued, in order to keep the financial statements from being misleading. If so, disclose the nature of the contingency and either estimate the amount of the loss or state that you cannot make such an estimate.

There is no need to disclose a loss contingency for an unasserted claim, unless it is probable that a claim will be asserted, and there is a reasonable possibility that there will be an unfavorable outcome.

CHAPTER 16

DEBT

What Is the Effective Interest Method of Accounting for Debt?

When an entity issues a bond, it is typically at a fixed, or stated, interest rate. If the investor believes that the rate is too high, then it will only pay a reduced price for the bond, thereby reducing the effective interest rate. Conversely, if the stated interest rate is too high, then the investor will be willing to pay more for the bond, thereby reducing the effective interest rate.

EXAMPLE 16.1

The Arabian Knights Security Company issues $1,000,000 of bonds at a stated rate of 8% in a market where similar issuances are being bought at 11%. The bonds pay interest once a year, and are to be paid off in ten years. Investors purchase these bonds at a discount in order to earn an effective yield on their investment of 11%. The discount calculation requires Arabian's controller to determine the present value of 10 interest payments at 11% interest, as well as the present value of $1,000,000, discounted at 11% for ten years. The result is as follows:

Present value of 10 payments of $80,000	= $80,000 × 5.8892	= $471,136
Present value of $1,000,000	= $1,000,000 × .3522	= $352,200
		$823,336
	Less: stated bond price	1,000,000
	Discount on bond	$176,664

The journal entry is:

Cash	823,336	
Discount on bonds payable	177,664	
Bonds payable		1,000,000

If investors buy a bond at an effective interest rate that differs from the stated rate, then the issuing entity should amortize the difference between the face value of the bond and the amount paid by investors, recognizing the amortization over the remaining life of the bond.

EXAMPLE 16.2

To continue with the preceding example, the effective interest method holds that, in the first year of interest payments, Arabian's controller would determine that the market interest expense for the first year would be $90,567 (bond stated price of $1,000,000 minus discount of $176,664, multiplied by the market interest rate of 11%). The resulting journal entry is:

Interest expense	90,567	
Discount on bonds payable		10,567
Cash		80,000

The reason why only $80,000 is listed as a reduction in cash is that the company only has an obligation to pay an 8% interest rate on the $1,000,000 face value of the bonds, which is $80,000. The difference is netted against the existing Discount on Bonds Payable account. The following table shows the calculation of the discount to be charged to expense each year for the full ten-year period of the bond, where the annual amortization of the discount is added back to the bond's present value, eventually resulting in a bond present value of $1,000,000 by the time principal payment is due, while the discount has dropped to zero.

Year	Beginning Bond Present Value[4]	Unamortized Discount	Interest Expense[1]	Cash Payment[2]	Credit to Discount[3]
1	$ 823,336	$176,664	$ 90,567	$80,000	$10,567
2	$ 833,903	$166,097	$ 91,729	$80,000	$11,729

3	$ 845,632	$154,368	$ 93,020	$80,000	$13,020
4	$ 858,652	$141,348	$ 94,452	$80,000	$14,452
5	$ 873,104	$126,896	$ 96,041	$80,000	$16,041
6	$ 889,145	$110,855	$ 97,806	$80,000	$17,806
7	$ 906,951	$ 93,049	$ 99,765	$80,000	$19,765
8	$ 926,716	$ 73,284	$101,939	$80,000	$21,939
9	$ 948,655	$ 51,346	$104,352	$80,000	$24,352
10	$ 973,007	$ 26,994	$107,031	$80,000	$26,994
	$1,000,000	$ 0			

(1) = Bond present value multiplied by the market rate of 11%
(2) = Required cash payment of 8% stated rate, multiplied by face value of $1,000,000
(3) = Interest expense reduced by cash payment
(4) = Beginning present value of the bond plus annual reduction in the discount

If the results of using a straight-line amortization method are not materially different from using the effective interest method, then it is acceptable to use the straight-line method.

How Should I Classify Debt that Has Covenants?

A loan may require periodic compliance with lender covenants. A covenant violation may give a lender the right to demand immediate payment of the loan.

You should classify a debt obligation as non-current, unless there has been a covenant violation that gives the lender the right to call the debt, and it is probable that the entity will not be able to comply with the covenant within the next 12 months. If both of these criteria have occurred, then classify the debt as a current liability.

You should not classify a debt as a current liability if the lender has waived the right to demand repayment for more than one year, the entity has cured the covenant violation, or it is probable that the entity will cure the violation within the specified grace period.

EXAMPLE 16.3

Hostetler Corporation has a $10 million long-term loan that requires compliance with a 2:1 current ratio at the end of each reporting quarter. At the end of the third quarter, Hostetler reports a 1.7:1 current ratio, which violates the covenant. The lender waives its right to call the debt for at least one year, but retains the future
(Continued)

covenant requirement. Hostetler's management does not feel that it can remedy the current ratio compliance issue within the next 12 months.

Though the lender has provided a waiver, Hostetler still cannot comply with the covenant, so it should classify the loan as a current liability.

How Should I Classify Debt that Has Subjective Acceleration Clauses?

There may be a subjective acceleration clause in a loan agreement that allows a lender to demand accelerated payment, usually if the entity has recurring losses or cash-flow problems. Depending on the circumstances, you may need to classify such debt as a current liability. However, if the lender has historically not accelerated the due dates of loans, and the financial condition of the entity is strong, it may not be necessary to reclassify the debt or disclose the situation.

How Should I Classify Debt that Is Due on Demand?

If a loan agreement contains a clause stating that the lender can demand payment at any time, then classify the debt as a current liability. This is the case even if there is no expectation that the lender will demand payment within the current year.

How Should I Classify Short-Term Debt that Is To Be Refinanced with Long-Term Debt?

An entity may expect to refinance its short-term debt with debt that will have a longer due date, thereby not requiring the use of working capital in the current year. You can record short-term debt as a long-term liability only if one of the following two conditions is met:

1. *Post-balance sheet activity.* After the date of the balance sheet but before issuance of the financial statements, the entity issues a long-term obligation or equity security in order to refinance the short-term obligation.

2. *Financing agreement.* Before the balance sheet is issued, the entity commits to a financing agreement, clearly stating that it can refinance the short-term obligation on a long-term basis. Further, this agreement does not expire within one year, is not cancelable by the lender within one year (except in response to a violation of the agreement), there is no violation as of the balance sheet date, there is no indication of a violation thereafter (or the entity has received a waiver for it), and the lender is financially capable of honoring the arrangement.

If the amount of long-term obligation that an entity enters into is less than the amount of the short-term obligation that it is intended to offset, then only exclude that portion of the short-term obligation from current liabilities that does not exceed the amount of the long-term obligation.

If the amount of funds available through the long-term obligation may vary (as would be the case if it is based on collateral whose value changes over time), then only exclude that amount of short-term obligation from current liabilities that equals a reasonable estimate of the minimum proceeds from the long-term obligation during the current fiscal year.

If an entity repays a short-term obligation before it obtains long-term refinancing, then you should record the short-term obligation as a current liability.

EXAMPLE 16.4

Chestnuts International, maker of hardwood furniture, has $5,000,000 of short-term obligation as of December 31. It intends to refinance the obligation with a long-term bond issuance. Once the bond issuance closes on January 31, Chestnuts finds that it has obtained $4,750,000. It uses the entire amount of the proceeds to pay down the short-term obligation. Chestnuts issues its fiscal year financial statements on February 1.

Because Chestnuts did not replace the short-term obligation with a sufficient amount of long-term obligation, it must still classify $250,000 of its short-term obligation as a current liability. However, it did obtain replacement financing for the remainder of the short-term obligation before the financial statements were issued, so it can reclassify the remaining $4,750,000 of the obligation as a long-term liability.

What Information Should I Disclose about Debt?

You should disclose the following information in the notes accompanying the financial statements:

- The aggregate amount of maturities and sinking fund requirements for each of the five years following the balance sheet date.
- If callable debt is classified as a long-term liability, disclose the circumstances.
- If a short-term obligation is excluded from current liabilities, describe the financing agreement and the terms of any refinancing.
- The existence of any subjective acceleration clauses, though not if the likelihood of acceleration is remote.
- The rights and privileges of the various securities outstanding.

 What Are Detachable Warrants?

Debt may be issued with detachable warrants, which may trade separately from the debt instrument. Since they are detachable, the two elements of a debt offering exist independently and should be treated as separate securities. A holder of a detachable warrant may eventually exercise it and purchase the entity's stock, or may allow it to expire.

The debt issuer includes the detachable warrants in its sale of the debt security in order to obtain a lower cash interest cost than would be possible without the warrants, while a buyer is interested in the profit it could earn by converting the warrants to stock if the entity's stock price rises.

 How Do I Account for Detachable Warrants?

You should allocate the proceeds from the sale of a debt instrument with detachable warrants between the two items, based on their freestanding relative fair values on the issuance date. Allocate the portion of the proceeds assigned to the warrants to paid-in capital, and the remainder to the debt instrument.

EXAMPLE 16.5

Hostetler Corporation issues $1 million of convertible debt that includes 200,000 detachable warrants. The fair value of the convertible debt without the warrants is $900,000 and the fair value of the detachable warrants is $300,000 without the debt. Based on their relative fair values, Hostetler assigns $750,000 to the debt (calculated as $900,000 ÷ ($900,000 + $300,000)) and $250,000 to the detachable warrants (calculated as $300,000 ÷ ($900,000 + $300,000)). The resulting journal entry is:

Cash	$1,000,000	
Additional paid-in capital		$250,000
Debt		750,000

What Is a Convertible Security?

A convertible security is a hybrid instrument that its holder can either convert into common stock or convert into cash–but not both, as is the case with a debt security having a detachable warrant.

The debt issuer includes the convertibility feature in a debt security in order to obtain a lower cash interest rate, and also may deliberately set a favorable conversion rate in order to encourage conversion of the debt into equity–thereby eliminating the need for repayment. The buyer is interested in convertible securities because of the possibility of earning a profit by converting them to stock if the entity's stock price rises.

How Do I Account for a Convertible Security?

You should allocate a portion of the proceeds from a convertible security to additional paid-in capital. The amount of the allocation is based on the intrinsic value of that feature on the issuance date. *Intrinsic value* is the difference between the conversion price and the fair value of the stock into which the security is convertible, multiplied by the number of shares into which the security is convertible.

If a convertible instrument includes multiple discounts at which conversion can occur, then calculate the intrinsic value using those conversion terms most beneficial to the investor.

However, if the issuing entity sells the convertible security at a price not significantly in excess of its face amount, then do not allocate any portion of the proceeds to additional paid-in capital.

EXAMPLE 16.6

Hephaestus Construction issues a convertible instrument for $900,000. The instrument is convertible three years after issuance at a conversion price of $12, which is also the fair value of the stock on the issuance date. Another provision of the agreement states that the conversion price will reset to $9 if Hephaestus does not go public and attain a per-share price of at least $15 within three years.

If there is no change in Hephaestus' current situation, then the conversion price will be $9 (that is, the company does not go public). Therefore, the intrinsic value of the conversion option is:

Convertible debt issuance amount	$ 900,000
÷ Conversion price if no change in circumstances	÷ $ 9/share
Number of shares issuable if no change in circumstances	100,000 shares
Initial conversion price	$12/share
− Conversion price if no change in circumstances	− 9/share
= Variance	$ 3/share
Intrinsic value (100,000 shares x $3/share)	$ 300,000

Do Issuance Costs Affect the Calculation of Intrinsic Value?

Intrinsic value is the difference between the conversion price and the fair value of the stock into which a security is convertible, and is the basis upon which to allocate a portion of the proceeds from a convertible security to additional paid-in capital. You should not allocate any costs associated with the issuance of convertible instruments to the calculation of the intrinsic value of a conversion option.

 ## How Do I Account for Contingently Adjustable Conversion Ratios?

If the conversion ratios in a convertible security agreement are adjustable based on future events, then do not calculate the intrinsic value of the security that is allocable to additional paid-in capital until the contingent event occurs. Then compute the number of shares that the investor will receive because of the new conversion price. Then compare this share total to the number that would have been received by the investor before the contingent event, and multiply the variance by the stock price on the commitment date to determine the incremental intrinsic value that is caused by resolution of the contingent event.

 ## How Do I Account for Unamortized Discounts Upon the Conversion of a Convertible Security?

If a convertible security is converted to equity, then credit the carrying amount of the debt, as well as any unamortized premium or discount, to the capital account. Do not recognize a gain or loss on the conversion.

 ## How Do I Account for Interest Forfeited as Part of a Debt Conversion?

An investor may convert a convertible instrument to equity some time after an interest payment date. If so, and the terms of the conversion state that any accrued but unpaid interest is forfeited, then you should accrue interest from the last payment date to the conversion date (net of income tax effects), and charge it to interest expense and credit it to capital.

 ## How Do I Account for an Inducement Offer?

If an entity offers an inducement to the holders of its convertible debt securities to convert them to equity, then recognize an expense equal to the fair value of the securities and other consideration transferred in the conversion transaction in excess of the fair value of securities issuable under the original conversion terms. Measure the fair value of the consideration transferred as of the date when the inducement offer is accepted by the investor.

EXAMPLE 16.7

The Ginseng Plus retail chain, purveyor of natural food supplements, issues a $1,000 face amount 7% convertible bond that matures in ten years. The carrying amount of the bond in Ginseng's financial statements is $1,000, and investors can convert it into Ginseng's common stock at a conversion price of $20 per share. At the beginning of Year 3, the convertible bond has a market value of $1,250. Ginseng induces investors to convert their bonds by reducing the conversion price to $10 if they convert within the next 30 days. The market price of Ginseng's common stock on the conversion date is $25.

The value of the securities issuable by Ginseng in accordance with the original conversion privilege is:

Face amount	$1,000
÷ Original conversion price	÷ $20/share
Number of shares issuable under original conversion privileges	50 shares
× price per common share	× $25
Value of securities issuable under original conversion privileges	$1,250

The value of the securities issued by Ginseng to investors is:

Face amount of convertible bond	$1,000
÷ New conversion price	÷ $10/share
Number of shares issued following conversion	100 shares
× price per common share	× $25
Value of securities issued	$2,500

Thus, the fair value of the incremental consideration offered by Ginseng is:

Value of securities issued	$2,500
Value of securities issuable under original agreement	1,250
Fair value of incremental consideration	$1,250

Based on the above information, Ginseng records the following entry for the conversion of the convertible debt to equity:

Convertible debt	$1,000	
Debt conversion expense	1,250	
Common stock		$2,250

What Is a Product Financing Arrangement?

A product financing arrangement is any of the following arrangements:

○ The sponsoring party sells a product to a third party and agrees to repurchase it in a related transaction.
○ The sponsoring party arranges to have a third party purchase a product on the sponsor's behalf, and agrees to purchase the product from the third party.
○ The sponsoring party controls how a product is dispositioned that was acquired by a third party.

The *sponsoring party* is the entity seeking to finance a product whose future use is pending. In brief, the sponsoring party agrees to either purchase or guarantee the purchase of a product, and at a predetermined price that is equal to the original sale price plus carrying and financing costs. The arrangement may involve a resale price guarantee, where the sponsoring party agrees to pay the difference between the specified price and the resale price for any products sold to third parties.

How Do I Account for Product Financing Arrangements?

You should account for a product financing arrangement as a borrowing, rather than a sale. The sponsoring entity owns the product, so it should report the product as an asset and the related obligation as debt. If another entity purchases the product on the sponsoring entity's behalf and the sponsoring entity agrees to purchase the product, then the sponsoring entity records an asset and the related liability as soon as the other entity purchases the product.

Any costs of the product in excess of the sponsoring entity's original production costs are financing and holding costs.

EXAMPLE 16.8

Manila Rope Company sells a portion of its inventory to Acme Financing, and in a related transaction agrees to repurchase it. In exchange for this transaction, Acme pays Manila $500,000. Upon receipt of these funds, Manila records the following entry:

Cash	500,000	
Debt – Product financing arrangement		500,000

Upon completion of the predetermined holding period, Manila buys back the inventory from Acme for $510,000. There are no holding costs. Manila records the following entry:

Debt – Product financing arrangement	500,000	
Interest expense	10,000	
Cash		510,000

How Do I Account for an Early Debt Extinguishment?

Consider the following factors when accounting for the early extinguishment of debt:

- ○ *Stock payment.* The debtor may exchange various classes of its stock for a reduced repayment of debt. If so, determine the reacquisition price of the extinguished debt by either the value of the stock issued or the value of the debt–whichever is more clearly evident.
- ○ *Gain or loss.* Record the difference between the cash acquisition price of the debt and its net carrying amount as a gain or loss.
- ○ *Exchange with different terms.* If there is an exchange of debt instruments with substantially different terms, treat the debt being replaced as a debt extinguishment. This may result in the recognition of a gain or loss. If the original and new debt instruments

are substantially different (their present values are different by at least 10%), then record a gain or loss measured as the difference between the fair value of the replacement debt and the carrying amount of the extinguished debt.

How Do I Account for Line of Credit or Revolving Debt Changes?

An entity may arrange with its lender to alter the terms of its line of credit or revolving debt. The result may be a new agreement or a traditional term-debt arrangement. The accounting for the change differs, depending on the following two scenarios:

1. *Greater borrowing capacity.* If the borrowing capacity of the new arrangement is greater than or equal to that of the old arrangement, then associate any unamortized deferred costs related to the old arrangement with the new arrangement.
2. *Lower borrowing capacity.* If the borrowing capacity of the new arrangement is less than that of the old arrangement, then write off any unamortized deferred costs related to the old arrangement in proportion to the decrease in borrowing capacity from the old arrangement. Amortize the remaining amount over the term of the new arrangement.

EXAMPLE 16.9

Tallahassee Trailers has a $10 million, three-year line of credit with its bank, of which one year has been completed. Given a decline in Tallahassee's financial situation, the bank presses for a reduced borrowing capacity. The parties agree to a revised line of credit having a maximum borrowing capacity of $5 million, and the remaining term is still two years. There are $40,000 of unamortized costs associated with the original line of credit.

There has been a 50% decline in borrowing capacity from the original arrangement, so Tallahassee writes off half of the $40,000 of unamortized costs associated with the original line of credit, and amortizes the remainder over the two-year term of the new arrangement.

What Is a Troubled Debt Restructuring?

A troubled debt restructuring occurs when a creditor for economic or legal reasons related to its debtor's financial difficulties grants a concession to the debtor that it would not normally consider. A debtor is experiencing financial difficulties when it is in default on any of its debt, is in bankruptcy, has securities that have been delisted, cannot obtain funds from other sources, projects that it cannot service its debt, or there is significant doubt about whether it can continue to be a going concern.

A concession may involve restructuring the terms of a debt (such as a reduction in the interest rate or principal due, or an extension of the maturity date) or payment in some form other than cash, such as an equity interest in the debtor.

A debtor that can obtain funds from sources other than the lender at market interest rates is generally not involved in a troubled debt restructuring. Further, you should not classify a debt restructuring as a troubled debt restructuring in any of the following situations:

- The fair value of the payment accepted by the creditor in full payment of the debt at least equals the carrying amount of the debt, as recorded by the debtor.
- The creditor reduces the interest rate on the debt to reflect either a decrease in market interest rates or reduced risk.
- The debtor issues new marketable debt having an effective interest rate near current market rates.

 ## How Do I Account for Troubled Debt Restructurings?

If the debtor restructures its debt, it should record a gain, which is the excess of the debt's carrying amount over the fair value of any assets transferred or the fair value of any equity interest granted to the creditor in full payment of the debt. If the fair value of the debt is more easily measurable than the fair value of the assets transferred, then use that number instead.

If there is a partial settlement of a debt, then you should *only* use the fair value of the assets transferred or the equity interest granted to measure the amount paid to the creditor.

The debtor should include the gain in net income in the period when the transfer occurs.

If there is only a modification of the terms of a troubled debt restructuring, rather than a transfer of assets or equity, then you should not change the carrying amount of the debt unless the carrying amount exceeds the total future cash payments under the new terms. However, if the total future cash payments are less than the carrying amount of the debt, then you should reduce the carrying amount to equal the total future cash payments specified under the new debt terms and recognize a gain in the amount of the reduction.

The debtor should not recognize a gain on a restructured debt when there are indeterminate future cash payments, so long as the maximum of the total future cash payments may still exceed the carrying amount of the debt.

EXAMPLE 16.10

The Powder Hound Snowmobile Company has a note payable with Forlorn Bank that has an outstanding balance of $240,000 and accrued interest payable of $15,000. Powder Hound finds itself in financial difficulties and works with Forlorn to restructure its debt. Forlorn agrees to accept from Powder Hound a warehouse building having a book value of $200,000 and a fair value of $210,000, which will fully settle the debt. Powder Hound records the following entry to record the settlement:

Note payable	240,000	
Interest payable	15,000	
Fixed assets – building	10,000	
Fixed assets – building		200,000
Gain on asset transfer		10,000
Gain on debt settlement		55,000

What Information Should I Disclose about a Troubled Debt Restructuring?

Include the following information about troubled debt restructurings in the notes accompanying the financial statements:

- ○ The principal terms changes for each restructuring
- ○ The aggregate restructuring gain
- ○ The aggregate gain or loss on the transfer of assets to the creditor
- ○ The per-share amount of the aggregate restructuring gain
- ○ The total amounts that are contingently payable on restructured debt, and the conditions under which these amounts will be either payable or forgiven

In addition, consider whether the terms of the restructured debt require a reclassification into or out of the current liabilities classification in the balance sheet.

CHAPTER 17

EQUITY

What Is Equity?

Equity is the difference between the total of all recorded assets and liabilities on the balance sheet.

What Is Additional Paid-In Capital?

Additional paid-in capital is any payment received from investors for stock that exceeds the par value of the stock. *Par value* is the stated value of a stock, which is recorded in the capital stock account. Equity distributions cannot drop the value of stock below this minimum amount.

What Is Stock?

The owners of common stock are the true owners of the corporation. Through their share ownership, they have the right to dividend distributions, vote on various issues presented to them by the Board of Directors, elect members of the Board of Directors, and to share in any residual funds left if the corporation is liquidated. If the company is liquidated, they will not receive any distribution from its proceeds until all creditor claims have been satisfied, as well as the claims of holders of all other classes of stock. There may be several classes of common stock, which typically have different voting rights attached to them; the presence of multiple types of common stock generally indicates that some shareholders are attempting some degree of preferential control over a company through their type of common stock.

Most types of stock contain a par value, which is a minimum price below which the stock cannot be sold. The original intent for using par value was to ensure that a residual amount of funding was contributed to the company, and which could not be removed from it until dissolution of the corporate entity. In reality, most common stock now has a par value so low (typically anywhere from a penny to a dollar) that its original intent no longer works. Thus, though the accountant still tracks par value separately in the accounting records, it has little meaning.

If an investor purchases a share of stock at a price greater than its par value, the difference is credited to an additional paid-in capital account. For example, if an investor buys one share of common stock at a price of $82, and the stock's par value is $1, then the entry would be:

Cash	82
Common stock – par value	1
Common stock – additional paid-in capital	81

What Are Retained Earnings?

Retained earnings are a company's accumulated earnings since its inception, less any distributions to shareholders.

Can I Appropriate Retained Earnings?

Yes. It is permissible to appropriate retained earnings for specific purposes, as long as you show the appropriation within the shareholders' equity section of the balance sheet.

You cannot charge costs or losses to a retained earnings appropriation.

What Is a Stock Split?

A stock split involves the issuance of a multiple of the current number of shares outstanding to current shareholders. For example, a one-for-two split of shares when there are currently 125,000 shares outstanding will result in a new amount outstanding of 250,000 shares. This is done to reduce the market price on a per-share basis. In addition, by dropping the price into a lower range, it can have the effect of making it more affordable to small investors, who may then bid up the price to a point where the split stock is cumulatively more valuable than the un-split stock.

A stock split is typically accompanied by a proportional reduction in the par value of the stock. For example, if a share with a par value of $20 were to be split on a two-for-one basis, then the par value of the split stock would be $10 per share. This transaction requires no entry on a company's books.

A reverse split may also be accomplished if a company wishes to proportionally increase the market price of its stock. For example, if a company's common stock sells for $2.35 per share and management wishes to see the price trade above the $20 price point, then it can conduct a ten-for-one reverse split, which will raise the market price to $23.50 per share while reducing the number of outstanding shares by 90%. In this case, the par value per share would be increased proportionally, so that no funds were ever removed from the par value account.

There is no accounting entry associated with a stock split, simply a notation in the financial statements that the number of shares has increased. However, if a split occurs without a change in the par value, then funds must be shifted from the additional paid-in capital account to the par value account.

EXAMPLE 17.1

If 250,000 shares were to be split on a one-for-three basis, creating a new pool of 750,000 shares, and the existing par value per share of $2 were not changed, then the accountant would have to transfer $1,000,000 (the number of newly-created shares times the par value of $2) from the additional paid-in capital account to the par value account to ensure that the legally mandated amount of par value per share was stored there.

 ## What Is a Stock Dividend?

A stock dividend is the issuance by a corporation of its common stock to its common shareholders without any consideration. If a corporation issues less than 25% of the previously outstanding shares, debit retained earnings for the fair market value of the shares to be paid, and credit the capital and additional paid-in capital accounts. If the issuance is for a greater proportion of the previously outstanding shares, then treat the transaction as a stock split.

 ## How Do I Account for a Stock Dividend?

When there is a stock dividend, you should transfer from retained earnings to the capital stock and additional paid-in capital accounts an amount equal to the fair value of the additional shares issued.

If a company is closely held, you can elect not to capitalize retained earnings, other than to meet legal requirements.

 What Is Treasury Stock?

If the Board of Directors elects to have the company buy back shares from shareholders, the stock that is brought in-house is called treasury stock.

 How Do I Account for Treasury Stock Using the Cost Method?

The most common method of accounting for an entity's purchase of its own stock is the *cost method*. Under this approach, the cost at which shares are bought back is listed in a treasury stock account. When the shares are subsequently sold again, any sale amounts exceeding the repurchase cost are credited to the additional paid-in capital account, while any shortfalls are first charged to any remaining additional paid-in capital remaining from previous treasury stock transactions, and then to retained earnings if there is no additional paid-in capital of this type remaining.

EXAMPLE 17.2		
The Board of Directors of Hostetler Corporation chooses to buy back 500 of its common shares at $60 per share. The entry is:		
Treasury stock	30,000	
Cash		30,000

If management later decides to permanently retire treasury stock that was originally recorded under the cost method, then it backs out the original par value and additional paid-in capital associated with the initial stock sale, and charges any remaining difference to the retained earnings account.

EXAMPLE 17.3

To continue with the previous example, if the 500 shares had a par value of $1 each, had originally been sold for $25,000, and all were to be retired, the entry would be as follows:

Common stock – par value	500	
Additional paid-in capital	24,500	
Retained earnings	5,000	
Treasury stock		30,000

If instead, Hostetler subsequently chooses to sell the shares back to investors at a price of $80 per share, the transaction is:

Cash	40,000	
Treasury stock		30,000
Additional paid-in capital		10,000

If treasury stock is subsequently sold for more than it was originally purchased, the excess amount may also be recorded in an additional paid-in capital account that is specifically used for treasury stock transactions; the reason for this segregation is that any subsequent sales of treasury stock for less than the original buy-back price requires the accountant to make up the difference from any gains recorded in this account. If the account is emptied and there is still a difference, then the shortage is made up from the additional paid-in capital account for the same class of stock, and then from retained earnings.

 ## How Do I Account for Treasury Stock Using the Constructive Retirement Method?

When there is no intention of ever re-selling treasury stock, it is accounted for at the point of purchase from shareholders under the *constructive retirement method*. Under this approach, the stock is assumed to be retired, so the original common stock and additional paid-in capital accounts are reversed, with any loss on the purchase being charged to the retained earnings account, and any gain being credited to the additional paid-in capital account.

EXAMPLE 17.4

Amalgamated Munitions Corporation buys back 500 shares at $60 per share. The original issuance price was $52, with a par value of $1. The corresponding journal entry is:

Common stock – par value	500	
Additional paid-in capital	25,500	
Retained earnings	4,000	
Cash		30,000

Under the constructive retirement approach, no treasury account is used, since the assumption is that the shares are immediately retired from use, rather than being parked in a treasury stock holding account.

How Do I Account for an Enforced Stock Buyback?

A special case arises when a company is forced to buy back shares at above-market prices under the threat of a corporate takeover. When this happens, the difference between the repurchase price and the market price must be charged to expense in the current period.

What Is a Stock Subscription?

Stock subscriptions allow investors or employees to pay in a consistent amount over time and receive shares of stock in exchange. When such an arrangement occurs, a receivable is set up for the full amount expected, with an offset to a common stock subscription account and the Additional Paid-in Capital account (for the par value of the subscribed shares). When the cash is collected and the stock is issued, the funds are deducted from these accounts and shifted to the standard common stock account.

EXAMPLE 17.5

The Slo-Mo Molasses Company sets up a stock subscription system for its employees and they choose to purchase 10,000 shares of common stock with a par value of $1 for a total of $50,000. The entry is:

Stock subscriptions receivable	50,000	
Common stock subscribed		40,000
Additional paid-in capital		10,000

When Slo-Mo receives the $50,000 cash payment, it offsets the Stock Subscriptions Receivable account, and shifts funds stored in the Common Stock Subscribed account to the Common Stock account, as noted in the following entry:

Cash	50,000	
Stock subscriptions receivable		50,000
Common stock subscribed	50,000	
Common stock		50,000

What Is a Share-Based Payment?

A share-based payment transaction occurs when the purchaser of goods or services pays the supplier with its own equity instruments. In such a case, the purchasing entity should recognize the fair value of the equity instruments granted, or the fair value of the consideration received (whichever is more reliably measurable) in the same period as if it had paid cash for the goods or services.

The purchaser should measure the value of the equity grant on the earlier of the date, when a commitment for performance is made, or when the supplier has completed performance. "Performance commitment" is deemed to have occurred if there is a sufficiently large disincentive for non-performance to make performance probable (as shown in Example 17.6).

If no specific further performance is required of the supplier at the time of the equity grant, then the purchaser should recognize the associated expense in the period of the grant. If the supplier still needs to fulfill a performance requirement prior to earning the equity instrument, then the purchaser should record the equity payment as a prepaid asset and charge it to expense as the supplier earns it.

EXAMPLE 17.6

Hephaestus Construction has retained Scribe & Sons to design its new corporate headquarters. Scribe agrees to accept 10,000 shares of Hephaestus $1 par

(Continued)

value common stock in exchange for its design services, though the award declines by half if Scribe cannot deliver the drawings as of the scheduled due date,
which is in six months. This is a sufficiently large disincentive for Hephaestus to judge that a performance
commitment has occurred as of the contract date.

On the contract date, Hephaestus measures the
value of the stock payment as of the performance
commitment date, when the price per share is $6. On
this date, the 10,000 shares are valued at $60,000. Dur-
ing each of the six months of the design process,
Hephaestus recognizes one-sixth of the $60,000 cost of
the stock grant with this entry:

Construction-in-progress	10,000	
Accrued liabilities		10,000

Scribe & Sons completes the drawings by the dead-
line, which triggers the final issuance of 10,000 shares
by Hephaestus, which also records this entry:

Accrued liabilities	60,000	
Common stock		50,000
Additional paid-in capital		10,000

 ## What Information Should I Disclose About Equity?

You should disclose the following information in the
notes accompanying the financial statements:

- *Securities privileges.* The rights and privileges associated with outstanding securities, such as dividend
  and liquidation preferences, participation rights,
  conversion prices, sinking fund requirements, and
  unusual voting rights.
- *Preferred stock redemptions.* The aggregate or per-
  share amounts at which the entity can call preferred
  stock, or at which the preferred stock is subject to re-
  demption through sinking-fund operations.
- *Preferred stock dividends.* The amount of cumulative
  preferred dividends, both in aggregate and per-share.
- *Contingently convertible securities.* If there are contingently convertible shares, disclose the events that
  would cause the contingency to be met, as well as

the nature and timing of those rights. Also, disclose the conversion price, the number of shares into which the securities are convertible, events which could change the contingency event, and the manner of settlement (such as cash or shares). Further, note whether the contingently convertible shares are included in the calculation of diluted earnings per share, and the reasons why or why not.

EXAMPLE 17.7

NOTE XX

Unibody Plastics Company is obligated to issue an additional 10,000 shares in aggregate to the holders of its contingently convertible securities for every incremental $1.00 decline in the price of its common stock from the period January 1, 20X1 through December 31, 20X1.

PART III

REVENUE AND EXPENSES

CHAPTER 18

REVENUE RECOGNITION

 What Is Revenue?

Revenue is the total amount of money received by an entity in exchange for the goods and services that it has provided to its customers.

 When Can I Recognize Revenue?

You should consider the following two factors when determining the proper date and amount of revenue to recognize:

- ○ *Is the sale realized or realizable?* A sale is realized when goods or services are exchanged for cash or claims to cash. You generally cannot recognize revenue until a sale is realized or realizable.
- ○ *Has the sale been earned?* A sale has been earned when an entity has substantially accomplished whatever is needed in order to be entitled to the benefits represented by the revenue.

More specifically, an entity can record revenue when it meets *all* of the following criteria:

- ○ The price is substantially fixed at the sale date.
- ○ The buyer has either paid the seller or is obligated to make such payment. The payment is not contingent upon the buyer reselling the product.
- ○ The buyer's obligation to pay does not change if the product is destroyed or damaged.
- ○ The buyer has economic substance apart from the seller.
- ○ The seller does not have any significant additional performance obligations related to the sale.
- ○ The seller can reasonably estimate the amount of future returns.

When Can I Recognize Service Revenue?

Service revenues differ from product sales in that revenue recognition is generally based on the performance of specific activities, rather than on the shipment of a product. There are four ways in which you can recognize service revenues. They are presented as follows, in ascending order from the most conservative to the most liberal approaches:

1. *Collection method.* Used when there is significant uncertainty about the collection of payment from customers.
2. *Completed performance method.* Used when the primary service goal is not achieved until the end of a contract, or if there are no intermediate milestones upon which revenue calculations can be based.
3. *Specific performance method.* Used when revenue is tied to the completion of a specific act.
4. *Proportional performance method.* Used when a number of specific and clearly identifiable actions are taken as part of an overall service to a customer. Rather than waiting until all services have been performed to recognize any revenue, this approach allows you to proportionally recognize revenue as each individual action is completed. The amount of revenue recognized is based on the proportional amount of direct costs incurred for each action to the estimated total amount of direct costs required to complete the entire service. However, if the service involves many identical actions (such as delivering the newspaper for a year), then you can base revenue on the proportion of actions completed thus far under the contract. Alternatively, if the service period is fixed but the amount of service provided cannot be determined (such as annual customer support for a software package), then you can ratably recognize service revenue over the service period.

EXAMPLE 18.1

A service contract for $100,000 involves the completion of a single step that requires $8,000 of direct costs to complete. The total direct cost estimate for the entire job is $52,000, so the amount of revenue that can be recognized at the completion of that one action is $15,385 (calculated as ($8,000/$52,000) × $100,000).

EXAMPLE 18.2

Quaker Software sells annual support agreements along with its software packages. A typical support agreement costs $2,400 per year. The company has no obligation other than to respond to customer calls, whose timing, duration, and frequency cannot be predicted. Accordingly, it ratably recognizes $200 of revenue per month for each agreement, which is $1/12^{th}$ of the total amount.

 ## How Do I Recognize Losses on Service Contracts?

If the amount of direct costs incurred on a service project plus the estimate of remaining costs to be incurred exceeds the net revenue estimate for a project, then charge the excess cost to expense, with the offsetting credit first being used to eliminate any deferred costs and any remainder being stored in a liability account.

EXAMPLE 18.3

Quaker Software expects to earn $100,000 in revenues from the sale of a new computer game it is developing. Unfortunately, its incurred direct expenses of $64,000 and estimated remaining costs of $50,000 exceed projected revenues by $14,000. The company had stored an additional $3,500 of incurred costs related to the project in an asset account. The following entry records the initial loss transaction:

Loss on service contract	14,000	
Unrecognized contract costs		3,500
Estimated loss on service contracts		10,500

As Quaker incurs actual losses in later periods, it debits the Estimated Loss on Service Contracts account to reduce the outstanding liability.

 ## What Is the Installment Method?

The installment method is an accounting calculation under which an entity recognizes the profit on an installment

EXAMPLE 18.4

The Gershwin Music Company sells musical instruments in bulk to school districts. Under one recent deal, it sold $10,000 of instruments to a district in Indiana at a gross profit of 30%. The district paid for the instruments in four annual installments that included 8% interest. The following table illustrates the recognition of both interest income and gross profit under the deal. Equal cash payments of $3,019.21 were made at the end of each year (column 1), from which interest income was separated and recognized (column 2), leaving an annual net receivable reduction (column 3). The gross profit on the deal (column 5) was recognized in proportion to the amount of accounts receivable reduction each year, which was 30% of column 3.

Date	(1) Cash Payment	(2) Interest @ 8%	(3) Receivable Reduction	(4) Receivable Balance	(5) Profit Realized
01/01/2010				$10,000.00	
12/31/2010	$3,019.21	$ 800.00	$2,219.21	$ 7,780.79	$ 665.76
12/31/2011	$3,019.21	$ 622.46	$2,396.75	$ 5,384.04	$ 719.02
12/31/2012	$3,019.21	$ 430.72	$2,588.49	$ 2,795.56	$ 776.55
12/31/2013	$3,019.20	$ 223.64	$2,795.56	$ 0.00	$ 838.67
		$2,076.83			$3,000.00

In short, Gershwin recognized 30% of the deferred gross profit contained within each cash payment, net of interest income. As an example of the journal entry made with each cash receipt, the company made the following entry to record the cash payment received on 12/31/2010:

Cash	3,019.21	
Interest income		800.00
Accounts receivable		2,219.21
Deferred gross profit	665.76	
Recognized gross profit		665.76

sale when it receives cash. The installment method is used when there is a long string of expected payments from a customer that are related to a sale, and for which the level of collectability of individual payments cannot be reasonably estimated. This approach is particularly applicable in the case of multi-year payments by a customer. Under this approach, revenue is recognized only in the amount of each cash receipt, and for as long as cash is received. Expenses can be proportionally recognized to match the amount of each cash receipt, creating a small profit or loss at the time of each receipt.

What Is the Cost Recovery Method?

The cost recovery method is the most conservative accounting calculation for installment sales, where the recognition of all gross profit is deferred until the entire cost of sales has first been recognized. This method effectively pushes all profit recognition out until near the end of a contract period.

How Do I Account for the Repossession of Goods Under an Installment Sale?

It is acceptable to only recognize bad debts under installment sales, since the seller can usually repossess the underlying goods. However, when the goods are repossessed, you should adjust their value to their fair market value, which in most cases calls for the recognition of a loss.

Should I Record Revenue at Gross or at Net?

Some companies that act as brokers will over-report their revenue by recognizing not just the commission they earn on brokered sales, but also the revenue earned by their clients. For example, if a brokered transaction for an airline ticket involves a $1,000 ticket and a $20 brokerage fee, the company will claim that it has earned revenue of $1,000, rather than the $20 commission. This results in the appearance of enormous revenue (albeit with very small gross margins), which can be quite misleading. Consequently, you should apply the following rules to see if the full amount of brokered sales can be recognized as revenue:

Example 18.5

Use the same assumptions just noted for the Gershwin Music Company under the installment method. Cash payments are the same, as are the interest charges and beginning balance. However, no gross profit or interest income is realized until all $7,000 of product costs have been recovered through cash payments net of interest income. Instead, interest income is shifted to a deferred account. To reflect these changes, column 5 shows a declining balance of unrecovered costs that are eliminated when the third periodic payment arrives. This allows Gershwin's controller to recognize a small amount of deferred interest income in the third year, representing the net amount of cash payment left over after all costs have been recovered. In the final year, all remaining deferred interest income can be recognized, leaving the deferred gross margin as the last item to be recognized.

Date	(1) Cash Payment	(2) Interest @ 8%	(3) Receivable Reduction	(4) Receivable Balance	(5) Unrecovered Cost	(6) Profit Realized	(7) Interest Realized
01/01/2010				$10,000.00	$7,000.00		
12/31/2010	$3,019.21	$ 800.00	$2,219.21	$ 7,780.79	$4,780.79		
12/31/2011	$3,019.21	$ 622.46	$2,396.75	$ 5,384.04	$2,384.04		
12/31/2012	$3,019.21	$ 430.72	$2,588.49	$ 2,795.56	$ –		$ 204.43
12/31/2013	$3,019.20	$ 223.64	$2,795.56	$ 0.00	$ –	$3,000.00	$1,872.40
		$2,076.83				$3,000.00	$2,076.83

201

EXAMPLE 18.6

The Hudson's Bay Trailer Company has repossessed a construction trailer, for which $40,000 of accounts receivable is still outstanding, as well as $10,000 of deferred gross profit. The trailer has a fair market value of $28,000, so the company records the following entry to eliminate the receivable and deferred gross profit, while recognizing a loss of $2,000 on the write-down of the construction trailer:

Deferred gross margin	10,000	
Finished goods inventory	28,000	
Loss on inventory write-down	2,000	
Accounts receivable		40,000

○ *Principal.* The broker must act as the principal who is originating the transaction.
○ *Risks.* The broker must take on the risks of ownership, such as bearing the risk of loss on product delivery, returns, and bad debts from customers.
○ *Title.* The broker must obtain title to the product being sold at some point during the sale transaction.

There are several key indicators in a transaction that reveal whether it should be recorded at gross or net. It should be recorded at gross if the following indicators are present:

○ The company adds value to products sold, perhaps through alteration or added services.
○ The company can establish a selling price to the customer.
○ The company is responsible to the customer for order fulfillment.
○ The company takes title to inventory before shipping it to the customer.

The transaction should be recorded at net if the answer to any of the preceding indicators is "no." In addition, it should be recorded at net if the following indicators are present:

○ The company earns a fixed fee (such as a commission payment) from a transaction.
○ The company only has one source of supplier for the product it sells.

○ The supplier cannot obtain payment from the company if the customer does not pay.

If a specific transaction contains indicators pointing in either direction, the decision to record at gross or net should be based on the preponderance of evidence pointing in a particular direction.

EXAMPLE 18.7

The Aboriginal Travel Agency (ATA), which sells trips to Australia, purchases blocks of tickets from the airlines and resells them to customers as part of its package deals. If it cannot find purchasers for the tickets, it must absorb the cost of the tickets. In this case, ATA should record as revenues the entire amount of the airline tickets, since it has taken title to the tickets, bears the risk of loss, and is originating the transaction.

ATA also reserves airlines seats on behalf of its clients, charging a $30 fee for this service. Since it is only acting as an agent for these transactions, it can only record the $30 fee as revenue, not the price of the airline tickets.

Should I Record an Out-of-Pocket Expense Reimbursement as Revenue?

Yes. If an entity bills its customers for out-of-pocket expenses incurred, such as for photocopying and delivery charges, you should record the billing as revenue. Do not record the billing as a reduction in expenses.

EXAMPLE 18.8

The Crosby Mayer legal firm charges a client for $552 in document delivery charges. It incorporates this charge into its standard monthly customer billing, crediting revenues for $552 and debiting receivables for $552.

Should I Record Shipping and Handling Costs as Revenue?

Shipping costs are those costs incurred to physically move a product from the seller's location to the buyer's location. Handling costs are those costs incurred to store, move, and prepare a product for shipment, and an entity usually incurs these costs between finished goods storage and delivery to the shipper. You should recognize all shipping and handling fees billed to customers as revenue.

Do not net any shipping and handling costs against revenues. Instead, record them in the cost of goods sold.

 ### Should I Reduce Revenue for Any Cash Paid to a Customer?

A vendor may give a customer a sales incentive or similar consideration. There are two ways to account for such a transaction:

1. *Revenue reduction.* If the transaction is essentially an adjustment of the prices of the vendor's products, then record the payment as a reduction of the vendor's revenue.
2. *Cost or expense.* If the transaction is a cost that the vendor incurs for something received from the customer, then the vendor records a cost or expense. This situation arises when the vendor receives an identifiable benefit *and* can estimate the fair value of the benefit. If the vendor pays more than the fair value of the benefit received, it must record the excess as a revenue reduction.

Example 18.9

Nocturnal Widget Company includes an advertising allowance on its invoices to customers. The customers are supposed to use these funds to advertise Nocturnal's products, and then submit documentation of their advertising expenditures to Nocturnal. If they provide no documentation, then Nocturnal eliminates the allowance on future invoices until it earns back the undocumented allowance. Nocturnal should charge the allowance to expense, since it is receiving an advertising benefit at least equal to the amount of the allowance.

EXAMPLE 18.10

Quaker Software sells software to its customers at list price, and then pays back a portion of sales at the end of each calendar year if the customers exceed certain sales volume milestones. The amount of these payments in the past year was $130,000, which Quaker should charge against its revenues, on the grounds that Quaker did not receive an identifiable benefit in return for the payments.

 ## How Do I Account for Construction Projects?

If an entity is working on long-term construction contracts where the specifications are provided by the customer and payments depend on performance, then you should consider using either the percentage of completion method or the completed contract method.

The percentage of completion method provides periodic recognition of income based on the status of uncompleted projects, though the accuracy of its results is dependent upon how well you estimate final costs. The completed contract method is based on the final results of a contract, rather than the estimates so prevalent in the percentage of completion method; however, it provides no information about financial performance prior to completion of a project.

No matter which method you choose, your basic assumption is that each construction contract is a profit center, so you should accumulate both revenue and costs by contract. There may be cases where you can cluster a group of related contracts together into a single profit center. All of the following conditions should be present before you do so:

- ○ The contracts are negotiated as a package with an overall profit margin objective.
- ○ The contracts constitute a single project.
- ○ The contracts involve interrelated construction work having substantial common costs.
- ○ The contracts are performed together under the same management and in the same general vicinity.
- ○ The contracts are with a single customer.

What Types of Construction Contracts Are There?

There are a multitude of possible payment systems built into construction contracts. The most common ones are:

- ○ *Cost-plus-fixed fee contract.* The contractor is reimbursed for costs incurred, plus a fixed fee.
- ○ *Cost-plus-incentive fee contract.* The contractor is reimbursed for costs incurred, plus a fee whose size is dependent upon the contractor meeting various goals.
- ○ *Firm-fixed-price contract.* The contractor is paid a fixed amount that is not subject to adjustment for any extra costs incurred.
- ○ *Fixed price contract with performance incentives.* The contractor is paid a fixed amount, plus a fee whose size is dependent upon the contractor meeting various goals.
- ○ *Time-and-material contract.* The contractor is paid on the basis of direct labor hours at fixed hourly rates, as well as the cost of materials.
- ○ *Unit-price contract.* The contractor is paid a specific fee for every unit of work completed.

What Is the Percentage of Completion Method?

The percentage of completion method is an accounting calculation under which a percentage of the income associated with a project is recognized in proportion to the estimated percentage of completion of the project. It is heavily used in the construction industry, where very long-term construction projects would otherwise keep a company from revealing any revenues on its financial statements until its projects are completed, which might occur only at long intervals. Under this approach, the accounting staff creates a new asset account for each project in which it accumulates all related expenses. At the end of each reporting period, the budgeted gross margin associated with each project is added to the total expenses accumulated in each account, and subtracted from the accumulated billings to date. If the amount of expenses and gross profit exceed the billings figure, then the company recognizes revenue matching the difference between the two figures. If the expenses and gross profit figure are less than the amount of billings, the difference is stored in a liability account.

EXAMPLE 18.11

The Hephaestus Construction Company is building a log cabin-style office building for a company specializing in rustic furniture. Thus far, it has accumulated $810,000 in expenses on the project and billed the customer $1,000,000. The estimated gross margin on the project is 28%. The total of expenses and estimated gross profit is therefore $1,125,000, which is calculated as $810,000 divided by (1 − 0.28). Since this figure exceeds the billings to date of $1,000,000, the company can recognize additional revenue of $125,000. The resulting journal entry is:

Unbilled contract receivables	125,000	
Contract revenue earned		125,000

Since Hephaestus must also recognize a proportional amount of expenses in relation to the revenues recognized, it should credit the construction-in-progress account and debit the cost-of-goods-sold account for $90,000. This cost of goods sold is derived by multiplying the recognized revenue figure of $125,000 by one minus the gross margin, or 72%.

Under an alternative scenario, Hephaestus has billed the customer $1,200,000, while all other information remains the same. In this case, the amount of revenue earned is $1,125,000, which is $75,000 less than the amount billed. Consequently, the company must record a $75,000 liability for the incremental amount of work it must still complete before it can recognize the remaining revenue that has already been billed. The resulting journal entry would be:

Contract revenue earned	75,000	
Billings exceeding project costs and margins		75,000

What Is the Cost-to-Cost Method?

The cost-to-cost method is used to measure the extent of progress toward completion, and as such is a useful calculation technique that supports the percentage-of-completion method. The calculation is to divide all costs incurred to date on a project by the total estimated project cost, in order to derive the overall project percentage of completion for incremental billing purposes.

Under this approach, you measure the percentage of completion by dividing the total amount of expenses incurred to date by the total estimated project cost. This method only works well if the total estimated project cost is regularly revised to reflect the most accurate expense information. Also, it tends to result in proportionately greater amounts of revenue recognition early in a project, since this is when most of the materials-related costs are incurred.

EXAMPLE 18.12

The Hephaestus Construction Company is building a hotel, and has elected to purchase the materials for the air conditioning system, costing $200,000, at the beginning of the project. The total estimated project cost is $2,000,000 and the amount billable to the customer is $2,500,000. After one month, Hephaestus has incurred a total of $400,000 in costs, including the air conditioning equipment. This is 20% of the total project cost, and would entitle Hephaestus to recognize $500,000 of revenue (20% of $2,500,000). However, because the air conditioning equipment has not yet been installed, a more accurate approach would be to exclude the cost of this equipment from the calculation, resulting in a project completion percentage of 10% and recognizable revenue of $250,000.

 ## What Is the Completed Contract Method?

Under the completed contract method, you should only recognize income when a contract is substantially complete (though you should recognize expected losses as soon as you are aware of them). You should consider a contract to be complete when the remaining costs and potential risks are insignificant.

Prior to recognition, you should accumulate all billings and costs on the balance sheet. If there is an excess of accumulated costs over related billings, then report the excess on the balance sheet as a current asset. If there is an excess of accumulated billings over related costs, then report the excess on the balance sheet as (in most cases) a current liability.

The completed contract method is most appropriate when there are minimal dependable estimates upon which to use the percentage-of-completion method. It also yields results similar to those of the percentage-of-completion method for very short-term contracts.

Example 18.13

Hephaestus Construction is building a research facility for a not-for-profit entity, whose cash flows are entirely based on donations, and so are highly uncertain. Given the level of uncertainty, Hephaestus elects to use the completed contract method to recognize revenues and expenses under the contract. During the project, Hephaestus gradually incurs $320,000 of costs, which it records as an asset on its balance sheet. Once the project is completed, Hephaestus bills the customer $380,000 and recognizes the entire $320,000 of costs as expense, resulting in a $60,000 profit.

 ## How Do I Account for a Revised Estimate on a Construction Project?

It is extremely common to adjust the original estimates of the total revenue or cost of a contract, as the contractor gathers more detailed information and the project progresses. You should account for these alterations as changes in the accounting estimate, which only require changes going forward; you should not make retroactive changes based on a revised estimate on a construction project.

 ## How Do I Account for a Change Order?

A change order is a modification of an existing contract that changes the contract's provisions for such items as alterations of project specifications and the period of completion. A change order may be *unpriced*, which means that the work is defined, but the contract price adjustment is not — it will be negotiated later.

If a change order is within the original scope of a contract, then no change in the contract price may be required.

If a change order is unpriced, you can account for it if the customer has approved its scope in writing, there is documentation of the change order costs, and the entity has a favorable history of negotiating change orders.

If a change order involves services that differ from those provided under the original contract, if its price is negotiated without regard to the original contract, or if the price/cost relationship significantly differs from that of the original contract, then account for the change order as a separate contract. If none of these scenarios are applicable, then combine the change order with the original contract for accounting purposes.

If the customer is disputing or has not approved a change order, then treat it as a claim (see the next question).

 ## How Do I Account for a Claim?

A claim is an amount in excess of the agreed contract price, or an amount that is not included in the contract price, that the contractor wishes to collect from the customer. The causes of a claim typically include delays caused by the customer, design errors, contract terminations, and the like.

You should not recognize the revenue associated with a claim unless it is probable that the claim will result in additional revenue *and* you can reliably estimate its amount. You can recognize claim revenue if *all* of the following conditions are present:

○ There is a legal basis for the claim.
○ The additional costs related to the claim are not the result of contractor deficiencies.
○ The costs noted in the claim are identifiable and reasonable.
○ Evidence supporting the claim is verifiable and not based on unsupported representations.

Even when a contractor's claim meets all of the preceding conditions, you should only record revenue from the claim to the extent that the contractor has incurred costs related to the claim, and then record any remaining revenue amount once the claim has been awarded.

 ## How Do I Recognize a Project Loss?

If the estimate of costs left to be incurred on a project plus actual costs already incurred exceeds the total revenue to be expected from a contract, then you should recognize the full amount of the difference in the current period as a loss, and present it on the balance sheet as a current liability. If you used the percentage of completion method on the project, then the amount recognized will be the total estimated loss on the project plus all project profits previously recognized. If, after the loss estimate has been made, and the actual loss turns out to be a smaller number, then recognize the difference in the current period as a gain.

EXAMPLE 18.14

The Hephaestus Construction Company's cost accountant has determined that its construction of a military barracks building will probably result in a loss of $80,000, based on his most recent cost estimates. The company uses the percentage of completion method, under which it had previously recorded gross profits of $35,000 for the project. Thus, the company must record a loss of $115,000 in the current period, both to record the total estimated loss and to back out the formerly recognized profit. The entry is as follows:

Loss on uncompleted project	115,000	
Estimated loss on uncompleted contract		115,000

How Do I Account for a Multiple-Element Arrangement?

A multiple-element arrangement contains several activities that independently generate revenue. There are three general rules governing revenue recognition for a multiple-element arrangement, they are:

1. Divide the arrangement into separate units of accounting. An item is considered a separate unit of accounting if it has value to the customer on a stand-alone basis; and, if there is a general right of return, then delivery is probable and substantially in the control of the vendor.

2. Allocate the revenue generated by the total arrangement to the separate units of accounting, based on their relative selling prices when they are sold separately or (if not yet sold separately) the price established by management.

3. Apply standard revenue recognition criteria to each separate unit of accounting.

EXAMPLE 18.15

Hostetler Corporation manufacturers a low-volume bottling line for brew pubs. The Mad Dog Brew Pub buys a bottling line from Hostetler for $150,000. This price includes installation, which third parties routinely perform for $20,000. Hostetler charges the same price even if a brew pub chooses not to use its installation services.

There are two units of accounting, which are the bottling line and the assembly labor. Hostetler allocates the purchase price as follows:

$17,647	= $150,000 × ($20,000 installation ÷ ($150,000 bottling price + $20,000 installation price))
132,353	= $150,000 × ($150,000 bottling price ÷ ($150,000 bottling price + $20,000 installation price))
$150,000	= Total

Hostetler can separately recognize the two units of accounting associated with this sale whenever they are completed.

How Do I Record Revenue When a Right of Return Exists?

If a sale transaction allows the buyer to return goods to the seller within a stated time period, then you should only recognize the transaction when you can reasonably estimate the amount of returns. If so, then estimate a sales return allowance at the time of the sale, and coincide this with the recognition of the sale. In practice, many companies do not record a returns allowance because the amount of sales returns is so small.

If you cannot reasonably estimate the amount of sales returns, then delay revenue recognition until the expiration date of the return privilege has passed.

When Can I Record Initiation Fees as Service Revenue?

A company may charge an initiation fee as part of a service contract, such as the up-front fee that many health clubs charge to new members. This fee should only be recognized immediately as revenue if there is a discernible value associated with it that can be separated from the services provided from ongoing fees that may be charged at a later date. However, if the initiation fee does not yield any specific value to the purchaser, then you can only recognize revenue from it over the term of the agreement to which the fee is attached. For example, if a health club membership agreement were to last for two years, then the revenue associated with the initiation fee should be spread over two years.

How Do I Account for Product Warranty and Maintenance Contracts?

If an entity sells a separate contract for an extended period of product warranty or maintenance, then you should recognize the revenue over the contract period in proportion to the amount of insurance protection provided by the entity. This typically results in straight-line recognition over the contract period.

How Do I Record Barter Transactions for Advertising Services?

A company may enter into a barter transaction to provide advertising services in exchange for receiving advertising services from its customer. This can involve the exchange of no cash at all, or approximately equal amounts of cash or other consideration. You can recognize revenue in such a transaction based on its fair value, but only if the fair value of the advertising surrendered in the transaction within the past six months is determinable based on the entity's historical practice of receiving cash for similar advertising. The advertising being used as a comparison

---

EXAMPLE 18.16

Stoked TV enters into an advertising barter transaction with Dude magazine, where Stoked advertises Dude on its cable network in exchange for similar coverage in Dude magazine. Stoked is providing Dude with five advertising spots of thirty seconds duration. Stoked normally provides such coverage at a rate of $10,000 per spot, and does so frequently with other parties who pay cash. Accordingly, Stoked TV can recognize the fair value of its advertising as revenue, which is $10,000 multiplied by five coverage spots, or $50,000.

should have similar characteristics to the bartered advertising, including such factors as circulation, timing, prominence, demographics, and advertising duration.

How Do I Record Revenue Collected for a Third Party?

You cannot recognize revenue if the related transactions do not occur on an entity's own account. For example:

○ *Agencies.* Amounts collected by an agent are on behalf of the principal, and so do not alter the equity of the agent. These amounts are therefore not revenue; the agent should instead record commissions received as revenue.

○ *Taxes.* Amounts collected on behalf of government entities, such as sales taxes and value added taxes, do not create economic benefits for the entity and do not alter its equity; therefore, such transactions are excluded from revenue.

What Revenue Recognition Information Should I Disclose?

You should disclose the following information about an entity's revenue recognition practices in the notes accompanying the financial statements:

○ *Advertising.* The amount of revenue and expense recognized from advertising barter transactions. If the fair value of the transactions is not determinable, also disclose the volume and type of advertising surrendered and received.

○ *Completed contract method.* If the entity uses the completed contract method, disclose the criteria used to determine contract completion, as well as any departure from this policy.

○ *Contract claims.* The amounts of any revenue recognized from contract claims.

○ *Gross revenue.* The gross transaction volume for those revenues reported net.

○ *Incentive programs.* The nature of any sales incentive programs and the amounts recognized in the income statement for those programs.

○ *Multiple-element arrangements.* The nature of these arrangements and the significant deliverables related to them, as well as the timing of delivery or performance. Also, their performance, cancellation, termination, and refund provisions, as well as a discussion of the factors used to determine selling prices, the timing of revenue recognition by unit of accounting, the general timing of revenue recognition for significant units of accounting, and the effect of changes in selling prices on the allocation of revenue to units of accounting.

- ○ *Percentage of completion method.* If the entity uses the percentage of completion method, disclose the methods for measuring progress toward completion, and also any departures from this policy.
- ○ *Policies.* The methods of determining revenue and the cost of earned revenue.
- ○ *Revisions.* The effect of estimate revisions, if material.
- ○ *Shipping and handling.* The classification of shipping and handling costs.
- ○ *Subsequent events.* Any events occurring after the date of the financial statements that are outside of the normal exposure and risk aspects of a contract.

CHAPTER 19

EMPLOYEE BENEFITS AND BENEFIT PLANS

What Are Vested Employee Benefits?

Vested employee benefits are benefits granted to employees that are not conditional on any future employment.

What Are Short-Term Employee Benefits?

Short-term employee benefits include:

○ *Absences.* Compensated absences where payment is settled within 12 months of when employees render related services. Examples are vacation, short-term disability, jury service, and military service.
○ *Base pay.* Wages and social security contributions.
○ *Non-monetary benefits.* Includes medical care, housing, cars, and various subsidies for other goods or services.
○ *Performance pay.* Profit sharing and bonuses payable within 12 months of when employees render related services.

The entitlement to compensated absences can be accumulating or non-accumulating. An *accumulating compensated absence* is carried forward and can be used in future periods. An accumulating compensated absence can be vesting, so that employees are entitled to a cash payment for unused entitlement when they leave the entity. If an accumulating compensated absence is non-vesting, then employees do not receive such a cash payment when they leave the entity.

How Do I Account for Short-Term Employee Benefits?

Recognize the cost of short-term employee benefits in the period incurred. There is no need to incorporate actuarial assumptions in these costs. Also, do not discount these costs with a present value calculation.

Record a short-term employee benefit as an accrued expense, after deducting any amount already paid. If the amount paid exceeds the undiscounted benefit cost, then record the overage as a prepaid asset to the extent that it will reduce the amount of a future payment or yield a cash refund.

 ## What Is a Compensated Absence?

A compensated absence is an employee absence, such as a vacation or holiday, for which an entity pays the employee.

 ## How Do I Account for a Compensated Absence?

An employer should accrue a liability for compensation due to employees for their future absences, but only if all of the following conditions are met:

- The payment obligation for future absences is based on employee services already rendered.
- The amount of the obligation can be reasonably estimated.
- Payment is probable.
- The obligation is for employee rights that vest or accumulate.

When calculating the amount of the accrual, you can factor in the amount of anticipated forfeitures. Also, you

---

EXAMPLE 19.1

The accrued vacation policy of Hostetler Corporation is to grant employees the vested right to two weeks of paid vacation at the beginning of their second year with the company. If they are terminated or leave the company at any time before the day on which the vesting occurs, Hostetler does not compensate them for any portion of the vacation time.

Despite the absence of vesting during the first year of employment, the vacation accrual is essentially earned by employees during their first year, so Hostetler should accrue the related compensation expense during the first year, less an allowance for forfeitures caused by turnover.

should record the accrual in the year in which employees earn the compensation.

However, if a compensated absence has non-vesting rights and the rights expire at the end of the year in which they are earned, then you do not have to accrue a liability for future absences.

EXAMPLE 19.2

Hostetler Corporation pays its employees 50% of their normal compensation if they are called for active military duty, and for the entire period of their military service. However, if they are not called for duty, then the benefit expires. Since the right expires, Hostetler should not accrue for this type of compensated absence.

 ## What Is a Sabbatical Leave?

A sabbatical leave is a compensated absence whereby an employee is entitled to paid time off after completing a designated period of work for an entity. While on sabbatical, the employee is still compensated, while not having to perform any duties for the entity.

 ## How Do I Account for Sabbatical Leave?

If an employer gives an employee sabbatical leave in order to perform public service or to in some way benefit the employer, then the leave is not attributable to services already rendered by the employee; therefore, the employer should not accrue a liability in advance of the leave. However, if the leave constitutes unrestricted time off, then it is attributable to services already rendered by the employee, and should be accrued over the prior service period.

 ## How Do I Account for Sick Pay Benefits?

An employer does not have to accrue for compensating employees for their absences due to illness. However, if an employer pays sick leave benefits to employees whose absences are not caused by illness, or if it allows them to use accumulated unused sick pay benefits prior to retirement (thereby accelerating their actual retirement), then it should account for such benefits as though they were compensated absences.

What Is a Rabbi Trust?

A rabbi trust is a trust set up to fund the compensation of a group of managers or highly-paid executives. The terms of the trust agreement must state that its assets are available to general creditors in the event of the employer's bankruptcy; otherwise, the trust will not qualify for income tax purposes. There are four variations on the rabbi trust concept:

○ Plan A: Does not allow diversification of plan assets and is settled with a fixed number of employer shares.
○ Plan B: Does not allow diversification of plan assets and is settled with cash or employer shares.
○ Plan C: Allows diversification of plan assets, but the employee has not diversified.
○ Plan D: Allows diversification of plan assets, and the employee has diversified, so it may be settled with cash, employer shares, or other assets.

How Do I Account for a Rabbi Trust?

The accounting for a rabbi trust varies, depending on which Plan type is involved (see the preceding question). The accounting for each Plan type is:

○ Plan A: Classify the employer stock held by the trust in equity in a manner similar to treasury stock (see the Equity chapter), and classify the deferred compensation obligation within the equity classification. Do not recognize subsequent changes in the fair value of the employer's stock.
○ Plans B and C: Classify employer stock held by the trust in equity in a manner similar to treasury stock (see the Equity chapter), and classify the deferred compensation obligation as a liability. Do not recognize subsequent changes in the fair value of the employer's stock. However, you should adjust the deferred compensation obligation to reflect the fair value of the amount owed by the employer to the employee.
○ Plan D: Classify the various assets held by the trust in accordance with the relevant Generally Accepted Accounting Principles (GAAP), and classify the deferred compensation obligation as a liability. You

should recognize subsequent changes in the deferred compensation obligation to reflect the fair value of the amount owed by the employer to the employee.

How Do I Account for Deferred Compensation?

You should accrue for the present value of future benefits that the employer expects to pay to an employee for deferred compensation. You should incorporate into this calculation an estimate of the life expectancy of the recipient, which is based on either mortality tables or on the estimated cost of an annuity contract.

EXAMPLE 19.3

Nocturnal Widget Company creates a deferred compensation contract for its employees, under which they become fully eligible for benefits ten years after entering into the contract. A provision of the contract states that, if an employee becomes disabled prior to the ten-year vesting date, then the contract will pay benefits at once.

The structure of this plan indicates that employees are rendering services for ten years that earn the contractual benefits, so Nocturnal should accrue the obligation over the ten-year period.

The cost of the contract to Nocturnal is $10,000 per employee. An employee becomes disabled after two years. Since Nocturnal had only accrued $2,000 through the disability date, it should immediately accrue the remaining $8,000 cost associated with the contract for that employee.

Another employee is expected to retire before reaching the end of the ten-year vesting period. In this case, Nocturnal does not have to accrue any obligation, since there is no expectation of payment to the employee.

How Do I Account for Termination Benefits?

Termination benefits are those benefits provided by an employer to its employees when it terminates their employment. If an employer offers termination benefits, it should recognize the expense when employees accept the benefits offer and the employer can reasonably estimate the amount of the benefits. If some portion of the payment involves future payments, then recognize the present value of those future payments.

If an employer offers special termination benefits in exchange for employees' voluntary termination of service, then it should not recognize the related expense as of the offer date based on the estimated acceptance rate.

 ## What Is a Defined Benefit Pension Plan?

In a defined benefit pension plan, the employer provides retirement income payments in future years after its employees retire or terminate their service with the employer. The amount of benefit that the employer pays is typically dependent upon such factors as employee survival rates, their years of service, and their compensation shortly before their retirement or termination of service.

A defined benefit pension plan requires the use of a fund, through which cash flows in the following pattern:

Beginning plan assets

\+ Earnings on invested plan assets

\+ Sponsor's contributions

− Benefits paid to plan participants

= Ending plan assets

 ## What Terminology Is Associated with Defined Benefit Pension Plans?

The following terms are commonly used when accounting for defined benefit pension plans:

○ *Accumulated benefit obligation.* The actuarial present value of benefits that are attributed by a pension benefit formula to employee services that have been rendered before a specific date. These attributed benefits are based on employee service and compensation before the specified date. It does not contain any assumption about future compensation levels.

○ *Actuarial present value.* The value of either a single payment or series of payments, adjusted for the time value of money and the probability of payment. Probability of payment is based on such factors as estimated death rates, disabilities, and retirements occurring prior to the expected payment date.

○ *Attribution.* The assignment of pension benefits and costs to periods of employee service.

○ *Net periodic pension cost.* The amount that an entity recognizes as the cost of its pension plan for a period. This cost is comprised of the service cost, interest cost, actual return on plan assets, gain or loss, and the amortization of prior service costs.

○ *Plan curtailment.* An event resulting in a significant reduction of the expected years of future service by current employees, or which eliminates the accrual of defined benefits for some portion of the future service of a significant number of employees.

○ *Prior service cost.* The cost of any benefits retroactively granted as part of a plan amendment. This cost is attributed by the pension benefit formula to employee services that were rendered in periods prior to the plan amendment.

○ *Projected benefit obligation.* The actuarial present value of all benefits attributed to employee service that was rendered before a specific date. This calculation includes estimations of future employee compensation levels.

○ *Service cost.* The actuarial present value of benefits attributed to services rendered by employees during a specific period.

○ *Unfunded projected benefit obligation.* The excess amount of the projected benefit obligation over plan assets.

○ *Vested benefit obligation.* The actuarial present value of vested benefits.

○ *Vested benefits.* Benefits which an employee is entitled to receive, irrespective of any remaining service to the employer.

What Methods Are Available for Attributing Pension Benefits and Costs to Periods of Employee Service?

There are two groups of methods used to attribute pension benefits and costs to periods of employee service. They are the benefit approach and the cost approach:

○ *Benefit approach.* The attribution of pension benefits and costs based on a distinct unit of benefit for each year of credited service. Each unit is then assigned an actuarial present value.

○ *Cost approach.* The attribution of pension benefits and costs as level amounts or as constant percentages of compensation.

In General, How Do I Account for a Defined Benefit Pension Plan?

You should recognize the excess of the projected benefit obligation over the fair value of a defined benefit plan's assets as a liability. This liability is the unfunded projected benefit obligation. If the reverse situation is the case, where the fair value of the plan's assets exceeds the amount of the projected benefit obligation, then recognize an asset that equals the overfunded projected benefit obligation. You should record periodic changes in this under-funded or overfunded balance in other comprehensive income.

You should include all of the following items in the net pension cost:

○ *Service cost.* The actuarial present value of those benefits attributed to services rendered by employees during the period.

○ *Interest cost.* Interest on the projected benefit obligation, which is a discounted amount.

○ *Actual return on plan assets.* The actual return on those invested assets that are part of the plan assets.

○ *Amortization of prior service costs or credits.* The cost or credit generated by plan amendments that alter benefits that were based on services provided in prior periods. This amount is amortized over multiple future service periods.

○ *Gains or losses.* A change in the value of either the projected benefit obligation or the plan assets that result from experience being different from expectations. These gains and losses include those items both realized (such as from the sale of securities) and from unrealized amounts. Gains and losses may be caused by refinements in your estimates, rather than from real changes in economic value.

EXAMPLE 19.4

Mr. Trent Nectar, president of Ambrosia Cuisine, will receive a benefit upon his retirement from Ambrosia of 20% of his final annual salary, for each of his remaining years of employment. He will retire in three years. Ambrosia expects his salary in each of the three remaining years to be $200,000, $220,000, and $240,000. The discount rate is 4%. The service cost, discounted pension liability, and interest cost associated with Mr. Nectar's retirement benefit follows:

Year	Salary	Service Cost*	Discounted Pension Cost	Interest Cost**	Year-end Liability***
1	$200,000	$24,000	$22,189	$ –	$22,189
2	220,000	24,000	23,077	888	46,154
3	240,000	24,000	24,000	1,846	71,077
		$72,000	$69,266	$2,734	

*20% of the final-year salary
**4% of the year-end liability
***Cumulative discounted pension cost plus cumulative interest cost

How Do I Attribute Pension Benefits to Employees in a Defined Benefit Plan?

You should attribute pension benefits to periods of employee service based on the plan's benefit formula. This typically involves attributing a dollar amount to an employee for a specific time period of service, reduced by the actuarial present value of that benefit.

EXAMPLE 19.5

The Rock Hard Candy Company has a defined benefit pension plan, under which it pays out a pension benefit of $25 per month for the remainder of each employee's life, for each year of service completed. Rock Hard's actuary calculates that the average employee has 180 months of life expectancy following retirement, and will have 20 years of service completed at retirement. The actuarial present value discount is 0.45%.

The calculation of pension benefits attributable to each of Rock Hard's employees is:

Pension benefit per month ×	$ 25
Years of service completed	× 20
= Payment per month per employee ×	$ 500
Average number of months life expectancy	× 180
= Gross pension payable ×	$90,000
Actuarial present value discount rate	× 0.45
	$40,500

The benefit formulas of some plans attribute a disproportionate share of the total benefits provided to later years of employee service, which essentially delays employee vesting. For example, the benefit formula may attribute no benefits for the first ten years of an employee's service. In such cases, accumulate the total projected benefit in proportion to the ratio of the number of completed years of service to the number that an employee will have completed as of the date when the benefit is fully vested for the first time.

If a benefit formula does not clearly specify how to relate a benefit to services rendered, then accumulate it using either of these two approaches:

1. If a benefit becomes vested after a certain number of years, attribute the benefit in proportion to the ratio of the number of completed years of service to the number that will have been completed when the benefit is fully vested for the first time.
2. If a benefit is not based on vesting (such as a disability benefit that is triggered upon actual disability during active employee service), then attribute the benefit in proportion to the ratio of completed years of service to total projected years of service.

How Do I Amortize Prior Service Costs?

You should calculate the amortization of prior service costs by assigning an equal amount to each future period of service for each employee active on the amendment date who you expect to receive benefits under the pension plan. If most or all of the plan participants are inactive, then instead amortize the prior service costs over the remaining life expectancies of the participants.

You should charge the cost of a benefit improvement to other comprehensive income as of the amendment date, and adjust other comprehensive income in each period as you amortize the prior service cost or credit.

To reduce the amount of computations required, it is acceptable to calculate a straight-line amortization over the average remaining service period of those employees expected to receive plan benefits.

In some situations, the expected future benefit period is less than the remaining service period of active employees. If so, you should accelerate the amortization to more closely match the expected benefit period.

Once you have set up the amortization schedule, you should not alter it unless either there is a curtailment of

EXAMPLE 19.6

Hostetler Corporation amends its pension plan to grant $32,000 of prior service costs to its 100 employees. Hostetler expects the employees to retire on the following schedule:

Group	Number of Employees	Expected Retirement Year
1	10	Year 1
2	20	Year 2
3	25	Year 3
4	30	Year 4
5	15	Year 5

Hostetler calculates the service years for each group and in total as follows:

	Service Years					
Year	Group 1	Group 2	Group 3	Group 4	Group 5	Total
Year 1	10	20	25	30	15	100
Year 2		20	25	30	15	90
Year 3			25	30	15	70
Year 4				30	15	45
Year 5					15	15
	10	40	75	120	75	320

The preceding table shows that there are 320 service years over which the $32,000 prior service cost should be allocated, which is $100 per service year. Hostetler then uses the following table to determine the annual amortization expense using the $100 charge per service year:

Year	Total Service Years	×	Cost per Service Year	=	Annual Amortization
1	100		$100		$10,000
2	90		100		9,000
3	70		100		7,000
4	45		100		4,500
5	15		100		1,500
	320				$32,000

EXAMPLE 19.7

The Rock Hard Candy Company grants a retroactive credit for prior service, under the terms of a plan amendment. The amendment creates a new cost for Rock Hard of $400,000, which is a charge to other comprehensive income and an increase in the pension liability. The active participants in the plan are expected to have an average of five additional years of service. Rock Hard elects to amortize the $400,000 expense over the five-year period, as noted in the following table:

Year	Beginning-of-Year Balance	Amortization	End-of-Year Balance
1	$400,000	$80,000	$320,000
2	320,000	80,000	240,000
3	240,000	80,000	160,000
4	160,000	80,000	80,000
5	80,000	80,000	0

benefits or the future benefit period is shorter than you originally estimated. Do not revise the schedule for normal variances in the expected service lives of employees.

How Do I Amortize Prior Service Credits?

A prior service credit arises when a pension plan amendment retroactively reduces benefits. You should record this reduction as a credit to other comprehensive income in the following two-stage process:

1. Reduce any remaining prior service cost included in accumulated other comprehensive income.
2. Amortize any remaining prior service credit as a component of net periodic pension cost, using the same calculation just noted for the amortization of prior service costs.

How Do I Account for Gains and Losses on a Pension Plan?

You can immediately recognize gains and losses, as long as you apply such recognition consistently, and apply it to *all* gains and losses on both a plan's assets and obligations.

If you do not elect to use immediate recognition of gains and losses, then recognize them as increases or decreases in other comprehensive income when they occur.

If you elect to include gains and losses in other comprehensive income, then you must amortize it if, at the beginning of the year, the net gain or loss exceeds 10% of the greater of the projected benefit obligation or the market-related value of plan assets. Then amortize the excess amount, divided by the average remaining service period of those active employees who are expected to receive plan benefits. The amortization must *always* reduce the balance at the beginning of the year. If most or all plan participants are inactive, then instead amortize over their remaining life expectancies.

 ### How Do I Account for Pension Costs Related to Future Compensation?

A pension benefit formula may define some portion of pension benefits as a function of future compensation levels. Future compensation levels are assumptions that are based to some extent on expected levels of inflation, productivity, seniority, promotions, and so forth.

When measuring the accumulated benefit obligation, which includes those employee services that occur before a specific date, do not estimate future compensation levels, with the exception of automatic cost-of-living increases.

 ### On What Basis Should I Develop Pension Plan Assumptions?

For each assumption that you incorporate into pension plan calculations, use the best estimate solely with regard to that single assumption. Also, you should assume that the plan will continue in effect, unless there is evidence that it will not continue. In addition, here are guidelines for particular assumptions:

○ *Discount rates.* Discount rates are used in the measurement of the projected, accumulated, and vested benefit obligations, as well as the service and interest cost components of net periodic pension cost. You can estimate these rates based on the current prices of annuity contracts that could be used to settle an obligation, or based on the rates of return on high-quality fixed-income investments.

○ *Expected long-term rate of return.* This return should reflect the average rate of earnings expected on those funds invested in order to provide for the benefits included in the projected benefit obligation.

 ## How Should I Measure Plan Assets?

Plan assets should be measured at their fair value. This rule applies to equity and debt securities, real estate, and other assets. When measuring investments, reduce their fair value by the amount of any brokerage commissions and other costs that an entity would normally incur in a sale (it is not necessary to include these costs if they are insignificant).

If an entity is using plan assets in plan operations, as might be the case for buildings, furniture and fixtures, and leasehold improvements, then measure these assets at their cost, less accumulated depreciation or amortization.

If a benefit plan buys annuity contracts to cover benefits earned by employees, then measure the contracts at their purchase cost. If benefits are covered by annuity contracts, then exclude those contracts from the projected benefit obligation and the accumulated benefit obligation.

 ## When Should I Measure Plan Assets?

You should measure plan assets and benefit obligations as of an entity's fiscal year-end balance sheet date. However, this does not mean that you must perform all measurement procedures on that date. It is also permissible to conduct measurements at an earlier date and project them forward to the fiscal year-end date to account for subsequent events.

When you present financial statements for interim periods, there are two alternatives for measuring plan assets:

1. Measure the plan assets and benefit obligations as of the end of each interim period.
2. Use the same asset or liability recognized in the previous year-end balance sheet, adjusted for subsequent contributions, benefit payments, and accruals of net periodic pension cost that exclude the amortization of amounts previously recognized in other comprehensive income.

 ## How Do I Account for More than One Plan?

If an entity has more than one defined benefit plan, you should separately determine their net periodic pension cost, liabilities, and assets.

How Do I Account for a Settlement?

You should measure the projected benefit obligation as of the date the settlement occurs, and determine the maximum gain or loss that may be recognized in earnings. You should recognize this maximum amount in earnings if the entire projected benefit obligation has been settled. If only a portion of the projected benefit obligation has been settled, then you should recognize in earnings the pro rata portion of the maximum amount equal to the percentage reduction in the projected benefit obligation.

 How Do I Account for a Benefit Curtailment?

If an entity curtails existing benefits in a defined benefit plan, this creates a gain. If the gain exceeds any net loss included in accumulated other comprehensive income, the excess is a curtailment gain.

If an entity curtails an aspect of a defined benefit plan that accelerates employees' earning of benefits, then this creates a loss. You should recognize a curtailment loss for the excess by which such a loss exceeds any gain recorded in accumulated other comprehensive income.

You should record a curtailment gain or loss in earnings when it is probable that a curtailment will occur, as well as when the amount can be reasonably estimated. If you intend to recognize a curtailment net gain, then only do so when the related employee terminations are complete, or when the board of directors approves a plan suspension.

EXAMPLE 19.8

Ambrosia Cuisine discontinues its Canola Oil production facility; the employees of that segment will earn no further benefits. Under current actuarial assumptions as of the curtailment date, Ambrosia has a defined benefit obligation with a present value of $100,000, plan assets having a fair value of $75,000, and net cumulative unrecognized actuarial gains of $5,000. The curtailment reduces the present value of the obligation by $10,000, to $90,000. 10% of the net cumulative unrecognized actuarial gains relate to the part of the obligation that was eliminated by the curtailment. These changes result in the post-curtailment figures in the following table:

(Continued)

	Prior to Curtailment	Curtailment Gain	Post Curtailment
Obligation present value	$100,000	$(10,000)	$90,000
Plan assets fair value	(75,000)	–	(75,000)
	25,000	(10,000)	15,000
Unrecognized actuarial gains	5,000	500	5,500
Net liability in statement of financial position	$ 30,000	$ (9,500)	$20,500

Ambrosia records the curtailment gain with the following entry:

Accrued pension cost	9,500	
Curtailment gain		9,500

Can I Use Approximations to Calculate Benefits?

Yes. You can use averages or computational shortcuts to reduce the cost of determining compensation expense, as long as you reasonably expect that the results will not be materially different from the results of a detailed calculation.

What Information Should I Disclose about a Defined Benefit Plan?

You should separately disclose for each pension plan the following information in an entity's financial statements or accompanying notes:

- ○ The benefit obligation, fair value of plan assets, and funded status of the plan.
- ○ The amount of employer contributions, participant contributions, and benefits paid.
- ○ Description of investment policies and strategies for the plan.
- ○ The fair value of each major category of plan assets.
- ○ The basis used to determine the expected long-term rate of return on assets.

- Information readers can use to assess the inputs and valuation techniques used to develop fair value measurements of plan assets at the reporting date.
- The net periodic benefit cost recognized.
- The accumulated benefit obligation.
- The benefits the entity expects to pay in each of the next five fiscal years, and in aggregate for the following five fiscal years.
- The best estimate for contributions to be paid to the plan during the next fiscal year.
- The post-retirement benefit assets and liabilities recognized in the balance sheet.
- The net gain or loss and net prior service cost or credit recognized in other comprehensive income for the period, as well as related reclassification adjustments to other comprehensive income.
- The amounts in accumulated other comprehensive income not yet recognized that are the various components of the pension liability.
- The amount in other comprehensive income in the reporting period that resulted from a change in the additional minimum pension liability recognized.
- The assumed health care cost trend rate for the next year that was used to measure the expected cost of benefits covered by the plan.
- The amount and types of employer securities included in plan assets, and significant transactions between the employer and the plan.
- The nature and effect of non-routine plan events, such as amendments, curtailments, and settlements.
- The amounts in accumulated other comprehensive income that you expect will be recognized in the next fiscal year.
- The amount and timing of any plan assets that you expect will be returned to the employer within the next 12 months.

The disclosure requirements are more extensive for the pension plans of publicly-held entities.

What Is a Defined Contribution Plan?

Under a defined contribution plan, each participant receives an individual account, to which are contributed amounts by the employer or employee, as well as investment earnings and forfeitures allocated to the account. The funds in the account are reduced by any administrative expenses charged to the plan.

How Do I Account for a Defined Contribution Plan?

Under a defined contribution plan, you should record the benefit cost in the amount of the contribution called for in each period. If the plan also calls for contributions in periods after employees retire, then accrue an estimate of this additional cost during the employee service period.

 ### What Information Should I Disclose about a Defined Contribution Plan?

You should disclose the amount of cost recognized for defined contribution pension plans, as well as for other defined contribution post-retirement benefit plans. Include a description of the effect of any significant changes during the period that impact comparability; possible changes include the rate of employer contributions, business combinations, and divestitures.

CHAPTER 20

STOCK COMPENSATION

 What Are Share-Based Payment Arrangements and Awards?

A share-based payment arrangement is one under which either an entity issues an award of equity shares, share options, or other such instruments to a supplier, or the entity incurs liabilities to a supplier where the liability amount is based on the price of the entity's shares or the liability may require settlement in the entity's shares.

A share-based award is the same as a share-based payment, except that the recipient in this case is an employee, and the payment is a form of compensation.

 What Is an Employee?

An employee is an individual over whom the grantor of share-based compensation exercises sufficient control to establish an employer-employee relationship based on common law.

A leased individual is an employee if he or she qualifies as a common law employee of the lessee, the lessee has the exclusive right to grant stock compensation to the individual, the lessee has the right to hire, fire, and control the activities of the individual, the individual can participate in the lessee's employee benefit plans, and the lessee agrees to remit to the lessor sufficient funds to cover the individual's complete compensation.

 What Is the Grant Date?

The grant date is the date on which an employer and employee mutually agree upon the key terms and conditions of a share-based payment award. On the grant date, the employer becomes obligated to issue equity instruments or transfer assets to the employee, contingent upon the employee rendering the required amount of service.

If the award is subject to shareholder approval, then do not consider the award to be granted until you have obtained this approval. However, if the approval is essentially a formality, then the grant date is not subject to shareholder approval.

If an award is of equity instruments, then the grant date is the first date on which an employee begins to benefit from, or be adversely affected by, any subsequent changes in the price of the employer's equity shares.

EXAMPLE 20.1

The Long Walk Shoe Company's president promises 50,000 stock options to Mr. Evans, who has just been hired as the company's new sales manager. According to the company's articles of incorporation, only the board of directors can approve equity issuances. The Board has authorized a subcommittee, the Equity Grant Committee, to make these authorizations on its behalf. The president promised the stock options on June 1, the Equity Grant Committee approves the transaction on July 1, and the Board formally approves the actions of the Equity Grant Committee on August 1.

The correct grant date for the stock options is July 1, which is the date when an authorized representative of the Board approves the grant.

 ## What Is Vesting?

When used in conjunction with share-based compensation, vesting is earning the right to a share-based award. The payment becomes vested on the date when the employee's right to receive the award is no longer contingent upon the satisfaction of any service or performance condition. A market-based condition is not a vesting condition. A common vesting condition requires the passage of time, so that a share-based award is vested once the required time period has been completed.

 ## What Are Non-Vested Shares?

Non-vested shares are those not yet issued by an entity, because the employee has not yet completed his or her service period. An employee cannot sell non-vested shares, since the employee must forfeit them if the service period is not completed.

How Do I Account for a Share-Based Award?

You should recognize the compensation cost of a share-based award to employees over the requisite service period. This period is the period over which an employee provides services in exchange for an award, and usually corresponds to the vesting period of the award. To account for such a payment, debit the related expense and credit either an equity or liability account, depending upon whether the award is to be classified as equity or a liability. An award settled in stock calls for a credit to an equity account, while an award settled in cash requires a credit to a liability account.

You should accrue an expense for a share-based award based on the probable outcome of a performance condition associated with the award. Thus, you should accrue the award if the employee will probably achieve the performance condition, and do not accrue the expense if it is not probable that the employee will achieve the performance condition.

The amount you accrue for a share-based award is measured based on the fair value of the equity instruments that the entity issues. You should measure the fair value on the grant date of the share-based award.

Example 20.2

The Wilkerson Supercomputer Company orders a specially-designed computer chip from a supplier, and receives delivery on July 31. The supplier has agreed to accept 10,000 of Wilkerson's ordinary shares as payment. The chips are custom-designed for Wilkerson, so it is impossible to directly determine their value. Instead, Wilkerson assigns a value to the transaction based on the market price of its shares on July 31 (the delivery date) of $5.50. Thus, Wilkerson records an expense of $55,000 on the delivery date.

If an employee pays for an equity instrument when it is granted, then the portion of the fair value of the instrument that you should attribute to employee service is net of the amount that the employee paid to the entity.

EXAMPLE 20.3

Hostetler Corporation issues 100 shares of its stock to Hugh Hostetler, a member of the founding family. On the grant date, the fair value of these shares was $50 each. Mr. Hostetler paid $10 to the company for each of the 100 shares. Thus, the amount that Hostetler Corporation's controller can attribute to Mr. Hostetler's employee services to the company is $4,000 ($5,000 share fair value - $1,000 employee payment).

How Does the Vesting of a Share-Based Award Impact the Recognition of Services?

If an entity settles a share-based payment in equity and the equity vests immediately, then the entity presumes that the related services have also been completed, and should recognize the full amount of the transaction at once.

If an entity settles a share-based payment in equity and the equity *does not* vest at once, then the entity presumes that the related services will be provided over the vesting period, and accordingly recognizes the services over the vesting period. There are three conditions under which you can estimate the vesting period:

○ *Fixed period.* If the vesting period is fixed in the agreement, then use the stated vesting period over which to recognize the related expense.

○ *Market condition.* If the vesting period is dependent upon a market condition, then estimate the expected vesting period, ratably recognize the expense over that period, and do not subsequently revise it.

○ *Performance condition.* If the vesting period is based upon the completion of a performance condition, then estimate the vesting period at the grant date, using the most likely outcome. You should revise the vesting period if subsequent information indicates that a different vesting period is more likely.

What if I Cannot Determine the Fair Value of a Share-Based Award?

You should base the fair value of a share-based award on the observable market price of an identical or similar equity instrument. If this information is not available, then estimate the fair value using a valuation technique that incorporates all of the substantive characteristics of the instrument underlying the award, including its exercise price, expected term, current price of the underlying shares, expected price volatility, expected dividends, and the expected risk-free interest rate over the expected option term. The types of information to use within the valuation calculation include the following:

- ○ *Exercise price.* This is located in the award documentation.
- ○ *Expected term.* The expected period of time that elapses before an employee elects to exercise an option is most easily derived (and justified) from historical experience. Exercising an option is correlated with the price of the underlying share. Other factors impacting the expected term are the expected volatility of the underlying stock price, the vesting period of the award, any blackout periods during which vesting is not allowed, employee age, and employee length of service.
- ○ *Current price of the underlying shares.* This information is readily available for publicly-traded equity instruments.
- ○ *Expected price volatility.* Price volatility is the amount by which a share price is expected to fluctuate during a period. Consider the historical volatility of a share, as well as its tendency to revert to a long-run average level. Ignore volatility within a time period when price volatility was caused by a specific event that is not expected to occur again.
- ○ *Expected dividends.* Consider an entity's historical pattern of changes in dividend payments.
- ○ *Expected risk-free interest rate.* If using a lattice model (as described later in this answer), incorporate the implied yield currently available from the

U.S. Treasury zero-coupon yield curve over the contractual term of the option. If using a different model, incorporate the implied yield currently available on U.S. Treasury zero-coupon issues with a remaining term equal to the expected term of the option.

Examples of valuation methods that can be used are the lattice model and the Black-Scholes-Merton formula. Descriptions of these two methods are as follows:

○ *Lattice model.* The lattice model can be designed to accommodate a variety of assumptions regarding expected volatility and dividend payments over the term of an option, as well as varying option exercise patterns.
○ *Black-Scholes-Merton formula (BSM).* The BSM formula assumes that the holder of an option exercises it at the end of the option's contractual term, and that expected volatility, expected dividends, and risk-free interest rates will be consistent over the term of the option.

Of these two valuation methods, the lattice model is more complex, but can be tailored to the specific circumstances of a share-based award, while the BSM formula's assumption of weighted-average conditions is not so precise, but does require less effort to construct.

Example 20.4 (Lattice Model)

Assume Manly Corporation grants an option on a $20 stock that will expire in one year. The option exercise price equals the stock price of $20. Also, assume there is a 50% chance that the price will jump 20% over the year and a 50% chance the stock will drop 20%, and that no other outcomes are possible. The risk-free interest rate is 4%. With these assumptions there are three basic calculations:

1. Plot the two possible future stock prices.
2. Translate these stock prices into future options values.
3. Discount these future values into a single present value.

The following lattice shows the outcome of these assumptions (Exhibit 20.1):

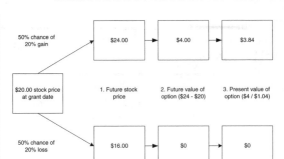

Exhibit 20.1 LATTICE MODEL

In this case, the option will only have value if the stock price increases, and otherwise the option would expire worthless and unexercised. In this example, there is a 50% chance of the option having a value of $3.84, and therefore the option is worth $1.92 at the grant date.

EXAMPLE 20.5 (BSM MODEL)

Manly Corporation's stock is currently selling at $40 and the standard deviation of prices over the past several years was $6.50, thus yielding an estimated volatility of $6.50/$40 = 16.25%. Assume the following facts:

S	=	$40
t	=	2 years
K	=	$45
r	=	3% annual rate
s	=	standard deviation of percentage returns = 16.25% (based on $6.50 standard deviation of stock price compared to current $40 price)

From the foregoing data, the factors d_1 and d_2 can be computed. The cumulative standard normal variates (N) of these values must then be determined (using a table or formula), following which the BSM option value is calculated, *before the effect of dividends*. In this example, the computed amounts are:

$N(d_1)$	=	0.2758
$N(d_2)$	=	0.2048

(Continued)

With these assumptions the value of the stock options is approximately $2.35. This is derived from the BSM as follows:

C		
	=	$SN(d_1) - Ke^{(-rt)}N(d_2)$
	=	$40(.2758) - 45(.942)(.2048)$
	=	$11.032 - 8.679$
	=	2.35

The foregone two-year streams of dividends, which in this example are projected to be $0.50 annually, have a present value of $0.96. Therefore, the net value of this option is $1.39 ($2.35 − .96).

Generally Accepted Accounting Principles (GAAP) does not state a preference for any particular valuation model.

 Can I Change Valuation Techniques?

Yes. You can change to a different technique to value a share-based award if you believe it will yield a better estimate of fair value. You may also use different valuation techniques for different share-based awards, using the same justification.

 How Do I Derive a Private Company's Stock Volatility?

A non-public entity may not be able to reasonably estimate the fair value of an award at its grant date, because the volatility of its shares may be difficult to determine. If so, a non-public entity should consider using the historical volatility of an industry sector index, or the average volatility of comparable entities.

If an entity operates in multiple industries, it could derive a suitable measure of volatility by using the historical volatilities of multiple industry sectors and weighting them based on the entity's participation in those industries. Conversely, it could choose to use the volatility of the industry sector that most closely represents its operations.

An entity should consistently use the same industry sector index or weighted-average participation in multiple indexes, unless a change in its operations warrants the use of a different index or index weighting.

EXAMPLE 20.6

Starling Airlines is a small nonpublic entity that operates local charter flights. It grants 25,000 stock options to its employees. Starling's controller locates an industry stock price volatility index for the airline industry, and uses it to derive an annualized historical stock price volatility of 38%. The controller includes this volatility and other factors in a Black-Scholes-Merton option-pricing calculation, yielding a value of $3.92 per share. When multiplied by the number of stock options granted, this results in a total compensation expense of $98,000. The vesting period is two years, so the company recognizes a related compensation expense of $49,000 per year for the two years of the vesting period.

How Do I Account for an Equity Instrument Whose Fair Value Is Not Reasonably Estimable?

If it is not possible to reasonably estimate the fair value of an equity instrument at its grant date, then continue to remeasure the instrument at each reporting date until the date of settlement. As the final compensation cost of the instrument, you should use the intrinsic value of the instrument on its settlement date. Intrinsic value is the difference between the price a party must pay for the right to receive shares, and the fair value of those shares.

The compensation cost in each period prior to settlement is the change in the intrinsic value of the instrument (which may be recognized over multiple reporting periods, depending on the duration of the underlying service requirement).

EXAMPLE 20.7

The Quack's Roast Duck franchise chain pays for the services of a legal firm with share options. Each option has an exercise price of $10 and a fair value of $15. The intrinsic value of each option is $5, which is the difference between its fair value and exercise price.

If it later becomes possible to determine the fair value of an equity instrument, you should continue to use the intrinsic value method for that instrument.

Can I Reduce the Share Option Expense by the Amount of Expected Forfeitures?

Yes. You should adjust the compensation expense accrual for the estimated rate of share option forfeitures. This forfeiture rate should be based on a combination of historical employee turnover rates and expectations for future forfeiture rates. You may adjust this rate over the vesting period, depending on actual experience rates over the course of the vesting period.

EXAMPLE 20.8

Industrial Donut Corporation issues 10,000 stock options having a fair value of $100,000, and which vest over three years. The company has experienced a historical forfeiture rate of 10%, and expects this rate to continue. Consequently, it expects to record a total compensation expense of $90,000 (net of expected forfeitures) over the three-year period.

After one year, actual forfeitures are substantially higher than expectations, so management changes the forfeiture rate to 40%, which will result in a total compensation expense of $60,000 over the three-year period. The company already recorded a compensation expense accrual of $30,000 in the first year, and now records an accrual of only $10,000 in the second year, resulting in a total two-year accrual of $40,000, which is appropriately two-thirds of the total expected compensation expense.

Should I Recognize an Expense for Unvested Forfeited Share-Based Compensation?

No. If share-based compensation includes a service or performance condition and the recipient does not fulfill the condition, you should not recognize any compensation cost for the compensation.

EXAMPLE 20.9

Kensington Properties grants 10,000 restricted stock units to Mr. Berthold, with a two-year cliff vesting period. On the grant date, the market price of the company's stock was $5; thus, the fair value of the restricted stock units was $50,000. Kensington's controller accrues a compensation expense of $25,000 in the first year of the vesting period, and another $25,000 in the second year of the vesting period. However, Mr. Berthold leaves the company two days prior to the cliff vesting date of the award. Since the award does not vest, the controller reverses the $50,000 of accruals.

 ## What Happens if I Modify the Terms of an Equity Instrument?

You may sometimes modify the terms and conditions of an equity instrument, such as altering an option exercise price or the vesting period. These changes can alter the fair value of the equity instrument. The primary measurement concept is to, at least, always recognize goods and services received based on the fair value of the equity instruments on their grant date, unless vesting is not yet complete. This applies even if the instruments are later modified, canceled, or replaced. In addition, you should recognize instrument modifications that incrementally *increase* the fair value of the instruments. Here are the key accounting issues related to terms modifications:

- ○ *Replacements.* If an entity grants new equity instruments to an employee and identifies them on the grant date as replacements for canceled instruments, then recognize the incremental increase (if any) of the fair value of the new instruments on their grant date over the old instruments immediately prior to their cancellation.
- ○ *Settlement.* If an equity instrument is settled during the vesting period, treat it as vesting acceleration, and immediately recognize all remaining expenses that would otherwise have been recognized later in the vesting period.

This answer has assumed that terms modifications are being applied to an equity instrument granted to an employee. If the grant is to a supplier, the accounting treatment is the same, except that you replace the grant date with the date when the entity obtains goods or services from the supplier.

EXAMPLE 20.10

Mr. Smith is the president of World Audio Distributors. World's board of directors granted him 100,000 restricted stock units (RSUs) on January 1 of Year 1, and they will fully vest on December 31 of Year 3. The RSUs were initially valued at $3.60 each, or $360,000 in total. Since Mr. Smith is assumed to be providing services during the vesting period, the company charges $10,000 to compensation expense in each of the 36 months.

After 10 months, the board of directors decides to modify the terms of the RSUs, so that they vest immediately. At this point, $260,000 of the related expense remains unvested, so World must charge the remaining $260,000 to expense as of the date of the modification.

At the date of modification, if the entity does not expect that the award would have vested under the original vesting conditions, then it should only recognize the cumulative compensation cost of the modified award.

EXAMPLE 20.11

Pilkington Pottery grants 10,000 restricted stock units to its most productive salesperson, which will cliff vest in three years, but only if the salesperson exceeds a sales quota of 15,000 units during the three-year period. After two years, it is apparent that the sales person will not meet the sales quota, so Pilkington does not accrue a compensation expense, on the assumption that the restricted stock units will not vest.

Pilkington's president modifies the grant terms to extend it by one year, in order to give an added incentive to the salesperson. Doing so greatly increases the probability of the salesperson meeting the vesting criteria, so Pilkington fully accrues the compensation expense associated with the grant over the remaining term of the agreement.

What Is a Reload Feature?

A reload feature is a provision for the automatic granting of additional options whenever an employee exercises previously granted options and uses the entity's shares, instead of cash, to satisfy the exercise price. At the time of such exercise, the entity automatically grants the employee a new option for the shares that he or she used to exercise the previous option.

 ## How Do I Account for a Reload Feature?

A reload feature automatically grants additional share options whenever an option holder exercises previously-granted options using an entity's shares to satisfy the exercise price. If a share option contains a reload feature, do not include it in an estimate of the fair value of options granted. Instead, account for it as a new option grant.

 ## How Do I Account for a Cash-Settled Share-Based Payment Transaction?

When an entity settles a share-based payment in cash, measure the goods or services received at the fair value of the offsetting liability. You should re-measure the liability's fair value at the end of each reporting period and at final settlement, and recognize in profit or loss any incremental changes in fair value following each measurement.

EXAMPLE 20.12

The Acme Roadrunner Tire Company grants 10,000 restricted share units (RSUs) to its chief executive officer, Mr. Coyote, under which Acme will pay Mr. Coyote, in cash, the net increase in the RSUs during their vesting period. The grant date is January 1, and the vesting date is December 31 of the same year. On January 1, Acme's stock sells for $5. On April 30, the share price has increased to $6, so Acme records compensation expense of $10,000. On October 31, the share price has dropped back to $5, so Acme reverses the $10,000 charge to compensation expense. On December 31, the settlement date, the share price has risen to $7, so Acme records compensation expense of $20,000 and pays the amount in cash to Mr. Coyote.

(Continued)

Acme's incremental income tax rate is 35%. The journal entries associated with this transaction are:

Compensation expense	20,000	
Share-based compensation liability		20,000
Deferred tax asset	7,000	
Deferred tax benefit		7,000

The final journal entry to record the payment to Mr. Coyote is:

Share-based compensation liability	20,000	
Cash		20,000

If employees must render services in exchange for cash-settled share-based payments, then recognize the services received and the offsetting liability as the employees render service. Again, you should re-measure the fair value of the instruments at the end of each reporting period and at settlement, and recognize any incremental changes in profit or loss.

EXAMPLE 20.13

Hephaestus Construction issues two grants to its chief executive officer, Ms. Charis. The first is restricted stock units (RSUs) worth $50,000 that vest immediately and that require cash payment. Since Ms. Charis has no service period requirement, Hephaestus should recognize the full amount of the compensation expense at once.

The second grant is for RSUs worth $100,000 that vest over 36 months, and which will be paid in cash. Due to the implied 36-month service period, Hephaestus should recognize the $100,000 compensation expense ratably over 36 months.

How Do I Account for a Non-Compete Agreement Linked to a Share-Based Award?

A share-based award may include a non-compete agreement. A non-compete agreement may actually be construed as a significant service condition, depending upon the facts and circumstances of the situation. If so, the compensation cost associated with the share-based award should be accrued over the duration of the non-compete agreement.

EXAMPLE 20.14

The Latham Lumber Company grants 50,000 restricted stock units (RSUs) to Emily Latham, its sales manager. The fair value of the grant is approximately five times her annual compensation, and is fully vested on the grant date. However, the company issues the RSUs to her on a delayed transfer schedule, at the rate of 10,000 RSUs per year for five years, and will only be transferred if she complies with the terms of the non-compete agreement. If Ms. Latham does not conform to the non-compete agreement, then she loses the right to the remaining RSUs. The company has a history of vigorously enforcing all prior non-compete agreements that were breached.

Given the company's history of enforcement of non-compete agreements, the matching of the transfer schedule to the terms of the non-compete agreement, and the size of the grant, it is evident that the grant is really intended to compensate Ms. Latham for her future service to the company. Accordingly, the company should recognize the expense associated with the share-based award over the five-year transfer schedule of the RSUs.

In Which Accounts Do I Record Share-Based Compensation?

When recording share-based compensation, you should debit a compensation expense account. The offsetting credit goes against the additional paid-in capital account.

When you record compensation expense related to share-based compensation, you should also create an accompanying journal entry to reduce income taxes, debiting the deferred tax asset account and crediting the deferred tax benefit account.

EXAMPLE 20.15

Katana Cutlery recognizes $100,000 of compensation expense related to share-based compensation. Katana's incremental income tax rate is 35%. Katana makes the following entry to record the expense recognition:

Compensation expense	100,000	
Additional paid-in capital		100,000
Deferred tax asset	35,000	
Deferred tax benefit		35,000

 ## What Happens to Vested Equity Instruments that Are Forfeited or Not Exercised?

There is no subsequent adjustment to total equity after the vesting date of an equity instrument. Thus, if an employee does not exercise share options or a supplier forfeits vested shares, you should not reverse the related amounts recognized for services received.

 ## When Do I Calculate the Cost of a Share-Based Payment?

You should calculate the cost of a share-based payment on the grant date. The grant date is usually the date on which the award is approved, as long as the award is a unilateral grant, and someone will communicate the terms and conditions of the award to the recipient within a short time period from the approval date.

 ## What if the Service Inception Date Is Prior to the Grant Date?

The service inception date is the beginning of the service period associated with a share-based payment. When the service inception date precedes the grant date, you should accrue the related compensation cost for all periods between the service inception date and the grant date, based on the fair value of the award on each successive reporting date.

Once the grant date arrives, lock in the fair value of the award on that date, and adjust the cumulative compensation cost to date based on the fair value of the award on the grant date. From the grant date onward, the fair value of the award is frozen at the fair value on the grant date.

 ## When Do I Account for Payroll Taxes Associated with Share-Based Payments?

You should recognize a liability for employee payroll taxes related to a share-based payment on the date when an event triggers the measurement and payment of the tax. This is generally the exercise date of the payment.

 ## How Do I Account for the Repurchase of a Vested Equity Instrument?

If an entity repurchases a vested equity instrument, account for the payment as a deduction from equity. If the payment exceeds the fair value of the equity instruments that the entity purchased as of the repurchase date, then recognize the excess as additional compensation expense.

 ## How Do I Account for the Cancellation of an Equity Instrument?

If an entity cancels an equity instrument, and there is no concurrent replacement by another award, then accelerate the recognition of any previously unrecognized compensation cost as of the cancellation date.

 ## What Is an Employee Stock Purchase Plan?

An employee stock purchase plan allows employees to buy shares of employer stock, usually under a subscription plan where a deduction is made from their pay and used to acquire stock at fixed intervals. Such a plan may include a discount from the market price on the purchase date.

 ## How Do I Account for an Employee Stock Purchase Plan?

You should not recognize any compensation expense associated with an employee stock purchase plan if the plan satisfies all of the following four criteria:

1. The terms of the plan are no more favorable than those available to all holders of the same class of shares, or the purchase discount does not exceed the discount that would have been given to raise a significant amount of capital in a public offering.
2. Substantially all employees meeting employment requirements can participate in the purchase plan.
3. Employees have no more than 31 days after the purchase price has been fixed in which to enroll in the plan.
4. Employees are permitted to cancel their participation in the plan before the purchase date and obtain a refund.

If there is a purchase discount of 5% or less, then you do not have to record a compensation expense in the amount of the discount. However, you should recognize the full amount of the discount as a compensation expense if the discount is greater than 5%, unless you can justify the greater discount.

EXAMPLE 20.16

The Nocturnal Widget Company has an employee stock purchase plan. Under the terms of the plan, employees can purchase shares for a 15% discount from the market price. Employees have $85,000 deducted from their pay, which is used to acquire company shares having a fair value of $100,000. Nocturnal cannot justify the 15% discount as being similar to the discount required to sell shares in a significant public offering, so it must record the entire $15,000 difference between the stock's fair value and its purchase price by employees as a compensation expense.

What Information Should I Disclose about Share-Based Payments?

You should disclose the following information about share-based payment arrangements in the notes accompanying the financial statements:

○ The nature of such arrangements and their effect on shareholders, including:

• The general terms of awards
• The number and weighted-average exercise prices of share options at the beginning of the year, end

of the year, exercisable at the end of the year, and for those that were granted, exercised, forfeited, or expired during the year

- The number and weighted-average grant-date fair value of equity options or other such instruments granted during the year
- The total intrinsic value of options exercised, share-based liabilities paid, and the fair value of shares vested during the year
- For any fully-vested share options, the number, weighted-average exercise price, aggregate intrinsic value, and weighted-average contractual terms remaining outstanding
- For those share options currently exercisable, the number, weighted-average exercise price, aggregate intrinsic value, and weighted-average contractual terms remaining outstanding
- The policy for issuing shares when a share option is exercised, including the source of those shares

EXAMPLE 20.17

Luminescence Corporation's 20X1 stock option plan, which is approved by its shareholders, permits the granting of stock options and shares to its employees for up to 12 million shares of common stock. Luminescence believes that these awards better align the interests of its employees with those of its shareholders. Luminescence grants stock options with an exercise price equal to the market price of its common stock at the average of its closing price for the preceding five business days; these awards vest based on five years of continuous service, and have five-year contractual terms. Share awards vest over two years. If there is a change in control, the terms of the employee stock option plan provide for accelerated vesting.

The fair value of each option award was estimated on the grant-date using a lattice-based option valuation model that incorporates the assumption noted below. Expected stock price volatilities are based on implied volatilities from traded options in Luminescence's stock and the historical volatility of this stock. Historical data was used to estimate the exercise of options, as well as employee terminations. The risk-free interest rate of periods within the contractual life of an option is based on the U.S Treasury yield curve that was in effect at the time of each grant.

(Continued)

	20X1	20X2	20X3
Expected volatility	15%–30%	17%–32%	19%–34%
Weighted-average volatility	23%	24%	25%
Expected dividends	2%	2%	2%
Expected term in years	5.0–7.0	4.8–6.8	4.6–6.6
Risk-free interest rate	3.0%–4.5%	3.2%–4.7%	3.4%–4.9%

A summarization of option activity under the employee share option plan as of December 31, 20X1, and changes that occurred during that year follows:

Options	Shares	Weighted-Average Exercise Price	Weighted-Average Remaining Contractual Term	Aggregate Intrinsic Value
Outstanding at 1/1/X1	1,000,000	$10.50		
Granted	250,000	11.00		
Exercised	(100,000)	9.50		
Forfeited or expired	(50,000)	11.25		
Outstanding at 12/31/X1	1,100,000	$10.85	4.8	$8,521,000
Exercisable at 12/31/X1	800,000	$10.00	2.9	$6,197,000

A summarization of the status of Luminescence's non-vested shares as of December 31, 20X1, and changes during the year ended December 31, 20X1 follows:

Non-Vested Shares	Shares	Weighted-Average Grant-Date Fair Value
Non-vested at 1/1/20X1	400,000	$9.75
Granted	250,000	11.00
Vested	(400,000)	10.50
Forfeited or expired	(50,000)	11.25
Non-vested at 12/31/20X1	200,000	$10.80

○ The effect on compensation cost of the arrangements, including:

- The method used to measure compensation costs
- Total compensation cost for share-based payment arrangements

- Description of significant modifications to the arrangements, including the number of employees affected and the resulting incremental change in compensation costs
- The compensation cost associated with non-vested awards that are not yet recognized, and the weighted-average period over which you expect to recognize the cost

EXAMPLE 20.18

As of December 31, 20X1, there was $2,160,000 of total unrecognized compensation cost related to non-vested share-based compensation arrangements granted under Luminescence's employee share option plan. That cost is expected to be recognized over a weighted-average period of 4.8 years.

During 20X1, the contractual life of 50,000 fully vested share options held by the senior management team was extended. Because of that modification, Luminescence recognized additional compensation expense of $82,000 for the year ended December 31, 20X1.

○ The method used to estimate the fair value of either the goods or services received, or the equity instruments granted, including:

- The significant assumptions used to estimate the fair value of awards
- The method used to estimate the fair value of awards

○ The cash flow effects of the arrangements, including:

- The amount of cash received from, and used to settle, the exercise of share options, as well as from similar instruments that were granted under share-based payment arrangements

You do not have to disclose the preceding information in interim financial reports.

CHAPTER 21

OTHER EXPENSES

 What Are Start-Up Activities?

Start-up activities are one-time actions related to opening a new facility, introducing a new product or service, conducting business in a new geographic region or with a new class of customers, starting a new operation, or initiating a new process in an existing facility.

 How Do I Account for Start-Up Costs?

You should charge all start-up costs to expense as incurred.

EXAMPLE 21.1

Hostetler Corporation is opening a new distribution center in British Columbia for its sports equipment subsidiary. The following table shows the proper accounting treatment for the various costs that it incurs as part of the start-up activities:

	Expense	Capitalize
Travel costs	X	
Employee salaries	X	
Feasibility studies	X	
Employee training	X	
Nonrecurring operating losses	X	
Building construction costs		X

What Is a Claims-Made Insurance Contract?

Under a claims-made insurance policy, an insurer provides coverage to an entity for only those claims reported during the term of the policy. Coverage typically includes claims made for which the underlying event occurred prior to the policy effective date but after the specified retroactive date.

An entity usually continues to buy claims-made coverage in multiple successive years. If it elects to stop such coverage (typically when operations cease), it may purchase *tail coverage*, which provides insurance coverage in subsequent periods against any previously unasserted claims.

How Do I Account for a Claims-Made Insurance Contract?

If a claims-made insurance policy includes a retroactive provision that provides coverage for claims arising in prior periods, then you should (if possible) separately account for this portion of the policy. If there is retroactive coverage but it is not possible to separately account for this portion of the policy, then account for the entire policy as a retroactive policy.

If you can reasonably estimate the amounts and timing of insurance recoveries under a retrospective policy, then recognize the policy cost over the estimated period over which you expect to recover the amounts due under the contract terms. If you cannot estimate the amount and timing of these recoveries, then recognize the policy cost in proportion to the actual recoveries as a percentage of total estimated recoveries.

If a claims-made policy does not contain a retroactive provision, then account for it on a prospective basis. For a prospective policy, you should ratably recognize the insurance expense over the coverage period. You should recognize tail coverage ratably over the period covered by the policy.

The following are indicators that a policy does not contain a retroactive provision:

○ The entity consistently buys claims-made coverage, and tail coverage is readily available.
○ The type of risk insured is inherently short-tailed, the policy term is for a limited time period, claims-made

---

EXAMPLE 21.2

The Grinch Toy Removal Company has obtained a directors and officer (D&O) insurance policy for many years, and intends to continue to do so in the future. The current policy contains no retroactive element. Grinch purchases a D&O policy on January 1 for $1,200,000, which provides coverage for the entire current calendar year. Grinch should recognize the policy cost on a straight-line basis over the year, at the rate of $100,000 per month.

---

is the most readily available type of coverage, *and* the occurrence date of the risk covered by the policy is unclear.

○ The policy contains an unambiguous trigger indicating claim coverage by the policy.

○ The premium charged for the policy does not significantly exceed the amount that a similar company would pay for a claims-made policy.

○ The premium is not based on estimates of specific, known events that are expected to be recovered under the policy.

○ The current-year premium does not significantly exceed the amount charged in previous years.

○ The policy is intended to cover insurance risk, and is not a financing arrangement.

○ If the policy contains a retroactive date, the duration of the retroactive coverage is short.

EXAMPLE 21.3

Armenian Imports enters into a directors and officers (D&O) insurance policy. Armenian includes in the insurer's D&O questionnaire a concern that a prior stock price decline could result in shareholder lawsuits. The parties agree that the policy will include coverage of any claims related to the stock price decline. By doing so, the premium price increases from $1 million to $15 million.

The policy contains a $14 million retroactive element, because it incorporates the expected cost of settling claims related to the stock price decline; the premium charged is essentially a financing of the unasserted claim. Thus, Armenian should split the insurance contract into its retroactive and prospective parts and account for them separately.

If some portion of a premium paid to an insurer is essentially a deposit, then you should record that portion of the payment as a deposit.

How Do I Account for an Incurred But Not Reported Claim?

You should recognize a liability for probable losses from incurred but not yet reported incidents, but only if the loss is both probable and can be reasonably estimated.

What Terms Are Associated with Contributions?

The following terms are commonly associated with contributions to a third party:

- ○ *Contribution.* The unconditional transfer of assets by an entity to a third party, or the cancellation of the third party's liabilities held by the entity. This is not an exchange transaction, where the parties exchange items of approximately equal value.
- ○ *Promise to give.* An agreement to contribute assets to another entity. This prospective contribution may be conditional upon the occurrence of an event.
- ○ *Unconditional promise to give.* An agreement to transfer funds that is contingent upon no more than the passage of time or the recipient's demand for performance.

How Do I Account for a Contribution?

You should recognize a contribution made as an expense in whichever period the related assets decline or liabilities increase (depending upon the type of contribution made). You should recognize an unconditional promise to give as soon as the agreement is legally binding.

If you transfer an asset to a third party as a contribution, you should recognize the asset at its fair value, rather than its carrying amount, and therefore recognize a gain or loss on the transaction.

How Do I Account for Property Taxes?

You should recognize on a straight-line basis a portion of property taxes in each month of the period covered by a property tax liability. Since an entity may not receive

EXAMPLE 21.4

The Ferranti Auto Design Laboratory donates the Aston Martin sports car in its lobby to the Auto Racing Museum. Ferranti had originally purchased the Aston Martin for $250,000, and then recorded $100,000 of accumulated depreciation. The automobile's fair value is now $450,000. Accordingly, Ferranti records the entry for the contribution:

Accumulated depreciation	100,000	
Charitable contribution expense	450,000	
Fixed assets – automobiles		250,000
Gain on contribution		300,000

notification of the exact amount of property tax due until late in a reporting period, it is acceptable to accrue an estimated property tax in earlier months, and then adjust the accrual to match the actual billing. You may include the property tax expense in the operating expenses category on the income statement, or as a separate deduction from income.

You should record accrued property taxes as a current liability.

What Activities Are Included in Advertising?

In general, advertising activities are those that promote an industry, entity, brand, product name, or specific products or services. The two main components of advertising are the cost to produce it (such as idea development, artwork, and printing) and communication (such as billboard space and television airtime).

Examples of types of advertising are buyer's guides, advertisements in newspapers and on television, reprints of advertisements, direct mail pieces, billboard advertisements, product catalogues, cooperative advertising, sponsorships, and point-of-sale materials.

How Do I Account for Advertising?

You should charge the cost of advertising to expense either as an entity incurs it or when advertising takes place for the first time. You should consistently apply whichever method you select.

If it becomes apparent that an advertising campaign will not occur, then expense all advertising costs associated with it at once.

If you produce sales brochures that are expected to be used over more than one reporting period, then it is acceptable to treat them as prepaid supplies and charge them to expense as they are used. However, if there is no expectation of using remaining stocks, then you should charge all remaining associated costs to expense at once.

EXAMPLE 21.5

The Nocturnal Widget Company is planning an advertising campaign for its new night vision goggle product line. The cost to produce the magazine advertisement is $25,000, which Nocturnal records as a prepaid asset. The company then buys an ad placement in a home security magazine for $10,000, which it also records as a prepaid expense. When the advertisement first runs in the magazine in the following month, Nocturnal charges the entire $35,000 to advertising expense.

What Information Should I Disclose About Advertising?

You should disclose the following information about advertising costs in the notes accompanying an entity's financial statements:

- ○ The accounting policy used to account for advertising (e.g., recognition as incurred or when advertising first occurs)
- ○ The total amount charged to advertising expense

What Is Business and Technology Reengineering?

Reengineering an entity's business and technology infrastructure includes software development, software acquisition and implementation, training, and ongoing support, as well as the purchase of office equipment, furniture, and work stations.

How Do I Account for Business and Technology Reengineering Costs?

You should charge all costs of business and technology reengineering to expense as incurred; the sole exception is property, plant, and equipment, which you should capitalize. Costs that can be capitalized include the costs of software design, coding, installation, testing, and data conversion.

If a business process reengineering project includes the acquisition, development, or implementation of internal-use software, you should charge these costs to expense as incurred, with the same exception for property, plant, and equipment.

The costs related to business and technology reengineering projects which should always be expensed include:

Request for proposal preparation	Determination of needed technology
Current state assessment	Selection of alternatives
Process reengineering	Training
Work force restructuring	Application maintenance
Conceptual formulation of alternatives	Ongoing support
Evaluation of alternatives	

CHAPTER 22

RESEARCH AND DEVELOPMENT EXPENSES

 What Is Research and Development?

Research is a planned search aimed at discovering new knowledge, with the hoped-for result that the new knowledge can be used to develop a new product, process, or technique, or to improve an existing product or process. Development is the translation of research findings into a new product or process, or to improve an existing product or process. Development includes such activities as designing and testing product alternatives, building prototypes, and operating pilot plants.

The following table notes which activities should (or should not) be considered research and development (R&D) activities:

Activity	R&D Activity	Not an R&D Activity
Laboratory research for the discovery of new knowledge	X	
Searching for applications of new research findings	X	
Conceptual formulation and design of possible products	X	
Product evaluation testing	X	
Modification of a product's formulation or design	X	
Building of preproduction prototypes	X	
Designing tools involving new technology	X	
Building and operating pilot plant	X	
Engineering activities to advance a product design	X	
Tools used to facilitate research and development	X	

(continued)

Activity	R&D Activity	Not an R&D Activity
Engineering follow-through on early commercial phase		X
Quality control during commercial production		X
Troubleshooting of problems during commercial production		X
Routine efforts to improve an existing product		X
Adapting a product to customer requirements		X
Periodic design changes to existing products		X
Routine design of molds, tools, and dies		X
Legal work on patent applications or litigation		X

How Do I Account for Research and Development Expenditures?

Most research and development activities cannot be directly linked to specific future benefits with any degree of certainty. Thus, they do not create a measurable asset, and so all costs associated with them should be charged to expense as incurred. More specifically, follow these guidelines:

- *Materials.* Capitalize as inventory when acquired or constructed, and recognize as an expense when used or deemed obsolete.
- *Equipment and facilities.* If equipment and facilities have no alternative future use other than in a specific research and development project, then charge their costs to expense as incurred. If there is an alternative future use, then capitalize their costs and depreciate them.
- *Personnel.* Charge the salaries and wages of those individuals working on research and development activities to expense as incurred.
- *Purchased intangible assets.* Capitalize the cost of only those purchased intangible assets relating to research and development activities that have alternative future uses. If there is no alternative future use, whether on other research and development projects or elsewhere, then charge their costs to expense immediately.
- *Contract services.* Charge the costs of others working on the entity's research and development projects to expense as incurred.
- *Indirect costs.* Include a reasonable allocation of indirect costs to research and development costs.

○ *Computer software.* If an entity acquires or builds software for use in a research and development project, charge its cost to expense as incurred unless the software has alternative future uses.

 ## What Information Should I Disclose about Research and Development Costs?

You should include in the notes accompanying an entity's financial statements, or in the financial statements themselves, the total amount of research and development costs charged to expense within the current reporting period.

 ## What Is a Research and Development Arrangement?

A research and development arrangement is used to finance the research and development of new products, frequently as a limited partnership. In a research and development partnership, the entity conducting the research may be the general partner. The limited partners may contribute funds, facilities, personnel, or intellectual property in exchange for an equity stake in the partnership. The entity performs the work under a contract with the partnership, with payment being either on a fixed fee basis or cost reimbursement plus a fee. Upon completion of the work, the partnership retains legal rights to the resulting technology.

The entity undertaking the research and development work for the partnership may incur an obligation to repay the partnership for some or all of the funds provided, or the only obligation may be to conduct the work on a best efforts basis.

In some arrangements, the entity has the right to either buy out the partnership's legal right to the technology, or obtain exclusive rights to it.

 ## How Do I Account for a Research and Development Arrangement?

The legal form of a research and development arrangement may vary from the substance of the arrangement. For example, an agreement to pay royalties may actually represent a debt repayment. Consequently, you should account for the transactions indicated by the substance of the arrangement, which may differ from the terms of the legal agreement.

The accounting for research and development arrangements under different scenarios is:

- ○ *Obligation to repay.* If the entity has an obligation to repay the funding to the partnership, irrespective of the results of the funded project, it should record a liability for the amount to be repaid, and charge research and development costs to expense as incurred.
- ○ *Obligation to perform contractual services.* If the financial risk associated with a project has been transferred to the partnership, then the entity should account for the project as a contract to perform services.
- ○ *Warrants.* If the entity issues warrants as part of a funding arrangement, then it should report a portion of the proceeds as paid-in capital, in the amount of the fair value of the warrants issued.

 ## What Information Do I Disclose about a Research and Development Arrangement?

If an entity accounts for its obligations under a research and development arrangement as a contract for services, then you should disclose:

- ○ The terms of significant research and development arrangements.
- ○ The amount of compensation recognized and costs incurred under the arrangements.

It may be appropriate to aggregate the disclosure for multiple similar arrangements.

EXAMPLE 22.1

Des Moines Agricultural Research enters into an R&D arrangement with a funding partnership. Under the terms of the agreement, the partnership pays Des Moines $15,000,000 for a research project involving soybean modifications for dry climates; also, the agreement stipulates that the partners in the partnership can require Des Moines to buy their interests in the partnership at a stipulated price per share, no matter what the outcome of the project may be. This arrangement is effectively an obligation to repay, so Des Moines should record the $15,000,000 as a liability.

CHAPTER 23

INCOME TAXES

What Is Taxable Profit?

Taxable profit is the profit or loss upon which income taxes are payable. The composition of taxable profit varies by taxation authority, so it will vary depending on the rules of the taxation authorities within which an entity is located or does business.

What Is Tax Basis?

The tax basis of an asset is the amount that will be deductible for tax purposes against any taxable economic benefits generated by the asset. If the economic benefits are nontaxable, then an asset's tax basis equals its carrying amount.

EXAMPLE 23.1

Bonifacio Bakeries owns an automated baking oven that cost $100,000 that it is depreciating on a straight-line basis over ten years. After three years, it has depreciated $30,000 of the baking oven's cost. The remaining $70,000 cost will be deductible in future periods. The baked goods that Bonifacio produces with the baking oven generate taxable revenue. Consequently, the remaining $70,000 cost of the baking oven is the tax basis of the asset, to be deducted against future revenues.

The tax basis of a liability is its carrying amount minus any amount related to that liability that will be deductible for tax purposes in the future. If an entity receives revenue in advance, its tax basis for the resulting liability will be its carrying amount, less any amount that will not be taxable in the future.

> ### EXAMPLE 23.2
>
> The Ginseng Plus retail chain records accrued expenses of $5,000. Ginseng reports its taxable results on a cash basis, so there is no tax basis for the accrued expenses. If Ginseng reported its taxable results on an accrual basis, the accrued expenses would have a tax basis of $5,000.

How Do I Recognize a Tax Liability?

You should record the current tax for current and prior periods as a liability, if not already paid. If you have paid more than the tax amount due in the current and prior periods, then record the excess as an asset.

What Is a Carryback and a Carryforward?

A carryback is a deduction or credit that can be carried back to reduce taxable income or taxes payable in a prior year. A carryforward is a deduction or credit that can be carried forward to reduce taxable income or taxes payable in a future year. In both cases, the carryback and carryforward amounts cannot be used in the current tax return, thereby making them available in other periods.

How Do I Recognize a Carryback Tax Loss?

If you record a tax loss that you can carry back to recover taxes paid in a previous period, you can recognize the eligible tax loss as an asset in the current period.

What Are Deferred Tax Assets and Liabilities?

A deferred tax liability is income taxes payable in a future period, while a deferred tax asset is income taxes recoverable in a future period that is caused by a deductible temporary difference, and the carryforward of either unused tax losses or unused tax credits.

What Is a Temporary Difference?

A temporary difference is the difference between the carrying amount of an asset or liability in the statement of

Example 23.3

Electro Tram has the following assets and liabilities at the end of its fiscal year (in thousands):

	Carrying Amount	Tax Basis	Temporary Difference
Cash	$3,500	$3,500	$ 0
Accounts receivable	8,000	8,500	(500)
Inventory	6,500	7,500	(1,000)
Plant and equipment	11,000	9,250	1,750
Accounts payable	2,000	2,000	0
			$250

In the table, the plant and equipment has a different valuation for tax purposes than for its carrying amount. Electro Tram has also made provisions for receivable bad debts of $500,000 and of $1 million for inventory obsolescence, neither of which are allowed in the current year for tax purposes, but which can be used in the future. These issues result in a net difference between Electro Tram's carrying amounts and tax basis of $250,000. Since the income tax rate is 35%, Electro Tram records a deferred tax provision of $87,500.

financial position and its tax basis. A temporary difference can be either of the following:

- ○ *Deductible.* A deductible temporary difference is a temporary difference that will yield amounts that can be deducted in the future to determine taxable profit or loss.
- ○ *Taxable.* A taxable temporary difference is a temporary difference that will yield taxable amounts in the future to determine taxable profit or loss.

In both cases, the differences are settled when the carrying amount of the asset or liability is recovered or settled.

Examples of temporary differences include:

- ○ Gains recognized for tax purposes later or earlier than they are recognized in financial income
- ○ Expenses deductible for tax purposes later or earlier than they are recognized in financial income
- ○ A reduction or increase in an asset's tax basis
- ○ Differences between the assigned values and tax bases of the assets and liabilities recognized in a business combination

EXAMPLE 23.4

Celtic Pottery Company has a taxable temporary difference when it depreciates an automated glazing machine using accelerated depreciation for tax purposes, but uses straight-line depreciation to determine its financial income.

Celtic also has a taxable temporary difference when it deducts rent expenses on a cash payment basis to calculate its tax profit, but records it as a prepaid expense to calculate its financial income.

EXAMPLE 23.5

Industrial Environmental has a deductible temporary difference when it deducts retirement benefit costs to calculate its financial income, but does not deduct it for tax profit purposes until Industrial pays the benefits.

Similarly, Industrial Environmental has another deductible temporary difference when it recognizes research costs as an expense to determine its financial income, but cannot include it in the tax profit calculation until a later period.

EXAMPLE 23.6

Meridian Vacuum Company has financial income of $500,000, as well as $60,000 of taxable temporary differences and $30,000 of deductible temporary differences. Its taxable income is:

Net profit	$500,000
Taxable temporary differences	(60,000)
Deductible temporary differences	30,000
Taxable profit	$470,000

Meridian is subject to a 30% income tax rate. It records the following income tax entry:

Income tax expense – current	141,000	
Income tax expense – deferred	9,000	
Deferred tax asset	9,000	
Deferred tax liability		18,000
Payables – income taxes		141,000

Because of temporary differences, the tax expense that an entity incurs in a reporting period is usually comprised of both current tax expense or income, and deferred tax expense or income.

 ## What Is a Taxable Temporary Difference?

A taxable temporary difference is a temporary difference that will result in taxable amounts in future years when the related asset or liability is recovered or settled.

EXAMPLE 23.7

Hephaestus Construction accounts for a long-term construction contract to erect a government facility on the percentage-of-completion method for its financial reporting, which yields income of $100,000 in the current year. However, it uses the completed contract method for tax purposes, which defers all of the current-year income until the contract is completed in the following year. This is a temporary taxable difference, since Hephaestus will have an obligation to pay taxes on the $100,000 of reported income in a later period.

 ## Does a Temporary Difference Arise from the Initial Recognition of an Asset or Liability?

A temporary difference can arise upon the initial recognition of an asset or liability. A common reason is that some portion of an asset is not deductible for tax purposes; if so, an entity recognizes any deferred tax liability or asset, and recognizes the resulting deferred tax expense or income in profit or loss.

EXAMPLE 23.8

The Smith & Wilberforce Pop-Gun Factory intends to acquire a conveyor belt which costs $40,000, use it for four years, and then dispose of it. Smith's controller assumes there will be no residual value. The tax rate is 35%. In the tax jurisdiction in which Smith is located, depreciation of the conveyor belt is not deductible for tax purposes. When it disposes of the conveyor, any
(*Continued*)

capital gain will not be taxable, nor will any capital loss be deductible.

After one year, Smith has depreciated $10,000 of the conveyor's cost, leaving a book value of $30,000. Smith earns taxable income of $30,000, and pays $10,500 of income taxes. Smith does not recognize the deferred tax liability of $10,500 because it results from the initial recognition of the conveyor.

How Do I Recognize Taxable Temporary Differences?

Recognize a deferred tax liability for all taxable temporary differences, except when the liability arises from the initial recognition of goodwill, or the recognition of an asset or liability that does not affect taxable profit or loss.

EXAMPLE 23.9

Masterson Brick Company has an asset that cost $15,000, and has a carrying amount of $10,000. Cumulative tax depreciation on the asset is $9,000, and the tax rate is 35%.

Masterson's tax basis in the asset is $6,000, which is the cost of $15,000 minus cumulative tax depreciation of $9,000. To recover the carrying amount of $10,000, Masterson must earn offsetting taxable income of $10,000; however, it can only deduct the remaining tax depreciation of $6,000. Thus, Masterson will pay income taxes of $1,400 ($4,000 × 35% tax rate) when it recovers the asset's carrying amount.

The difference between the carrying amount of $10,000 and the tax basis of $6,000 is a taxable temporary difference of $4,000. Consequently, Masterson recognizes a deferred tax liability of $1,400 ($4,000 × 35% tax rate), which represents the income taxes it must pay when it recovers the asset's carrying amount.

A temporary difference may arise when an entity includes income or expense in accounting profit in one period, but in taxable profit in a different period. This results in a *timing difference*.

EXAMPLE 23.10

Ram-Jet International incurs a large amount of development costs for its hypersonic ramjet engine. In the current year, it capitalized $28 million of development costs and will amortize it over future periods to determine its accounting profit. However, the tax jurisdiction in which Ram-Jet is located requires that all development costs be deducted as incurred to derive taxable profit.

The $28 million of development costs have no tax basis, since Ram-Jet has already deducted them from its taxable profit. The temporary difference is the difference between the carrying amount of $28 million and their tax basis of zero.

What Is a Deductible Temporary Difference?

A deductible temporary difference is a temporary difference that will result in deductible amounts in future years.

EXAMPLE 23.11

The Unibody Plastics Company recognizes a liability of $100,000 for accrued warranty costs on its children's toy products. The product warranty costs are not deductible for tax purposes until Unibody actually pays a warrant claim. The tax rate is 35%.

The tax basis of the accrued liability is zero, while the carrying amount of the liability is $100,000. This results in a deductible temporary difference of $100,000. Thus, Unibody recognizes a deferred tax asset of $35,000 ($100,000 × 35% tax rate), provided that it is more likely than not that Unibody will earn a sufficiently large enough taxable profit in the future to benefit from this reduction in tax payments.

How Do I Initially Recognize Income Tax Expense?

You should calculate income tax expense based on the provisions of those tax laws applying to an entity. Income tax expense in any reporting period is the amount of income taxes currently payable or refundable under applicable tax laws, plus the sum of any deferred tax expense or benefit that can be used in the period. Use the following five steps to determine the amount of any deferred tax expense:

1. Identify all existing temporary differences, operating losses, and tax credit carryforwards, their amounts, and their remaining length (for carryforwards).
2. Calculate the deferred tax liability for taxable temporary differences, at the tax rate applicable to the entity.
3. Calculate the deferred tax asset for any deductible temporary differences and operating loss carryforwards, at the tax rate applicable to the entity.
4. Measure the deferred tax assets for any tax credit carryforwards.
5. Reduce deferred tax assets by a valuation allowance if it is more likely than not that some or all of the deferred tax assets will not be realized. Set the valuation allowance at a level where the deferred tax asset is reduced to an amount that is more likely than not to be realized.

 ## When Should I Use a Valuation Allowance?

A valuation allowance is used to reduce a deferred tax asset to an amount that is more likely than not to be realized. You are less likely to need a valuation allowance when:

○ The existing sales backlog indicates that the entity will generate more than enough income to realize the deferred tax asset.
○ An excess of appreciated asset value over assets' net basis is sufficient to realize the deferred tax asset.
○ There is a strong earnings history, and evidence indicating that the loss causing the future deductible amount was an aberration.

Conversely, a valuation allowance will likely be needed in any of the following situations:

○ There is a history of operating losses, or of letting tax credit carryforwards expire unused.
○ Losses are expected in the near future.
○ If current circumstances are not favorably resolved, they could negatively impact profits in future years.

○ The carryback and/or carryforward period is so brief that the entity's realization of the deferred tax asset may be limited.

Of all of the factors noted here, the existence of a cumulative loss in recent periods will likely result in the need for a valuation allowance.

How Do I Incorporate Graduated Tax Rates Into Tax Calculations?

If an entity's income will likely expose it to multiple tax rates within a graduated tax rate structure, then you should measure a deferred tax liability or asset with the average graduated tax rate that applies to the entity's estimated annual taxable income.

Should I Anticipate the Effects of Future Tax Changes in Tax Laws?

No. You should not record the effects of tax law changes if those changes have not yet been enacted.

How Do I Account for a Change in Tax Laws or Rates?

You should recognize the effect of a change in tax laws or tax rates as of the date when the changes are enacted. If there is a retroactive change in tax rates, then you should also recognize that effect when the changes are enacted (which will impact any temporary differences in existence on the enactment date).

You should account for the effect of changes in tax laws or rates within the income from the continuing operations section of the income statement.

What Is the Alternative Minimum Tax?

The alternative minimum tax was established under the Tax Reform Act of 1986, and is essentially a minimum tax system that may require a tax payment even when normal tax calculations do not indicate a payment. Thus, an entity's federal income tax liability is the greater of the tax computed under the regular tax system or the alternative minimum tax system. If an entity pays a tax under the alternative minimum tax system that is greater than the amount called for under the regular tax system, the difference is a credit that you can carry forward indefinitely and use to reduce federal taxes in a future year (though not below the amount of the alternative minimum tax in the years when it is used).

You should record a tax credit generated by an alternative minimum tax payment as a deferred tax asset.

 What Is Tax Planning?

A tax planning opportunity is an action an entity must take to create or increase taxable income in a period before the expiration of a tax loss or tax credit carryforward. Examples of tax planning are:

- ○ *Asset swap.* Selling an asset that generates non-taxable income and using the funds to buy another asset that generates taxable income.
- ○ *Asset sale.* Selling an asset that has appreciated, and for which the tax base has not been adjusted to reflect the appreciation. A variation on this approach is the sale and leaseback transaction (see the Leases chapter).
- ○ *Deduction deferral.* Delay the recognition of some deductions from taxable profit that can be deferred.
- ○ *Recognition basis.* Elect to recognize interest income for the calculation of taxable profit on either a received or receivable basis.

Tax planning may shift an entity's estimated future taxable income between future years, or it may shift the estimated timing of future reversals of temporary differences.

EXAMPLE 23.12

Franciscan Friars' Discrete Tanning has a $50,000 operating loss carryforward that will expire unused at the end of the following year. To make use of the carryforward, it implements a tax planning strategy to sell the installment sales receivables on its tanning bed products in the following year, thereby accelerating the future reversal of taxable temporary differences to generate gains on the installment sales. The company can then offset the operating loss carryforward against these gains to reduce its taxable income.

How Do Tax Status Changes Alter Income Tax Recognition?

An entity may experience a change in its tax status, such as when it gains or loses tax incentives by moving to a different location. If so, include these tax effects in profit or loss for the period, unless the consequences relate to transactions and events that will alter equity or other comprehensive income.

What Is a Tax Position?

A tax position is a position that an entity takes in a previously filed tax return or which it expects to take in a future tax return, which it uses to measure current or deferred income tax assets and liabilities. A tax position can yield a permanent reduction or deferral of income taxes payable.

Examples of tax positions are the decision to not file a tax return, to shift income between tax jurisdictions, and to classify a transaction as tax-exempt.

When Do I Record a Tax Position?

You should record the effects of a tax position when it is more likely than not that the position will be sustained upon examination by a taxing authority. *More likely than not* is defined as being more than 50% likely to occur.

How Do I Account for a Tax Position?

You should initially and subsequently measure a tax position at the largest amount of tax benefit that is more than 50% likely to be realized.

EXAMPLE 23.13

The Nocturnal Widget Company has determined that a tax position it has taken, involving $50,000, qualifies for recognition and should be measured. Nocturnal determines that the amounts and probabilities of the possible estimated outcomes are as follows:

(Continued)

Possible Estimated Outcome	Individual Probability of Occurrence (%)	Cumulative Probability of Occurrence (%)
$50,000	10	10
35,000	15	25
25,000	30	55
10,000	10	65
5,000	15	80
0	20	100

The largest benefit amount immediately above the 50% threshold is $25,000, so Nocturnal should recognize a tax benefit of $25,000 in its financial statements.

You should re-measure a tax position if there is new information that leads to a different conclusion regarding the tax position. However, you should not re-measure a tax position if you are simply conducting a re-evaluation or re-interpretation of information that was available in a previous financial reporting period.

You should derecognize a previously recognized tax position as soon as it is no longer more likely than not that the tax position would be sustained by tax authorities.

EXAMPLE 23.14

The Nutmeg Spice Company takes a tax position under which it amortizes the cost of an asset that it acquired for $100,000 on a straight-line basis for five years, as opposed to a ten-year amortization period for financial reporting purposes. After two years, Nutmeg has deducted 40% of the cost of the asset in its income tax return and 20% in its financial statements, which represents a deferred tax liability of $20,000; this is the difference between the financial reporting and tax bases of the asset.

Nutmeg evaluates its tax position on this matter annually, and, based on recent tax court rulings, concludes after two years that the tax position no longer meets the more-likely-than-not threshold. Consequently, it immediately recognizes a tax liability for the $20,000 difference between the two amortization methods, resulting in the elimination of the temporary difference.

How Do I Account for the Cessation of Taxable Status?

If an entity's status changes from that of a taxable to a non-taxable entity, you should eliminate all deferred tax liabilities and assets as of the date when the entity ceased to be a taxable entity.

You should record the effect of recognizing or derecognizing tax assets and liabilities in the income from the continuing operations section of the income statement.

How Do I Account for Interest and Penalties on Underpaid Income Taxes?

You should begin recognizing interest expense on underpaid income taxes as of the first period in which it would begin accruing under the tax laws.

If a tax position will not avoid payment of penalties, then recognize an expense for the amount of the penalty in the period in which the entity takes the tax position in a tax return. It may be necessary to continue reviewing tax positions, and recognize the expense in a later period, when you judge that the entity can no longer avoid the payment of penalties.

If you have been accruing interest and penalties on tax positions that were *not* more likely than not to be upheld by a tax authority, and the position is now more likely than not to be upheld, then you should derecognize the accrued expense in the current period.

You can record interest expenses either within the interest expense or income tax classifications on the income statement, in accordance with corporate policy. Similarly, you can record penalties either within the penalties expense or income tax classifications on the income statement, as authorized by corporate policy.

Should I Discount Deferred Tax Assets and Liabilities?

No. Discounting a deferred tax asset or liability requires a present value analysis that contains detailed payment and/or payout schedules. Given the uncertainty and complexity of future tax scenarios, it is difficult to create reliable discounted information, and so do not report deferred tax assets or liabilities in this manner.

How Should I Present Income Tax Information in the Financial Statements?

Follow these guidelines for presenting income tax information in the financial statements:

○ In the balance sheet, you should separately report the amounts of deferred tax liabilities and assets as current and non-current amounts.

○ Allocate the valuation allowance for a specific tax jurisdiction between the current and non-current deferred tax assets for that jurisdiction.

○ Offset the deferred tax liabilities and assets only for a particular tax jurisdiction and for a specific tax-paying component of an entity. Present these offsetting amounts separately for current and non-current amounts.

○ Do not offset the deferred tax liabilities and assets for different tax-paying components of an entity, or for different tax jurisdictions.

How Should I Allocate Income Taxes?

You should allocate income tax expense or benefit among the following categories on the income statement:

○ Continuing operations
○ Discontinued operations
○ Extraordinary items
○ Other comprehensive income
○ Items charged or credited directly to shareholders' equity

You should allocate income taxes to continuing operations based on the tax effect of the pretax income or loss from continuing operations, adjusted for the income tax effects of:

○ A change in judgment about the realization of deferred tax assets in future years
○ Changes in tax laws or rates
○ Changes in tax status
○ Tax-deductible dividends paid to shareholders

You should allocate income taxes to other comprehensive income or to related components of shareholders' equity for the following items:

○ Adjustments to the opening balance of retained earnings for changes in accounts principles or an error correction
○ Gains and losses included in comprehensive income, but which are excluded from net income
○ A change in contributed capital
○ Expenses for employee stock options recognized differently for financial reporting and tax purposes
○ Dividends paid on unallocated shares held by an employee stock ownership plan and that are charged to retained earnings
○ Deductible temporary differences and carryforwards existing at the date of a quasi-reorganization
○ Changes in the tax bases of assets and liabilities caused by transactions with shareholders

If there are two or more items other than continuing operations to which income taxes can be allocated, you should first calculate the amount of income taxes to be allocated to continuing operations. Then allocate the remaining amount of income taxes to the other items in proportion to their individual effects on income tax expense or benefit for the year.

If you change a valuation allowance because of a change in judgment regarding the realization of deferred tax assets in future years, allocate the change to continuing operations.

EXAMPLE 23.15

The Nutmeg Spice Company has an ordinary loss from continuing operations of $200,000, and an extraordinary gain of $500,000 that is a capital gain. The tax rate for ordinary income is 35% and the tax rate for capital gains is 15%.

The total tax expense is $45,000 ($300,000 taxable profit × 15% capital gains tax rate), which Nutmeg allocates in the following manner:

○ The $200,000 loss from continuing operations offsets an equal amount of capital gains that would otherwise be taxed at the 15% rate. Consequently, Nutmeg allocates $30,000 of tax benefit to continuing operations.
○ The remaining incremental tax expense is $15,000, which Nutmeg allocates to the extraordinary items line item.

What Situations Result in Tax Asset or Liability Recognition Outside of Profit or Loss?

You should recognize current taxes and deferred taxes outside of profit or loss if the tax relates to items that are recognized outside of profit or loss. Thus, if an item is recognized in other comprehensive income, then also recognize the related current and deferred taxes in other comprehensive income. Similarly, if an item is recognized in equity, then also recognize the related current and deferred taxes in equity.

An example of an item recognized in other comprehensive income is foreign exchange differences caused by translating the financial statements of a foreign operation. An example of an item recognized in equity is an adjustment to the opening equity balance caused by a change in accounting policy or the correction of an error.

If it is difficult to determine the amount of current and deferred tax relating to items recognized outside profit or loss, then use a reasonable pro rata allocation of the current and deferred tax. This situation can arise, for example, when there are graduated rates of income tax, and you cannot determine the rate at which a specific component of taxable profit or loss has been taxed.

 What Is Ordinary Income?

Ordinary income is the income from continuing operations before income taxes, excluding extraordinary items, discontinued operations, and the cumulative effect of changes in accounting principles.

 What Tax Rate Should I Use for Recording Income Taxes in Interim Periods?

During interim reporting periods, you should compute income taxes or benefits based on the estimated annual effective tax rate for ordinary income. If there are other items than ordinary income, then compute their tax rate separately and apply it only when those items occur. You should continue to estimate the annual effective tax rate in each successive interim period, and revise the year-to-date income tax expense or benefit accordingly. If it is not possible to estimate the tax rate, then use the actual effective tax rate for the year to date.

You should include the tax benefit of an operating loss carryforward in the estimated annual effective tax rate if you expect to realize the tax benefit as a result of ordinary income.

 ## How Do I Account for the Tax Effect of Losses in Interim Periods?

If an entity has a loss earlier in a fiscal year, you should recognize the tax effect of the loss only when you expect that the tax benefit will either be realized during the year or recognizable as a deferred tax asset at the end of the year.

EXAMPLE 23.16

Caribbean Surfboard has a history of recording losses in its first quarter, when sales in temperate regions are at their lowest, and then higher seasonal revenue levels in the second and third quarters. In the first quarter of the current year, it records a $50,000 loss, but expects a $125,000 profit in the following quarter; this is a pattern similar to what has occurred in prior years. Based on this history of seasonality, realization of the tax loss is more likely than not, so Caribbean records the tax effect of the loss in the first quarter of the year.

In a later interim period, you can recognize the tax effects of losses in an earlier interim period, if their realization later becomes more likely than not.

If you do not recognize the tax benefit of an operating loss in the early part of a year because it is more likely than not that the entity will not realize the benefit, then you should not record income tax on subsequent income until the unrecognized tax benefit associated with the earlier ordinary loss has been completely offset.

 ## What Tax Rate Information Should I Disclose for Interim Periods?

If there is a significant variation in the customary percentage of income tax expense to pretax income, then you should disclose the reasons for the variation in the financial statements for interim periods.

What Income Tax Information Should I Disclose?

You should disclose the following information in the notes accompanying the financial statements:

- The total of all deferred tax assets.
- The total of all deferred tax liabilities.
- The total valuation allowance recognized for deferred tax assets, and the total net change during the year for the total valuation allowance.
- The amounts and expiration dates of operating loss and tax credit carryforwards.
- If there is a change in tax status subsequent to year-end, disclose the change in status and the effects of that change.
- The types of significant temporary differences.
- The current tax expense and the deferred tax expense.
- Investment tax credits.
- Government grants that are recognized as a reduction of income tax expense.
- The benefits of operating loss carryforwards.
- Adjustments for enacted changes in tax laws or rates, or caused by a change in the tax status of an entity.
- Adjustments to the beginning-of-year valuation allowance balance.
- The amount of income tax expense or benefit allocated to continuing operations and to other items.
- The nature of reconciling items causing a difference between the actual tax expense and the amount to be expected from statutory rates. No numerical reconciliation is required.
- Reconciliation of the total amounts of unrecognized tax benefits at the beginning and end of the period, including such factors as changes in tax benefits, interest, and penalties.
- For tax positions where there is a reasonable possibility of significant changes to unrecognized tax benefits within 12 months, note the nature of the uncertainty and estimate the reasonably possible range of change.
- The tax years remaining subject to examination by major tax jurisdictions.
- The accounting policy for recognizing interest and penalties related to tax positions.
- The accounting policy for handling investment tax credits.

A public entity should also disclose the tax effect for each type of temporary difference and carryforward causing deferred tax liabilities and assets. It should also disclose a reconciliation of the income tax expense from the expected amount based on statutory rates.

EXAMPLE 23.17

The Nutmeg Spice Company files income tax returns in the U.S. federal jurisdiction, and in various states and foreign jurisdictions. Nutmeg is no longer subject to U.S. federal, state, and local income tax examinations by tax authorities for years before 20X1. The Internal Revenue Service (IRS) is currently conducting an examination of Nutmeg's U.S. federal income tax returns for 20X2, which we expect will be completed in the second quarter of 20X5. As of December 31, 20X4, the IRS has proposed several significant adjustments to Nutmeg's transfer pricing tax positions relating to spice transfers from its Malaysian subsidiary. Management is evaluating the proposed adjustments; if accepted, Nutmeg does not anticipate that the adjustments would result in a material change in its financial position. It is possible that Nutmeg will make an additional tax payment in the range of $12 million to $18 million by the end of 20X5.

A reconciliation of the beginning and ending amounts of unrecognized tax benefits follows:

(000s)	20X4	20X3
Balance at January 1	$21,000	$18,000
Additions caused by tax positions related to the current year	7,000	5,000
Additions for the tax positions of prior years	9,000	2,000
Reductions for tax positions of prior years	(6,000)	(3,000)
Settlements	(4,000)	(1,000)
Balance at December 31	27,000	21,000

On December 31, 20X4 and 20X3, there were $13.5 million and $10.5 million of unrecognized tax benefits that if recognized, would affect the effective tax rate.

Nutmeg recognizes accrued interest related to unrecognized tax benefits in interest expense, and recognizes accrued penalties in operating expenses. During the years ended December 31, 20X4 and 20X3,

(Continued)

Nutmeg recognized approximately $400,000 and $250,000 in interest and penalties. Nutmeg had approximately $1,200,000 and $750,000 accrued at December 31, 20X4 and 20X3 for the payment of interest and penalties.

EXAMPLE 23.18

The Nutmeg Spice Company has recorded a deferred tax asset of $3.5 million, which reflects the benefit of $10 million in loss carryforwards, which expire between 20X5 and 20X9. Realization of this deferred tax asset is dependent upon generating sufficient taxable income prior to expiration of the loss carryforwards. Although realization is not assured, management believes it is more likely than not that all of the deferred tax asset will be realized. The amount of the deferred tax asset considered realizable could be reduced if Nutmeg's estimates of future taxable income during the carryforward period are reduced.

PART IV

SPECIAL TRANSACTIONS

CHAPTER 24

ACCOUNTING CHANGES AND ERROR CORRECTIONS

 What Is an Accounting Change?

An accounting change can be a change in accounting principle, accounting estimate, or the reporting entity. In more detail:

○ A *change in accounting principle* is a change from one generally accepted accounting principle (GAAP) to another generally accepted accounting principle. A change in accounting principle does not occur when there is an initial adoption of an accounting principle caused by transactions occurring for the first time.

○ A *change in accounting estimate* is a change that adjusts the carrying amount of an existing asset or liability, or which alters subsequent accounting for either existing or future assets or liabilities. Accounting estimates that are commonly changed include reserves for uncollectible receivables, warranty obligations, and inventory obsolescence.

○ A *change in reporting entity* is a change that results in financial statements that are effectively those of a different reporting entity. This usually involves changing from individual to consolidated reporting, or altering the subsidiaries that make up a group of entities whose results are consolidated.

 When and How Should I Change an Accounting Principle?

You should only change an accounting principle if the change is required by a new accounting codification update, or if you can justify use of the new principle because it is preferable.

When you implement a change in accounting principle, you should apply it retroactively, so that it is incorporated into all prior periods. This requirement does not apply if it is impractical to implement.

When applying a change in accounting principle retroactively, you must reflect in the asset and liability carrying amounts the cumulative effect of the change, due to the new principle, on periods prior to those presented. If this cumulative effect calls for an offsetting adjustment, then adjust the opening balance of retained earnings. You must also adjust the financial statements of each prior period presented, so that they incorporate the period-specific effects of the new accounting principle.

If it is not practicable to determine the period-specific effects of the accounting principle, then apply the cumulative effect as of the beginning of the earliest period to which you can apply the new principle, with an offsetting entry to beginning retained earnings for the same period.

When Is a Retrospective Principle Reapplication Considered Impracticable?

You do not have to apply a change in accounting principle retroactively if it is impracticable to do so. Retroactive application is considered impracticable under any of the following circumstances:

- ○ You are unable to apply the requirement after making every reasonable effort to do so.
- ○ Retrospective application requires information about management's intentions in a prior period that you cannot independently substantiate.
- ○ The retrospective application requires significant estimates, and it is impossible for you to distinguish objectively the supporting information needed to calculate those estimates, and which would have been available when the financial statements for that period were issued.

What if I Make a Change in Accounting Principle in an Interim Period?

If you make a change in accounting principle in an interim period, you must also retrospectively apply it to any prior interim periods in the current fiscal year. There is no impracticability exception for these interim periods—you

EXAMPLE 24.1

Chicago Pottery Company originally tracked its hand-thrown ceramic products in inventory on an individual basis. However, with increased sales volume, this method proves impractical to continue, so Chicago elects to change its accounting method to the first-in, first-out (FIFO) method.

Chicago presents two years of financial statements. For Year 1, the impact of the change was an inventory increase of $28,000, and the impact in Year 2 was an inventory decrease of $12,000. The changes to Chicago's income statement are as follows:

| | Year 1 | | | Year 2 | | |
	Prior to Adjustment	Adjustment	Restated	Prior to Adjustment	Adjustment	Restated
Revenue	$2,475,000		$2,475,000	$3,100,000		$3,100,000
Cost of sales	1,485,000	$(28,000)	1,457,000	1,860,000	$+12,000	1,872,000
Other expenses	750,000		750,000	868,000		868,000
Net profit*	$ 240,000	$(28,000)	$ 268,000	$ 372,000	$ 12,000	$ 360,000

*No impact on income taxes is assumed in this example.

Note A: On January 1, 20X1, Chicago Pottery Company changed its method of valuing its inventory to the FIFO method, whereas it valued inventory in all prior years using the specific identification method. The new method of accounting was adopted by Chicago in order to streamline inventory tracking and costing systems, and comparative financial statements of prior years have been adjusted to apply the new method retrospectively.

must retrospectively apply the change in accounting principle to them. Thus, it is best to adopt any accounting changes during the first interim period of a fiscal year, thereby avoiding any retrospective interim period adjustments.

How Do I Disclose a Change in Accounting Principle?

Disclose the following information in the period in which you make a change in accounting principle:

- ○ The nature of the change and the reason for it, stating why the newly adopted principle is preferable.
- ○ The prior period information that has been adjusted.
- ○ The effect of the change on income from continuing operations, net income, per share amounts, and any other affected financial statement line item, both for the current period and any prior periods that were impacted.
- ○ The cumulative effect of the change on retained earnings as of the beginning of the earliest period presented.
- ○ If retrospective application is not practicable, then disclose the reasons why it is not practicable. Also describe the alternative method used to report the change.

If you issue both interim and annual financial statements, then disclose this information in both cases.

How Does a Change in Accounting Estimate Impact Financial Reporting?

The financial effect of a change in accounting estimate only impacts the period in which you implement the change, and future periods. You do not retrospectively adjust financial statements for a change in accounting estimate.

EXAMPLE 24.2

Glass Lamination International uses vacuum deposition to deposit a thin-film coating on periscope lenses. It originally depreciates the vacuum deposition equipment using an estimated useful life of ten years, with no residual value. Thus, it depreciates the $10,000,000 carrying amount of the equipment at the rate of $1,000,000 per year.

After five years, Glass Lamination determines that the equipment now has a remaining useful life of eight years. It therefore depreciates the remaining carrying amount of $5,000,000 at a revised rate of $625,000 per year. There is no retrospective change in prior periods.

How Do I Disclose a Change in Accounting Estimate?

If you record a change in accounting estimate, then you should also disclose the impact on income from continuing operations, net income, and per share amounts. Disclosure is only required if the change in estimate is material. However, you should disclose a change in estimate when the impact in the current period is not material, but there is a material effect in later periods.

It is not necessary to disclose changes in estimates that are made in the ordinary course of accounting, such as for changes in the reserve for uncollectible accounts.

How Do I Disclose a Change in Accounting Entity?

When there is a change in reporting entity, you should describe the nature of the change, the reason for it, and the effect of the change on both income and earnings per share.

What Is an Error Correction and How Do I Report It?

An error correction is the correction of an error in previously issued financial statements. This can be an error in the recognition, measurement, presentation, or disclosure in financial statements that are caused by mathematical mistakes, mistakes in applying GAAP, or the oversight of facts existing when the financial statements were prepared. It is not an accounting change.

You should restate prior period financial statements when there is an error correction. Restatement requires that you do all of the following:

○ Reflect the cumulative effect of the error on periods prior to those presented in the carrying amounts of assets and liabilities as of the beginning of the first period presented.
○ Make an offsetting adjustment to the opening balance of retained earnings for that period.

○ Adjust the financial statements for each prior period presented, to reflect the error correction.

If the financial statements are only presented for a single period, then reflect the adjustment in the opening balance of retained earnings.

 ## What if I Correct an Accounting Error in an Interim Period?

If you correct an item of profit or loss in any interim period other than the first interim period of a fiscal year, and some portion of the adjustment relates to prior interim periods, then do all of the following:

○ Include that portion of the correction related to the current interim period in that period.
○ Restate prior interim periods to include that portion of the correction applicable to them.
○ Record any portion of the correction related to prior fiscal years in the first interim period of the current fiscal year.

 ## When Is an Accounting Error Material?

You should determine the materiality of an accounting error based on its relationship to estimated income for the full year and to its effect on the trend of earnings. If an error is material in respect to an interim period, but not to the results of the full fiscal year, then disclose it in the interim period.

 ## How Do I Disclose an Error Correction?

When you restate the financial statements to correct an error, disclose the following:

○ That the previously issued financial statements have been restated.
○ The nature of the error.
○ The effect of the correction on each affected financial statement line item and earnings per share for each prior period presented.
○ The cumulative effect of the correction on retained earnings as of the beginning of the earliest period presented.
○ If there is a correction to prior interim periods of the current fiscal year, then disclose for each prior interim period the effect on income and earnings per share.

Example 24.3

Baroque Furniture Company acquires Chestnut Hardwood. Two years later, Baroque discovers that it has not amortized any of the intangible assets that it booked as a result of the acquisition. The amortization expense should have been $30,000 in the first year (a partial year) and $75,000 in the second year. The changes to Baroque's income statement are as follows:

	Year 1			Year 2		
	Prior to Adjustment	Adjustment	Restated	Prior to Adjustment	Adjustment	Restated
Revenue	$5,220,000		$5,220,000	$5,612,000		$5,612,000
Cost of sales	3,760,000		3,760,000	4,040,000		4,040,000
Gross margin	1,460,000		1,460,000	1,572,000		1,572,000
Amortization	0	$30,000	30,000	0	$75,000	75,000
Other expenses	897,000		897,000	882,000		882,000
Other income before taxes	563,000		533,000	690,000		615,000
Income taxes	195,000	(10,000)	185,000	240,000	(25,000)	215,000
Net profit	$ 368,000	$20,000	$348,000	$ 450,000	$50,000	$ 400,000

(Continued)

Baroque adds the following disclosure to its financial statements:

The amortization of intangible assets acquired as part of the Chestnut Hardwood acquisition was not included in the financial statements for Year 1 or Year 2. The financial statements for the past two years have been restated to correct this error. The effect of the restatement on those financial statements is summarized below:

	Year 1	Year 2
Increase in amortization expense	$(30,000)	$(75,000)
Decrease in income tax expense	10,000	25,000
Decrease in profit	$(20,000)	$(50,000)
Decrease in equity	$(20,000)	$(50,000)

CHAPTER 25

BUSINESS COMBINATIONS

 What Is a Business Combination?

A business combination is a transaction in which the acquirer obtains control of another business (the acquiree). A *business* is an integrated set of activities and assets that can provide a return to investors in the form of dividends, reduced costs, or other economic benefits.

A business combination is not the formation of a joint venture, nor does it involve the acquisition of assets that do not constitute a business.

 In a Business Combination, Who Is the Acquirer?

It is not always clear who is acquiring whom in a business combination. The following are indicators of which entity should be considered the acquirer:

- The entity whose owners receive the largest portion of the voting rights of the combined entity
- The entity whose owners hold the largest minority voting interest in the combined entity
- The entity whose owners have the ability to elect, appoint, or remove a majority of the combined entity's governing body
- The entity whose former managers dominate the management of the combined entity
- The entity paying a premium over the fair value of the equity interests of the other combining entity
- The entity whose relative size is significantly larger than the other combining entity

 What Is Goodwill?

Goodwill is an asset that is not individually identified, is separately recognized, and which represents the future economic benefits arising from other assets acquired in a business combination.

How Do I Account for a Business Combination?

You should use the *acquisition method* to account for a business combination. Specifically, follow these five steps:

1. *Identify the acquirer.* This is the entity that gains control of the acquiree.
2. *Determine the acquisition date.* This is when the acquirer gains control of the acquiree, which is usually the deal closing date, but which could be another date if so stated in the purchase agreement.
3. *Recognize and measure identifiable assets acquired and liabilities assumed.* These must be part of the business combination transaction, rather than from separate transactions. Measure these assets and liabilities at their fair values as of the acquisition date. This recognition should include the identification of identifiable intangible assets. More specifically:

   a. *Leases.* Recognize an intangible asset if the terms of an acquiree operating lease are favorable compared with the market terms of similar leases, or recognize a liability if the terms of such a lease are unfavorable when compared to the market terms of similar leases.

EXAMPLE 25.1

Starling Airlines acquires Puffin Airways, which includes Puffin's valuable gate leases at Denver International Airport. Puffin pays $100,000 per year to lease the gates, whereas the market price of such a lease is currently $350,000 per year. The lease is a fixed rate for the next ten years. Starling can record the lease differential as an intangible asset.

---

   b. *Reacquired rights.* If the acquirer reacquires a right that it had previously granted to the acquiree (such as a technology license), it should recognize the reacquired right with a settlement gain or loss.
   c. *Contingent consideration.* If the acquiree had a contingent consideration agreement with a third party, and the acquirer takes over the agreement,

the acquirer should measure the agreement at its fair value on the acquisition date.

d. *Defined benefit pension plans.* Recognize an asset or liability, depending on the funding status of the acquiree's defined benefit pension plan.

e. *Employee benefits.* Recognize a liability for any employee benefits assumed.

f. *Held for sale assets.* Measure an acquiree's assets designated as held for sale at their fair value, less costs to sell.

g. *Indemnifications.* The acquiree provides an indemnification to the acquirer for various issues related to the acquired business. For example, the acquiree may provide an indemnification against excessive accounts receivable bad debts. This is an indemnification asset, which the acquirer recognizes at its fair value at the same time it recognizes the indemnified item. However, do not recognize an indemnification if the related asset is not recognized.

4. *Recognize and measure any non-controlling interest in the acquiree.* Measure this non-controlling interest at its fair value, or using other valuation techniques.

5. *Recognize and measure either goodwill or the gain from a bargain purchase.* Measure goodwill as follows:

+ Consideration paid, measured at fair value on the acquisition date

+ Non-controlling interests in the acquiree

+ Fair value of acquirer's previously-held equity interest in the acquiree

− Net of identifiable assets and liabilities acquired

= Goodwill

A *bargain purchase* occurs when the above calculation yields a negative goodwill amount. When this occurs, first review the goodwill calculation to ensure that all items were included. If they were, then recognize the gain resulting from the bargain purchase in profit or loss as of the acquisition date.

EXAMPLE 25.2

Wilson Ross, a publicly-held consulting firm, acquires Finnegan Beagle, which is also a publicly-held consulting firm. The price to buy Finnegan is $7 million.
(Continued)

Wilson identifies assets at Finnegan having a fair value of $8 million, intangible assets with a value of $1 million, as well as $2 million of liabilities and $500,000 of contingent liabilities. Wilson also owned an existing stake in Finnegan that has a fair value on the acquisition date of $3 million. Wilson calculates the goodwill associated with the business combination as follows:

+ Purchase price	$7,000,000
+ Liabilities	2,000,000
+ Contingent liabilities	500,000
+ Existing stake in Finnegan	3,000,000
− Assets	(8,000,000)
− Intangible assets	(1,000,000)
= Goodwill	$3,500,000

Do I Include Expected Costs in Assumed Liabilities?

If you expect to incur a cost as a result of a business combination, but there is no obligation to do so, then do not include it in the initial accounting for a business combination.

EXAMPLE 25.3

Amundsen Salvage acquires Scott Reclamation. Amundsen expects to sell off one of Scott's salvage tugboats and terminate the employment of its crew, but is under no obligation to do so. Thus, Amundsen does not assume a liability for the tugboat elimination as part of its accounting for the business combination.

What Is Contingent Consideration?

Contingent consideration is an obligation of the acquiring entity to transfer additional assets or equity interests to the former owners of the acquiree, as part of a contract to change control over the acquired entity, but only if specified future events occur or conditions are met.

How Do I Account for Contingent Consideration?

If there is additional consideration payable by the acquirer based on conditions not yet met, the acquirer recognizes its fair value as of the acquisition date.

EXAMPLE 25.4

Rotary Mower Company, maker of the world's only lawn mower that runs on a Wankel rotary engine, acquires Turbofan Concepts, maker of the only jet-engine powered lawn mower (for really big lawns). Rotary Mower includes in the purchase agreement a contingent consideration payment of $4 million, payable over the next four years, if Turbofan achieves specific levels of profitability in each period. Rotary's management believes that Turbofan will meet these targets, so it recognizes the full amount of the contingent consideration as of the acquisition date.

What Are Examples of Intangible Assets?

Some intangibles that you can record as part of a business combination include:

- ○ Marketing-related intangible assets

  - Trademarks
  - Newspaper mastheads
  - Internet domain names
  - Noncompetition agreements

- ○ Customer-related intangible assets

  - Customer lists
  - Order backlog
  - Customer relationships

- ○ Artistic-related intangible assets

  - Performance events
  - Literary works
  - Musical works
  - Pictures
  - Motion pictures and television programs

○ Contract-based intangible assets

- Licensing agreements
- Service contracts
- Lease agreements
- Franchise agreements
- Broadcast rights
- Employment contracts
- Use rights (such as drilling rights or water rights)

○ Technology-based intangible assets

- Patented technology
- Computer software
- Trade secrets (such as secret formulas and recipes)

Can I Record an Intangible Asset for the Assembled Workforce?

No. The assembled workforce is not considered an identifiable asset, so you cannot recognize it separately from goodwill.

How Do I Account for an Asset Acquisition?

An acquirer may selectively buy the assets of another entity, rather than buying the legal entity that controls the assets. If paid in cash, you should recognize an acquired asset based on its cost to the acquiring entity (which can include the transaction cost to the acquirer). If not paid in cash (such as with debt or equity), then you should measure the acquired assets at either the fair value of the assets acquired or the cost to the acquiring entity, whichever is more reliably measurable.

What Is a Step Acquisition?

A step acquisition occurs when the acquiring entity obtains control over an entity for which it already held a non-controlling interest.

EXAMPLE 25.5

Nocturnal Widget Company has owned 30% of the common stock of Acme Widget Company for five years. It now acquires an additional 32% of Acme's common stock, thereby achieving control over Acme with a total of 62% ownership.

How Do I Account for a Step Acquisition?

An entity may already have a non-controlling equity interest in an acquiree, and then acquires a controlling interest in the acquiree. This is called a *step acquisition*. In this situation, the acquirer should re-measure its existing equity interest in the acquiree as of the date when it obtains control over the acquiree, and recognize any gain or loss in profit or loss.

If the acquirer had recognized any changes in the value of its non-controlling interest in other comprehensive income, it should now shift that amount into profit or loss.

What Is a Reverse Acquisition?

A reverse acquisition is an acquisition in which the entity issuing securities is designated as the acquiree for accounting purposes. An example of a reverse acquisition is when a privately-owned entity wants to become publicly-owned, and does so by arranging for a public entity to acquire its equity interests in exchange for the equity interests of the public entity.

How Do I Account for a Reverse Acquisition?

In a reverse acquisition, the acquirer for accounting purposes normally issues no consideration for the acquiree; instead, the acquiree issues its stock to the owners of the acquirer. Thus, the fair value of the consideration transferred as of the acquisition date is based on the number of shares that the legal subsidiary would have had to issue in order to give the owners of the legal parent the same percentage equity interest in the combined entity.

When you issue the consolidated financial statements of the combined entities, the statements should be under the name of the legal parent (which is the acquiree for accounting purposes). State in the accompanying footnotes that the financial statements are a continuation of the financial statements of the legal subsidiary (the acquirer for accounting purposes), though they are adjusted to reflect the legal capital of the entity designated as the acquiree for accounting purposes.

Example 25.6

Iberian Tile acquires 100% of Tango Mural Company in two stages, as noted in the following table:

Acquisition Date	% Acquired	Purchase Payment	Net Assets Fair Value
January 1, 20X1	15%	$ 2,000,000	$12,000,000
July 1, 20X2	85%	13,000,000	14,000,000
Totals	100%	$15,000,000	

Iberian calculates the goodwill from the two transactions as follows:

Acquisition Date	(A) Purchase Payment	(B) % Acquired	(C) Net Assets Fair Value	A − (B × C) Goodwill
January 1, 20X1	$2,000,000	15%	$12,000,000	$ 200,000
July 1, 20X2	13,000,000	85%	14,000,000	1,100,000
				$1,300,000

The before-and-after statements of financial position for Iberian and Tango, with adjustments, are as follows:

	(A) Iberian	(B) Tango	(C) Adjustments	A + B +/− C Consolidated
Cash	$ 400,000	$ 150,000		$ 550,000
Accounts receivable	9,250,000	7,000,000		16,250,000
Property, plant, and equipment	8,200,000	5,700,000	+ $2,000,000 (Note 1)	15,900,000
Investment in Tango	2,000,000	0	− $2,000,000 (Note 2)	0
Goodwill	0	0	+ $1,300,000 (Note 3)	1,300,000
Total assets	$19,850,000	$12,850,000		$34,000,000
Accounts payable	1,900,000	850,000		2,750,000
Revaluation surplus	0	0	+ $1,300,000 (Note 4)	1,300,000
Retained earnings	7,500,000	5,100,000		12,600,000
Issued equity	10,450,000	6,900,000		17,350,000
Liabilities and equity	$19,850,000	$12,850,000		$34,000,000

(1) Add back excess of $14,000,000 fair value on acquisition date over initial net assets (cash + accounts receivable + PP&E − accounts payable).
(2) Eliminate minority interest, since now own 100% of Tango.
(3) See preceding goodwill calculation table.
(4) Iberian's share of the increase in the net assets of Tango, as per the preceding goodwill calculation table.

308 Business Combinations

Example 25.7

Cheshire Corporation is a privately held entity, and wishes to become a public company by acquiring Hillsmere Enterprises through a reverse merger transaction. The balance sheets of Cheshire and Hillsmere immediately prior to the business combination follow:

(000s)	Hillsmere (Legal Parent, Accounting Acquiree)	Cheshire (Legal Subsidiary, Accounting Acquirer
Current assets	$1,900	$1,700
Noncurrent assets	2,600	4,000
Total assets	4,500	5,700
Current liabilities	1,300	1,600
Noncurrent liabilities	1,400	2,100
Total liabilities	2,700	3,700
Shareholders' equity		
Retained earnings	1,600	1,600
Issued equity		
1,000 common shares	200	–
2,000 common shares	–	400
Total shareholders' equity	1,800	2,000
Total liabilities and shareholders' equity	$4,500	$5,700

On March 31, 20X1, Hillsmere issues two shares of its common stock in exchange for each share of Cheshire's common stock. Thus, Hillsmere issues 4,000 of its shares in exchange for all 2,000 of Cheshire's common shares outstanding. As a result of the stock issuance, there are now 5,000 shares of Hillsmere stock outstanding, of which 4,000 shares, or 80% of the total, are held by Cheshire shareholders, with the remaining 20% still held by Hillsmere's shareholders.

On the acquisition date, the quoted market price for a share of Hillsmere stock is $15. The appraised fair value of a share of Cheshire stock on that date is $30.

If the situation had been reversed and Cheshire were issuing shares, then Cheshire would need to issue 500 shares in exchange for the outstanding Hillsmere shares in order to arrive at the same 80%/20% ownership ratio. Thus, the fair value of the consideration that was paid to Hillsmere's shareholders was

$15,000 (500 shares × $30 fair value/share of Cheshire stock).

The fair value of Hillsmere's assets and liabilities on the acquisition date equal their carrying amounts, except that the fair value of its noncurrent liabilities has been reduced by $200,000.

The next step is to determine the amount of goodwill arising from the business combination, which is the excess of the consideration effectively transferred, less the net amount of Hillsmere's assets and liabilities, which is calculated as follows:

Consideration effectively transferred		$15,000
Recognized values of Hillsmere assets and liabilities:		
Current assets	$1,900	
Noncurrent assets	2,600	
Current liabilities	(1,300)	
Noncurrent liabilities	(1,200)	(2,000)
Goodwill		$13,000

These calculations result in the following consolidated balance sheet immediately after the business combination:

Current assets ($1,900 + $1,700)	$ 3,600
Noncurrent assets ($2,600 + $4,000)	6,600
Goodwill	13,000
Total assets	23,200
Current liabilities ($1,300 + $1,600)	2,900
Noncurrent liabilities ($1,200 + $2,100)	3,300
Total liabilities	6,200
Shareholders' equity	
Retained earnings	1,600
Issued equity ($15,000 + $400)	15,400
Total shareholders' equity	17,000
Total liabilities and shareholders' equity	$23,200

The consolidated financial statements of the combined entities should include all of the following items:

○ The assets and liabilities of the legal subsidiary, measured at their pre-combination amounts.
○ The assets and liabilities of the legal parent, measured as noted previously for an acquired entity.

- The retained earnings and other equity accounts of the legal subsidiary before the combination.
- The equity interest, which is calculated by adding the issued equity interest of the legal subsidiary just before the business combination to the fair value of the legal parent.
- The equity structure of the consolidated financial statements reflects the equity structure of the legal parent, so you should restate the legal structure of the legal subsidiary using the exchange ratio established in the purchase agreement to reflect the number of shares issued by the legal parent in the reverse acquisition.
- Any non-controlling interest's proportionate share of the legal subsidiary's pre-combination carrying amounts of retained earnings and other equity interests.

If you include comparative information in the financial statements for prior periods, you should retroactively adjust them to show the legal capital of the legal parent entity.

How Do I Account for Acquisition-Related Costs?

An acquirer incurs a variety of acquisition-related costs to complete a business combination. Examples of these costs are advisory fees, finder's fees, legal and accounting expenses, valuation services, and the costs of maintaining an internal acquisitions department. You should charge all of these costs to expense in the period incurred.

What Is the Measurement Period?

The measurement period is the period following the acquisition date, which the acquirer uses to adjust the provisional amounts that it initially recognizes for a business combination. This typically includes the finalization of the identification of the acquiree's assets and liabilities, non-controlling interests, and goodwill. The measurement period does not exceed one year from the acquisition date.

During the measurement period, it is acceptable to recognize additional assets or liabilities associated with the business combination, as long as the additions are based on facts and circumstances that existed as of the acquisition date, and which would have resulted in the recognition of those items at the acquisition date.

Example 25.8

Hostetler Corporation acquires Allspice Distributors on December 31, 20X1. Hostetler hires a valuation expert to appraise the Allspice assets acquired, but the expert's report is not yet complete as of the issuance date of Hostetler's 20X1 financial statements. Accordingly, Hostetler records an estimate of $2,500,000 for the assets in its 20X1 financial statements, and then later revises this figure down to $2,300,000 to match the amount in the valuation expert's appraisal report.

If you recognize a provisional amount for an asset, liability, or non-controlling interest and later need to alter it, the offsetting adjustment is to goodwill.

You should also revise comparative information for previous periods presented in the financial statements, so that adjustments are reflected in all comparative periods. If a change is to an asset that is being depreciated or amortized, retrospectively adjust the depreciation and amortization to reflect the revisions to the provisional amount.

 ## What if the Initial Measurement Is Not Completed in the Initial Reporting Period?

If the acquirer cannot complete the accounting for a business combination within the initial reporting period, then report provisional amounts for any incomplete items. During the measurement period, the acquirer should retrospectively adjust the initial provisional amounts as it obtains new information that affects the measurement of the business combination. This can involve the recognition of additional assets or liabilities.

The measurement period ends as soon as the acquirer either:

○ Finishes collecting information about the facts and circumstances existing at the acquisition date.
○ Determines that no more information is obtainable.
○ One year passes from the acquisition date.

How Do I Subsequently Account for a Business Combination?

You should adjust for the following items after the initial recordation of a business combination:

- ○ *Reacquired rights.* If you recognized an intangible asset because of a reacquired right, then amortize it over the remaining contractual period for which the right was granted.
- ○ *Indemnification rights.* Continue to re-measure indemnification rights on subsequent reporting dates, based on management's assessment of collectability. The acquirer should derecognize this asset if it loses the right to it.
- ○ *Acquired leasehold improvements.* Amortize any leasehold improvement acquired in a business combination over the shorter of the useful life of the assets or a time period that includes required lease and renewal periods that are considered to be reasonably assured.
- ○ *Contingent consideration.* If there is contingent consideration that you initially classified as an asset or liability, you should re-measure it at its fair value on each reporting date, until the situation has been resolved, and in most cases should recognize any changes in fair value in earnings.

What Is Pushdown Accounting?

Pushdown accounting is the process of using the acquiring entity's basis of accounting to prepare the financial statements of the acquired entity. Pushdown accounting is not required for entities that are not registrants with the Securities and Exchange Commission (i.e., public entities).

What Information Should I Disclose about a Business Combination?

You should disclose the following information about each business combination in the notes accompanying the financial statements:

- ○ The name and description of the acquiree
- ○ The acquisition date
- ○ The percentage of voting equity acquired
- ○ The primary reasons for the business combination

- How the acquirer obtained control over the acquiree
- Acquisition-related costs, the amount recognized as expense and where they are reported in the income statement, and the amount not recognized as an expense
- If achieved in stages, the fair value of the acquirer's equity interest in the acquiree just before the acquisition date
- The amount of any indemnification assets, a description of the arrangement, and an estimate of the range of outcomes
- The fair value of acquired receivables, disclosed by major class
- The amounts of major asset classes acquired and liabilities assumed
- The amount and nature of any recognized contingencies
- The fair value of any non-controlling interest in the acquiree, and how that amount was measured
- The factors making up the goodwill recognized
- The fair value of the payment made, by major class of assets paid or liabilities incurred
- The amount recognized for contingent consideration agreements, as well as a description of the agreement, how it is calculated, and an estimate of the range of possible outcomes
- The amount of goodwill expected to be tax deductible
- If there was a bargain purchase, note the amount of any gain recognized, where this amount is located in the income statement, and describe why the transaction resulted in a gain

If the acquirer is a publicly-held company, disclose the following additional information:

- The amounts of acquiree revenue and expense included in the acquirer's consolidated financial statements
- The revenue and earnings of the combined entities as though the acquisition had occurred at the beginning of the acquirer's fiscal year
- The amount of goodwill by reportable segment

If individual acquisitions are immaterial, it is not necessary to report the above information for each acquisition separately. Instead, aggregate the information within the disclosures accompanying the financial statements.

CHAPTER 26

DERIVATIVES

 What Is a Derivative?

A derivative is a financial instrument or other contract whose value changes in relation to changes in an underlier, such as a security price, commodity price, interest rate, credit rating, exchange rate, or climactic condition. It also requires either a small or no initial investment, and settlement is based on the net difference between the final positions of the parties. It allows an entity to speculate on or hedge against future changes in market factors at minimal initial cost. Examples of derivatives are call options, put options, forwards, futures, and swaps.

A non-financial instrument may also be a derivative, as long as it is subject to potential net settlement (not delivering or taking delivery of the underlying non-financial item) and it is not part of an entity's normal usage requirements.

EXAMPLE 26.1

Baroque Furniture Company enters into a contract to purchase gold at a fixed price on a future date. Baroque plans to sell a quantity of leftover gold from its gold-leaf operation on that future date, and intends to use the purchase contract to hedge the price it expects to be paid from the transaction. In this case, the gold purchase contract is a derivative transaction.

However, if Baroque had simply placed an order for the future delivery of gold, with the expectation of integrating the gold leaf into its faux-medieval furniture, then the transaction would not qualify as a derivative.

Example 26.2

Acme Investments is a speculator. On January 1, Acme enters into a soybean futures contract to purchase a number of bushels of soybeans on November 30, and intends to net settle the contract at that time. There is no up-front cost to enter into the contract. On June 30, the fair value of the contract has increased by $50,000. Acme creates the following entry at that time:

Derivative asset	50,000	
Gain		50,000

 ## What Is an Embedded Derivative?

An embedded derivative is part of a financial instrument that also includes a non-derivative host contract. The embedded derivative requires that some portion of the contract's cash flows be modified in relation to changes in a variable, such as an interest rate, commodity price, credit rating, or foreign exchange rate. If a derivative is contractually transferable separately from the contract, then it is not an embedded derivative.

 ## When Do I Separate An Embedded Derivative from the Host Contract?

You should separate an embedded derivative from the host contract and account for the derivative separately only when it meets all of these criteria:

- ○ The economic characteristics and risks of the derivative are not closely related to those of the host contract.
- ○ A separate instrument with the same terms and conditions as the embedded derivative would be classified as a derivative instrument.

If a contract contains an embedded derivative, an entity can irrevocably elect to measure the entire hybrid financial instrument at its fair value, and recognize any changes in fair value within earnings in all future periods.

If you cannot reliably identify and measure an embedded derivative, then you should measure the entire hybrid financial instrument at its fair value, and recognize any changes in fair value within earnings in all future periods.

EXAMPLE 26.3

Acme Investments buys a convertible bond issued by Toledo Motors. Each bond contains a debt instrument and an option to buy one share of Toledo equity after two years have passed, at a fixed price of $10 per share. Acme's total investment is $100,000 and the estimated fair value of the equity conversion option is $800. Acme should separate the equity conversion option from the bond and account for the option separately as a derivative with the following entry:

Investment	99,200	
Derivative asset	800	
Cash		100,000

 ## What Is a Hedging Instrument?

A hedging instrument is a designated financial instrument whose fair value or related cash flows should offset changes in the fair value or cash flows of a designated hedged item. A *fair value hedge* is a hedge of the exposure to changes in the fair value of a recognized asset or liability that are attributable to a specific risk. A *cash flow hedge* is a hedge of the exposure to variability in the cash flows of a specific asset or liability, or of a forecasted transaction, that is attributable to a particular risk. A *hedged item* is an asset, liability, commitment, highly probable transaction, or investment in a foreign operation that exposes an entity to changes in fair value or cash flows, and is designated as being hedged.

 ## What Is Hedging?

Hedging is a risk reduction technique whereby an entity uses a derivative or similar instrument to offset future changes in the fair value or cash flows of an asset or liability. A *hedged item* can be any of the following individually or in a group with similar risk characteristics:

- ○ Highly probable forecast transaction
- ○ Net investment in a foreign operation
- ○ Recognized asset
- ○ Recognized liability
- ○ Unrecognized firm commitment

Hedge effectiveness is the amount of changes in the fair value or cash flows of a hedged item that are offset by changes in the fair value or cash flows of a hedging instrument.

Hedge accounting involves matching a derivative instrument to a hedged item, and then recognizing gains and losses from both items in the same period.

EXAMPLE 26.4

Acme Investments has invested $100,000 in a hedged item, and designates a derivative to hedge this investment. At the end of one year, Acme experiences a gain of $8,000 on the derivative and a loss of $10,000 on the hedged item. The net difference of the gain and loss is a $2,000 loss, which Acme records in earnings.

When Does a Hedging Relationship Qualify for Hedge Accounting?

A hedging relationship only qualifies for hedge accounting if it meets all of the following criteria:

- *Documentation.* You must formally designate a hedge at its inception, as well as document the hedging relationship, the entity's risk management objective, its strategy for undertaking the hedge, and additional requirements specific to cash flow hedges and fair value hedges.
- *Eligibility of hedged items.* Only specific types of hedged items qualify for hedge accounting.
- *Eligibility of hedging instruments..* Either all or a portion of the hedging instrument must be designated as a hedging instrument, as well as other criteria that are specific to different types of hedges.
- *Hedge effectiveness.* You expect the hedge to be highly effective in offsetting any changes in the fair value or cash flows attributable to the hedged risk.

If you do not initially establish a hedging relationship, then you should record all subsequent gains or losses caused by changes in fair value in earnings.

How Frequently Should I Verify Hedge Effectiveness?

You should verify the effectiveness of a hedge at least quarterly. If the hedge has not been highly effective in having achieved offsetting changes in fair values or cash flows through the date of the periodic assessment, then it ceases to qualify for hedge accounting.

How Do I Account for a Fair Value Hedge?

A fair value hedge is a hedge of an asset's or liability's exposure to changes in its fair value, which is attributable to a particular risk, and which could affect profit or loss.

You should record a gain or loss on re-measurement of a fair value hedge in earnings. Also, recognize in earnings the gain or loss on the hedged item that is attributable to the hedged risk, while also adjusting the carrying amount of the hedged item.

If a fair value hedge is fully effective, the gain or loss on the hedging instrument should exactly offset the gain or loss on the hedged item attributable to the hedged risk. If there is a difference appearing in earnings, it is caused by hedge ineffectiveness.

EXAMPLE 26.5

Acme Investments buys a bond having a face value of $100,000 and paying interest of 4%, and records the purchase as an available-for-sale asset. The 4% rate paid by the bond matches the current market rate. If interest rates increase, the value of the bond will decline, so Acme enters into an interest rate swap, where it swaps the fixed interest payments it receives from the bond issuer for floating interest payments from a third party. Acme appropriately documents the interest rate swap as a hedge of the bond.

Market interest rates subsequently increase, reducing the fair value of the bond by $3,000, so Acme records the following entry:

Hedging loss (hedged item)	3,000	
Available-for-sale asset		3,000

Acme also records an increased value for the swap, which was positively impacted by the same increase in interest rates:

Swap asset	3,000	
Hedging gain (hedging instrument)		3,000

(Continued)

> Since the changes in fair value of the bond and the interest rate swap exactly offset each other, there is no net gain or loss, and the hedge is 100% effective.

You should discontinue hedge accounting if the hedging instrument expires or you sell, terminate, or exercise it. You should also discontinue hedge accounting if the entity revokes the hedging designation, or the hedge no longer meets the hedge accounting criteria.

If you adjust the carrying amount of a hedged asset held for sale, the adjustment remains part of the carrying amount of the asset until the entity sells it; at the point of sale, you should recognize the entire carrying amount of the hedged asset as the cost of the item sold.

If you adjust the carrying amount of a hedged interest-bearing financial instrument, you should amortize the adjustment to earnings. An example of such amortization is noted in the next question, using the effective interest method.

 ## What Is the Effective Interest Method?

The effective interest method is a technique for calculating the amortized cost of a financial asset or liability, and which allocates interest income or expense over the relevant period. The calculation includes all fees and points paid, and all premiums and discounts. The *effective interest rate*, which is used in the calculation, exactly discounts estimated future cash payments or receipts over the expected life of the instrument.

EXAMPLE 26.6

Svelte Equipment Company, which makes fine chrome-plated weight lifting equipment, acquires a debt security having a stated principal amount of $100,000, which the issuer will repay in three years. The debt has a coupon interest rate of 5%, which it pays at the end of each year. Svelte acquires the debt for $90,000, which is a discount of $10,000 to the principal amount of $100,000. Svelte classifies the investment as held-to-maturity, and records this entry:

Held-to-maturity investments	90,000	
Cash		90,000

Based on a cash outflow of $90,000 to acquire the investment, three interest payments of $5,000 each, and a principal payment of $100,000 upon maturity, Svelte calculates an effective interest rate of 8.95%. Using this interest rate, Svelte calculates the following amortization table:

Year	(A) Beginning Amortized Cost	(B) Interest and Principal Payments	(C) Interest Income [A × 8.95%]	(D) Debt Discount Amortization [C − B]	Ending Amortized Cost [A + D]
1	$90,000	$5,000	$8,055	$3,055	$93,055
2	93,055	5,000	8,328	3,328	96,383
3	96,383	105,000	8,617	3,617	100,000

Using the table, Svelte makes the following entries at the end of each of the next three years:

Year 1:

Cash	5,000	
Held-to-maturity investment	3,055	
Interest income		8,055

Year 2:

Cash	5,000	
Held-to-maturity investment	3,328	
Interest income		8,328

Year 3:

Cash	105,000	
Held-to-maturity investment		96,383
Interest income		8,617

How Do I Account for a Cash Flow Hedge?

A cash flow hedge is a hedge exposure to cash flow variability. In general, you should account for a cash flow hedge by recognizing the portion of the gain or loss on the hedging instrument in other comprehensive income, but only to the extent of the gain or loss that is effective. You should record the ineffective part of the gain or loss on the hedging instrument in earnings. You should re-classify gains or losses in other comprehensive income into earnings when the hedged transaction results in either the acquisition of an asset or the incurrence of a liability, and doing so affects earnings (such as when an entity recognizes a cost of sales, or incurs interest expense). More specific accounting applies to the following four situations:

1. If the risk management strategy for a hedging relationship excludes a certain component of the gain or loss, or related cash flows on the hedging derivative, recognize the excluded gain or loss component in earnings.

2. Adjust the accumulated other comprehensive income associated with a hedged transaction to an amount that is the lesser of 1) the cumulative gain or loss on the derivative from hedge inception, less any gains or losses on that derivative already reclassified into earnings; or 2) the cumulative gain or loss on the derivative needed to offset the cumulative change in expected future cash flows on the hedged transaction from hedge inception, less any gains or losses on that derivative already reclassified into earnings.

3. Recognize a gain or loss in earnings for any remaining gain or loss on the hedging derivative, or to adjust other comprehensive income to the amount just derived in item #2.

4. For foreign currency hedging, if hedge effectiveness is based on total changes in an option's cash flow, then reclassify an amount from other comprehensive income to earnings that adjusts earnings for the amortization of the cost of the option.

You should reclassify a gain or loss previously recognized in other comprehensive income into earnings in the same period when the hedged forecast transaction affects earnings.

EXAMPLE 26.7

Herndon Hydroelectric orders a turbine from a supplier in Germany for €250,000, for delivery to its Virginia facility on November 30, which is 90 days in the future. Herndon's functional currency is the U.S. Dollar. Currently, Herndon expects to pay $180,000 for the turbine, which reflects the current dollar/Euro exchange rate. However, if the Euro strengthens against the dollar within the next 90 days, Herndon will have to pay more dollars for the purchase.

To avoid this exchange rate risk, Herndon enters into a forward contract to purchase €250,000 on November 30 for $180,000. Herndon appropriately designates the forward contract as a hedge of its exposure to increases in the dollar exchange rate.

After one month, the Euro has increased in value against the dollar, so that the €250,000 would require $185,000 on the open market, which represents a $5,000 increase in the value of the forward contract. Herndon records the change in value with this entry:

Forward asset	5,000	
Equity		5,000

Herndon settles the forward contract on November 30 with this entry:

Cash	5,000	
Forward asset		5,000

Herndon then pays $185,000 for the turbine on November 30, and reduces the carrying amount of the machine with the following entry, which shifts the deferred gain from equity to the cost of the turbine:

Equity	5,000	
Machinery		5,000

You should terminate cash flow hedge accounting when the entity sells, terminates, or exercises the derivative instrument, the hedging arrangement no longer meets the hedging criteria, or the entity removes the hedging designation. If so, you should leave any gains or losses from the derivative in other comprehensive income, and reclassify it into earnings when the hedged forecasted transaction affects earnings (usually when the transaction is settled). Alternatively, you can designate a new hedging relationship with a different hedging instrument.

How Do I Account for a Net Investment Hedge?

A hedge of a net investment relates to an investment in a foreign operation. Hedge accounting can only be applied to the foreign exchange differences arising between the functional currencies of the foreign operation and the parent entity. The parent entity can hedge an amount equal to or less than the carrying amount of the net assets of the foreign operation.

You should account for it by recognizing the portion of the gain or loss on the hedging instrument in other comprehensive income, but only to the extent of the gain or loss that is effective. You should record the ineffective part of the gain or loss on the hedging instrument in earnings.

If the entity disposes of the foreign operation, then you should shift the related amount of the gain or loss previously recognized in other comprehensive income into earnings.

EXAMPLE 26.8

Toledo Motors invests 50 million Singapore dollars in an automobile production facility in Singapore, which it plans to sell in five years, likely at an amount that will recoup its original investment. To hedge the investment, Toledo borrows 50 million Singapore dollars and designates the loan as a hedge of the net investment.

Over the next five years, there is a 500,000 Singapore dollar foreign currency gain on the loan. Toledo defers the gain in equity, and then uses it to offset the 500,000 Singapore dollar foreign exchange loss when it sells the Singapore facility at the end of five years.

Can I Designate a Portion of a Financial Item as a Hedged Item?

You can hedge the risks associated with a portion of a financial asset's or financial liability's cash flows or fair value, as long as you can measure the effectiveness of the hedge.

Can I Cluster Similar Assets and Liabilities into Groups of Hedged Items?

You can aggregate similar assets or similar liabilities and hedge them as a group. However, you can only do so if the individual items in each group share the risk exposure that you are designating as being hedged.

How Do I Account for Intra-Entity Hedging Instruments?

Only a derivative instrument with an unrelated third party can be designated as a hedging instrument. Thus, it is not possible to designate as a hedging instrument an instrument that originates within a consolidated group.

What Is a Held-to-Maturity Investment?

A held-to-maturity investment is a long-term security that its holder has elected to hold until its date of maturity.

What Is an Available-for-Sale Investment?

An available for sale financial asset is a non-derivative asset that is designated as available for sale. It is not classified as a held-to-maturity or trading security.

EXAMPLE 26.9

Branxholm Industries invests $100,000 in an equity instrument that is traded on the New York Stock Exchange. Branxholm has also invested $75,000 in an equity instrument that is not actively traded. Branxholm also makes a strategic investment of $250,000 in the equity of a key supplier, which it does not intend to sell. Branxholm does not designate these investments as trading securities.

Branxholm should designate all of these investments as available-for-sale.

How Do I Account for a Derivative Instrument?

You should recognize all of an entity's derivative instruments in its balance sheet, using their initial fair value.

You should subsequently measure all derivative instruments at their fair values. If a derivative was initially designated as being in a hedging relationship, then you should record any gains or losses on changes in fair value within other comprehensive income. If there is no hedging relationship, then you should record any gains or losses on changes in fair value in earnings. The following more specific rules override the preceding general instructions:

- *Held-to-maturity investments.* If there is a change in fair value of a forward contract or purchased option, do not recognize it unless there is an other-than-temporary decline in the fair value; if such is the case, recognize the loss in earnings.
- *Available-for-sale investments.* Record changes in the fair value of a forward contract or purchased option to shareholders' equity, unless the decline in fair value is other-than-temporary; if such is the case, recognize the loss in earnings.
- *Trading securities.* Record changes in the fair value of a forward contract or purchased option in earnings.

 ## What Information Should I Disclose about Derivatives?

You should disclose the following general information about derivatives in the notes accompanying an entity's financial statements:

- How and why the entity uses derivatives (including the objectives and strategies associated with the derivatives program)
- How derivatives and hedged items are accounted for
- How derivatives and hedged items affect the entity's financial position, financial performance, and cash flows
- The volume of activity in the entity's derivatives program

You should disclose the preceding information separately for fair value hedging instruments, cash flow hedging instruments, foreign currency hedging instruments, and all other derivatives.

In addition, you should disclose the following quantitative information by contract type:

- The fair value amounts of derivatives in the balance sheet, and in which line items they are located
- The amounts of any gains and losses on derivatives and related hedged items, reported separately for fair value hedges, cash flow hedges, and all other hedges

If you include derivative-related information in more than one footnote to the financial statements, then cross-reference the information between the various footnotes.

DISCLOSURE EXAMPLE 26.10 FAIR VALUE OF DERIVATIVE INSTRUMENTS AT DECEMBER 31, 20X1

(000s)	Asset Derivatives		Liability Derivatives	
	Balance Sheet Location	Fair Value	Balance Sheet Location	Fair Value
Hedging Instruments				
Interest rate contracts	Other assets	$29,000	Other liabilities	($15,000)
Foreign exchange contracts	Other assets	10,000	Other liabilities	(5,000)
Commodity contracts	Other assets	9,000	Other liabilities	(4,000)
Total		$48,000		($24,000)
Non-Hedging instruments				
Interest rate contracts	Other assets	$ 5,000	Other liabilities	($3,000)
Foreign exchange contracts	Other assets	12,000	Other liabilities	(6,000)
Commodity contracts	Other assets	3,000	Other liabilities	(2,000)
Total		$20,000		($11,000)
Total derivatives		$68,000		($35,000)

DISCLOSURE EXAMPLE 26.11 THE EFFECT OF TRADING ACTIVITIES FOR THE YEARS ENDED DECEMBER 31, 20X2 AND 20X1

Type of Instrument (000s)	20X2	20X1
Commodity	$ 59,000	$ 51,000
Credit	12,000	29,000
Equity	41,000	38,000
Fixed income/interest rate	5,000	7,000
Foreign exchange	35,000	22,000
Other	11,000	5,000
Total	$163,000	$152,000
Line Item in Statement of Financial Performance	20X2	20X1
Principal/proprietary transactions	$100,000	$105,000
Asset management income	39,000	47,000
Other income	24,000	–
Total	$163,000	$152,000

What Additional Information Should I Disclose about Fair Value Hedges?

You should disclose the following information about fair value hedges in the notes accompanying the financial statements, as well as any related derivatives disclosures noted above:

- ○ The net gain or loss recognized in earnings for hedge ineffectiveness, and any component of a derivative instrument's gain or loss excluded from the assessment of hedge effectiveness
- ○ The net gain or loss recognized in earnings when a hedged firm commitment no longer can qualify as a fair value hedge

What Additional Information Should I Disclose about Cash Flow Hedges?

You should display within a separate classification in the statement of comprehensive income an entity's net gain or loss on derivative instruments designated as cash flow hedges. In addition, you should disclose the following information in the notes accompanying the financial statements:

- ○ The transactions resulting in the reclassification of gains or losses from other comprehensive income to earnings
- ○ The estimated amount of gains or losses in other comprehensive income that you expect will be reclassified into earnings within the next 12 months.
- ○ The maximum time period over which the entity is hedging its exposure to future cash flows for forecasted transactions
- ○ The amount of gains or losses that were reclassified into earnings because of the discontinuance of cash flow hedges because it is probable that the originally forecasted transactions will not occur during the specified time period
- ○ The beginning and ending accumulated derivative instrument gain or loss, net changes caused by current period hedging activities, and the net amount of any reclassification into earnings

CHAPTER 27

FAIR VALUE

 What Is Fair Value?

Fair value is the price that would be received to sell an asset or that would be paid to transfer a liability in an orderly transaction between market participants (an orderly transaction allows for normal marketing activities; it is not a forced liquidation or distress sale). The following assumptions are incorporated into the determination of fair value:

○ *Price.* The price is determined in an orderly transaction between market participants.
○ *Principal market.* The transaction occurs in the principal market for the asset or liability or in the most advantageous market, from the perspective of the reporting entity.
○ *Market participants.* The fair value would be determined based on the assumptions used by market participants to price the asset or liability.
○ *Application to assets.* The highest and best use of the asset by market participants is assumed, even if the intended use by the reporting entity is different. The highest and best use provides maximum value to market participants.
○ *Application to liabilities.* The liability to a counterpart is not settled; it continues subsequent to the transaction.
○ *The asset or liability.* Since a fair value measurement is for a specific asset or liability, the measurement should include consideration of the asset's or liability's condition, location, and restrictions on its use or sale.

 What Types of Markets Are There?

An *active market* is a market for an asset or liability where transactions occur with sufficient frequency and volume

EXAMPLE 27.1

Allspice Distributors acquires a plot of land as part of its acquisition of Nutmeg Corporation. The land is currently zoned for industrial use, and Nutmeg had been planning to build a spice warehouse on the site. However, an adjacent plot has just been developed for residential use, which implies a significantly higher value for the acquired land. Based on the adjacent development and recent zoning changes, Allspice decides that the land could instead be developed for residential use, which is the highest and best use of the land. Accordingly, Allspice assigns a fair value to the land that is higher than would be the case if it assumed industrial usage instead.

to provide pricing information. A *brokered market* is a market where brokers match buyers with sellers but do not trade on their own accounts. A *dealer market* is a market where dealers are ready to trade on their own accounts, thereby providing liquidity to the market. In a dealer market, bid and ask prices are more readily available than closing prices. An over-the-counter market is a dealer market. An *exchange market* is a market in which closing prices are readily available and are usually representative of fair value. The New York Stock Exchange is an exchange market. The *most advantageous market* is the market where the reporting entity can sell an asset for the maximum price or transfer a liability for the minimum price. The *principal market* is the market where the reporting entity can sell an asset or transfer a liability with the greatest volume and level of activity for the asset or liability.

Which Assets and Liabilities Are Measured at Fair Value?

Fair value principles do not apply to non-financial assets or non-financial liabilities, unless an entity recognizes such items as being at fair value on a recurring basis.

What Assumptions Do I Use to Measure Fair Value?

Assumptions used to measure fair value are known as *inputs*, and they are divided into the following three levels of inputs, with Level 1 inputs being of the highest informational quality and Level 3 inputs being of the lowest quality:

- ○ *Level 1 inputs.* Quoted prices in active markets for identical assets or liabilities that the reporting entity can access at the measurement date. This represents the most reliable evidence of fair value, so you should use it to determine fair value whenever possible.
- ○ *Level 2 inputs.* Inputs other than the quoted prices listed under Level 1, which are either directly or indirectly observable. Level 2 inputs include:
  - Quoted prices for similar assets or liabilities in active markets
  - Quoted prices for identical or similar assets or liabilities in non-active markets, such as those where there are few transactions, prices are not current, or where price quotations vary substantially
  - Inputs other than quoted prices are observable (i.e., obtained from independent sources), such as interest rates, volatilities, the severity of losses, credit risk, and default rates

An example of a Level 2 input is the price per square foot for a building, which is derived from prices in transactions involving similar buildings in similar locations.

- ○ *Level 3 inputs.* Inputs are not observable, so an entity must make assumptions about the assumptions that market participants would use in pricing an asset or liability. One should incorporate risk into these assumptions. An entity may use its own data when developing assumptions, as well as any information about market participant assumptions that is reasonably available without an excessive amount of cost and effort. An example of a Level 3 input is the expected cash flows from an entity's own data, used to develop the asset retirement obligation associated with an asset purchase.

If you make an adjustment to a fair value that was determined under Level 1 inputs because of factors specific to an asset or liability, this adjustment automatically makes the measurement a lower-level measurement than Level 1. Similarly, if you make a significant adjustment to a fair value that was derived from Level 2 inputs, this may shift the measurement to a Level 3 measurement.

What Information Do I Use if Bid and Ask Prices Are Available?

If you are measuring fair value based on bid and ask prices, it is permissible to use bid prices to value assets and ask prices to value liabilities, though you may alternatively use whatever price within the bid-ask spread that is most representative of fair value under the circumstances.

What Valuation Techniques Are Available?

The following methods can be used to value an asset or liability:

- ○ *Cost approach.* This technique is based on the amount that would currently be required to replace the service capacity of an asset.
- ○ *Income approach.* This technique converts future cash flow or earnings information into a discounted present value.
- ○ *Market approach.* This technique uses prices generated by market transactions that involve identical or comparable assets or liabilities. It may involve the use of market multiples that are derived from a set of comparables.

EXAMPLE 27.2

Allspice Distributors has a spice packaging machine that it has customized in order to integrate it with incoming and outgoing processes. The machine does not generate cash flow by itself, only as part of a larger group of assets, so it is inappropriate to derive its value using the income approach. However, Allspice can use the cost approach to determine what it would cost to currently acquire and modify similar equipment having comparable utility. Allspice has a valuation specialist conduct the review, who considers the condition of the existing packaging machine, and derives a fair value in the range of $115,000 to $130,000.

Despite the level of customization of the packaging machine, there are similar machines on the market today. Accordingly, Allspice's valuation specialist also uses the market approach, obtaining quotes for similar machines, and adjusting these prices for the differences between the Allspice machine and the comparison models. The valuation specialist's estimate reflects the price that Allspice would receive for the packaging machine in its current condition and location, resulting in a fair value in the range of $105,000 to $118,000.

Allspice decides that, based on the reliability of the inputs, the fair value indicated by the cost approach more closely approximates fair value, and so ascribes more weight to the results of the cost approach than the market approach in determining the fair value of the machine.

Can I Use Multiple Valuation Techniques?

You can use a single valuation technique to value an asset or liability when there are quoted prices in an active market for identical items. If not, then you can use multiple valuation techniques. If you use multiple techniques to determine fair value, then evaluate and weight the results, considering the reasonableness of the range of fair values indicated by the results. The fair value that you settle upon should be the point within the range of results that is most representative of fair value in the circumstances.

Can I Change Valuation Techniques?

You should consistently apply valuation techniques. However, a change in valuation techniques may be appropriate if the result is a measure that is either equally or more representative of fair value. The decision to change valuation techniques is particularly relevant when the circumstances change, such as when information used as input to the old valuation technique is no longer available, or if new information becomes available that can be used in a different valuation technique.

If you do change to a new valuation technique, account for it as a change in accounting estimate, which calls for changes in present and future periods; you should not make changes to prior accounting periods.

Do Asset and Liability Restrictions Impact Their Fair Values?

Most liabilities contain a restriction that requires the reporting entity to settle the transaction, and which also states that the entity must take some action in order to be relieved of this obligation. This restriction varies from the kind imposed on an asset, which typically restricts its marketability. It is not common to have a restriction on an asset, while it is nearly universal to have a restriction attached to a liability. Consequently, the presence of a restriction on a liability is assumed, and so does not affect its price, while the presence of a restriction on an asset is not assumed, and so does affect its price. In essence, restrictions tend to impact the fair values of assets more than the fair values of liabilities.

 ## When Might a Transaction Price Vary from Its Fair Value?

A transaction price might vary from an item's fair value when the transaction is between related parties, when it occurs under duress, or when the market in which it is bought or sold is not the most advantageous market.

 ## What Information Do I Disclose about Fair Value?

The main objectives of fair value disclosure are to reveal the inputs used to measure fair value, and to show the effect on earnings of measurements that are based on Level 3 inputs. To meet these objectives, you should disclose the following information in the notes accompanying the financial statements:

○ Fair value measurements at the reporting date.
○ In aggregate, where fair value measurements fall within the fair value hierarchy, segregating measurements for Level 1, Level 2, and Level 3 inputs.
○ For Level 3 inputs, a reconciliation showing beginning and ending balances, gains and losses for the period, purchases, sales, issuances, settlements, and transfers in or out of Level 3.
○ The total gains or losses included in earnings that are attributable to the change in unrealized gains or losses for those assets or liabilities still held as of the report date. Also note where these gains or losses are reported in the income statement.
○ The valuation techniques used to measure fair value. Discuss any changes in valuation techniques during the period.
○ If you measure the fair value of some assets or liabilities on a non-recurring basis, then disclose the fair

value measurements recorded during the period, the reasons for the measurements, the level within the fair value hierarchy where the measurements fall (by Level 1, 2, or 3), a description of the information used for Level 3 inputs, the valuation techniques used, and any changes in those techniques during the reporting period.

The above disclosures should be broken down into the major categories of an entity's assets and liabilities.

		EXAMPLE OF DISCLOSURES 27.3 QUANTITATIVE DISCLOSURES ABOUT FAIR VALUE INVESTMENTS		
	Fair Value Measured at Reporting Date Using:			
(000s) Description	**12/ 31/ XX**	**Quoted Prices in Active Markets for Identical Assets (Level 1)**	**Significant Other Observable Inputs (Level 2)**	**Significant Unobser- vable Inputs (Level 3)**
Trading securities	$290	$200	$ 90	
Available- for-sale securities	120	100	20	
Derivatives	300	150	90	$ 60
Venture capital invest- ments	50			50
Total	$760	$450	$200	$110

What Is the Fair Value Option?

Any entity has the option to measure the following assets and liabilities at their fair values:

- A financial asset and financial liability
- A firm commitment that involves only financial instruments
- A written loan commitment
- The rights and obligations under certain insurance contracts

---

EXAMPLE OF DISCLOSURES 27.4   RECONCILIATION OF FAIR VALUE OF ASSETS AND LIABILITIES USING LEVEL 3 INPUTS

(000s)	Fair Value Measurements Using Level 3 Inputs		
	Derivatives	Venture Capital Investments	Total
Beginning balance	$20	$60	$80
Total gains or losses (realized/ unrealized)			
Included in earnings (or changes in net assets)	8	(5)	3
Included in other comprehensive income	10		10
Purchases, issuances, and settlements	(5)	3	(2)
Transfers into or out of Level 3		7	7
Ending balance	$33	$65	$98

- ○ The rights and obligations under a warranty that requires the provision of goods or services, and which permits the warrantor to settle by paying a third party to handle the warranty
- ○ Certain financial instruments that have been separated from an embedded non-financial derivative

An entity cannot measure the following assets and liabilities at their fair values:

- ○ An investment in a subsidiary that the entity must consolidate
- ○ An interest in a variable interest entity that the entity must consolidate
- ○ Most types of employee and plan obligations for pension and other post-retirement benefits, as well as deferred compensation arrangements
- ○ Deposit liabilities
- ○ Financial instruments that are classified as a component of shareholders' equity

What Are the Rules for Using the Fair Value Option?

If you choose to measure eligible items at their fair value, you must do so:

- ○ Instrument by instrument
- ○ Only to an entire instrument and not to specified risks, cash flows, or portions of the instrument

Once you elect to measure items at their fair value, the decision is irrevocable; you must then continue to measure the items at their fair value.

You can choose the fair value option on an election date. The election date is when one of the following occurs:

- ○ The entity first recognizes the eligible asset or liability
- ○ The entity enters into a firm commitment
- ○ The accounting treatment for an investment changes because it either becomes eligible for the equity method of accounting or the investor stops consolidating the results of a subsidiary but retains an equity interest in it
- ○ There is an event requiring initial measurement at fair value, but not subsequently (such as a business combination)

With minor exceptions, you can elect to use the fair value option for a single eligible item, and not elect to use it for other identical items.

How Do I Subsequently Account for Items Under the Fair Value Option?

Once you have elected to use the fair value option for a specific item, you should report unrealized gains and losses related to it in earnings at each subsequent reporting date.

What Fair Value Information Do I Disclose on the Balance Sheet?

If you report assets and liabilities under the fair value option, you should separate their fair values from the carrying amounts of similar assets and liabilities that are measured using another measurement attribute. You can do this by either parenthetically disclosing the amount measured at fair value in the same balance sheet line item containing the aggregate asset or liability amount, or by presenting two separate line items, one for fair value items and one for those items having non-fair-value carrying amounts.

What Information Do I Disclose about the Fair Value Option?

You should report the following fair value information in the notes accompanying the financial statements:

- The fair value of financial instruments for which it is practicable to estimate their value
- The methods and assumptions used to estimate fair values
- Any changes in the methods and assumptions used to estimate fair values during the period
- If it is not practicable to estimate fair values, disclose information pertinent to estimating fair value, and the reasons why it is not practicable to estimate fair value
- Management's reasons for electing the fair value option
- If management elects the fair value option for some but not all eligible items, state the reasons for partial election
- The amounts of gains or losses from fair value changes included in earnings during the period, and in which income statement line item those gains or losses are reported
- For those liabilities whose fair values were significantly affected by changes in credit risk, disclose the fair value gains and losses attributable to credit risk, the reasons for those changes, and how the gains and losses were determined

The preceding requirements are optional for those non-public entities whose total assets are less than $100 million, and which (with minor exceptions) have no derivative instruments.

EXAMPLE OF DISCLOSURES 27.5
We used the following methods and assumptions to estimate the fair value of each of the following classes of financial instruments:

○ *Cash and short-term investments.* The carrying amount approximates fair value of the short maturity of these instruments.
○ *Long-term investments.* We estimate the fair values of some investments based on quoted market prices for those or similar investments. For other investments for which there are no quoted market prices, we cannot make a reasonable estimate of fair value without incurring excessive costs. We have provided the following information that is pertinent to the value of an unquoted investment:

- *Long-term debt.* We estimate the fair value of our long-term debt based on quoted market prices for the same or similar issues.
- *Foreign currency contracts.* We estimate the fair value of foreign currency contracts by obtaining quotes from brokers.

The estimated fair values of our financial instruments follow:

	20X2		20X1	
(000s)	Carrying Amount	Fair Value	Carrying Amount	Fair Value
Cash and short-term investments	$2,100	$2,100	$1,800	$1,800
Long-term investments for which it is:				
Practicable to estimate fair value	15,400	15,000	14,200	13,600
Not practicable*	2,400	2,400	2,400	2,400
Long-term debt	(3,900)	(3,700)	(4,100)	(4,300)
Foreign currency contracts	(1,000)	(800)	500	100

*It was not practicable to estimate the fair value of an investment in an oil drilling company, of which we own 10% of the outstanding shares, since the stock is not traded. We carry that investment at its original cost of $2.4 million.

CHAPTER 28

FOREIGN CURRENCY MATTERS

 What Is a Foreign Currency?

A *foreign currency* is a currency other than an entity's functional currency. An entity's *functional currency* is the currency of the primary economic environment in which it generates and expends cash. An entity's *reporting currency* is the currency in which it reports its financial results.

 What Is an Exchange Rate?

An exchange rate is the ratio between a unit of one currency and a unit of another currency that can be exchanged as of a specific point in time. The *spot exchange rate* is the exchange rate at which a currency can be delivered immediately. The *closing rate* is the spot exchange rate at the end of a reporting period.

 How Do I Identify a Foreign Entity's Functional Currency?

An entity may have foreign operations that are largely self-contained and integrated within their local economic environments, and which primarily generate and expend a foreign currency. For this type of foreign operation, the foreign currency is the functional currency.

An entity may have foreign operations that are primarily an extension of the parent entity's operations, and for which the parent provides financing in dollars. For this type of foreign operation, the dollar is the functional currency.

EXAMPLE 28.1

Chillo Ice Cream Company, based in the United States, has a subsidiary in Chile, to which it ships its products for sale through a number of retail outlets.
(Continued)

The local subsidiary only sells the imported ice cream and then remits receipts back to corporate headquarters, so Chillo should treat the functional currency of its Chilean operation as U.S. Dollars.

Chillo also owns Sorvete Firma, which is located in Brazil. Sorvete manufactures its own ice cream, markets it throughout Brazil, accumulates cash reserves and borrows funds in Brazilian reals, and rarely remits funds back to corporate headquarters. In this case, the functional currency for Sorvete is Brazilian reals.

What Happens if I Change the Functional Currency of a Foreign Entity?

Once you decide upon the functional currency to use for a subsidiary, you should continue to use it consistently, unless there is a significant change in the economic facts and circumstances that clearly indicate a change in the functional currency. If you do change the functional currency, *do not* restate previously issued financial statements to reflect the change.

If you change the functional currency from the reporting currency to a foreign currency, report the change attributable to current-rate translation of non-monetary assets as of the date of the change in other comprehensive income. Conversely, if you change the functional currency from a foreign currency to the reporting currency, do not remove translation adjustments for prior periods from equity; also, the translated amounts for non-monetary assets become the accounting basis for those assets.

How Do I Initially Account for a Foreign Currency Transaction?

On the date when you recognize a transaction that is denominated in a foreign currency, measure it in the recording entity's functional currency. To do so, apply the spot exchange rate between the functional currency and the foreign currency as of the transaction date.

If there is a change in the exchange rates between the two currencies during the period between when the transaction is denominated and when it is settled, then record the difference as a foreign currency transaction gain or loss in whichever period the exchange rate changes, through and including the final settlement date.

EXAMPLE 28.2

Rainier Designs is an American exporter of climbing equipment, whose functional currency is the U.S. dollar. On November 30, it sells an order of ice climbing gear to a German outdoor retail chain that is denominated in Euros, in the amount of €80,000. The spot rate on the November 30 shipment date was $1: €1.25, so Rainier records the following entry in dollars (calculated as €80,000 ÷ $1.25 exchange rate).

Accounts receivable	$64,000	
Sales		$64,000

The receivable is still outstanding on December 31, which is Rainier's fiscal year-end. On December 31, the exchange rate has changed to $1: €$1.15, so the receivable is now worth $69,565 (calculated as €80,000 ÷ $1.15 exchange rate). This represents a foreign exchange gain of $5,565, which Rainier records with this entry:

Accounts receivable	$5,565	
Foreign currency exchange gain		$5,565

The customer wires payment to Rainier on the following day, when the exchange rate remains at $1: €1.15. Rainier records the following entry to recognize the receipt of cash:

Cash	$69,565	
Accounts receivable		$69,565

Can I Record Foreign Exchange Rate Changes in Revenues?

No. An entity records revenues at the initial point of sale, and does not change it again, no matter what happens to foreign exchange rates between the initial sale and the settlement of payment terms. The reason is that the time period between the initial sale date and the payment date is a financing decision, not a sales decision, and so any foreign exchange gains or losses incurred during that interval should not be reflected in sales.

How Do I Translate the Financial Statements of a Foreign Subsidiary into the Currency of the Parent?

When deciding how to translate the financial statements of a foreign subsidiary into the currency of the entity's parent, use the *current rate* translation method when a currency besides the U.S. dollar is the primary currency used by a subsidiary. You usually select this approach when a subsidiary's operations are not integrated into those of its U.S.-based parent, if its financing is primarily in that of the local currency, or if the subsidiary conducts most of its transactions in the local currency.

However, you cannot use this method if the country in which the subsidiary is located suffers from a high rate of inflation, which is defined as a cumulative rate of 100% or more over the most recent three years. In this case, use the *re-measurement method* instead. If the local economy is considered to no longer be inflationary, then you can change the reporting method back to the current rate method; when this happens, convert the financial statements of the impacted subsidiary back into the local currency using the exchange rate on the date when the determination is made.

Use the re-measurement method when the U.S. dollar is designated as the primary currency in which transactions are recorded at a foreign location. Another clear indicator of when this method is used is when the subsidiary has close operational integration with its U.S. parent, or when most of its financing, sales, and expenses are denominated in dollars.

The following decision tree clarifies how to select the correct translation method:

How Do I Use the Current Rate Method?

To use the current rate translation method, first determine the subsidiary's functional currency. This should be the currency in which the bulk of the entity's transactions and financing is used. Next, convert all of the subsidiary's transactions to this functional currency. You should

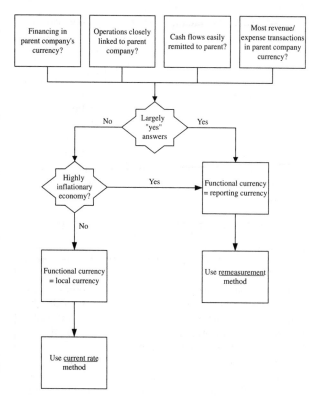

Exhibit 28.1   TYPE OF TRANSLATION METHOD DECISION TREE

continue to use the same functional currency from year to year in order to provide a reasonable basis of comparison when multiple years of financial results are included in the corporate parent's financial results.

Next, convert all assets and liabilities of the subsidiary to U.S. dollars at the current rate of exchange as of the date of the financial statements. The following conversion rules apply:

○ Convert revenues and expenses that have occurred throughout the current fiscal year at a weighted-average rate of exchange for the entire year. A preferable approach is to convert them at the exchange rates in effect on the dates when they occurred, but this is considered too labor-intensive to be practical in most situations.

○ Convert stockholder's equity at the historical rate of exchange. However, record changes to retained earnings within the current reporting period at the weighted average rate of exchange for the year, since they are derived from revenues and expenses that were also recorded at the weighted average rate of exchange.

o Record dividends declared during the year at the exchange rate on the date of declaration.

o Store any resulting translation adjustments in the equity section of the corporate parent's consolidated balance sheet. This account is cumulative, so you should separately report in the footnotes to the financial statements the change in the translation adjustments account as a result of activities in the reporting period.

EXAMPLE 28.3

A division of the Oregon Clock Company is located in Mexico. This division maintains its books in pesos, borrows pesos from a local bank, and conducts the majority of its operations within Mexico. Accordingly, its functional currency is the peso, which requires the parent's accounting staff to record the division's results using the current rate method.

The peso exchange rate at the beginning of the year is assumed to be .08 to the dollar, while the rate at the end of the year is assumed to be .10 to the dollar. For the purposes of this example, the blended full-year rate of exchange for the peso is assumed to be .09 to the dollar. The Mexican division's balance sheet is shown below, followed by its income statement. For simplicity, the beginning retained earnings figure is zero, implying that the company is in its first year of existence.

BALANCE SHEET CONVERSION

	Pesos	Exchange Rate	U.S. Dollars
Assets			
Cash	427	.08	34
Accounts Receivable	1,500	.08	120
Inventory	2,078	.08	166
Fixed Assets	3,790	.08	303
Total Assets	7,795		623
Liabilities & Equity			
Accounts Payable	1,003	.08	80

Notes Payable	4,250	.08	340
Common Stock	2,100	.10	210
Additional Paid-In Capital	428	.10	43
Retained Earnings	14	Note 1	0
Translation Adjustments	—	—	−50
Total Liabilities & Equity	7,795		623

Note 1: As noted in the income statement.

INCOME STATEMENT CONVERSION

	Pesos	Exchange Rate	U.S. Dollars
Revenue	6,750	.09	608
Expenses	6,736	.09	607
Net Income	14		1
Beginning Retained Earnings	0		0
Add: Net Income	14	.09	0
Ending Retained Earnings	14		0

How Do I Use the Re-measurement Method?

Under the re-measurement method, you translate not only cash, but also any transactions that will be settled in cash (mostly accounts receivable and payable, as well as loans) at the current exchange rate as of the date of the financial statements. You should settle all other assets and liabilities (such as inventory, prepaid items, fixed assets, trademarks, goodwill, and equity) at the historical exchange rate on the date when these transactions occurred.

There are a few cases where the income statement is impacted by the items on the balance sheet that have been translated using historical interest rates. For example, the cost of goods sold will be impacted when inventory that has been translated at a historical exchange rate is liquidated. When this happens, the inventory valuation at the historical exchange rate is charged through the income statement. The same approach is used for the depreciation of fixed assets and the amortization of intangible items.

Other income statement items primarily involve transactions that arise throughout the reporting year of the subsidiary. For these items, it would be too labor intensive to determine the exact exchange rate for each item at the time it occurred. Instead, determine the weighted average exchange rate for the entire reporting period, and apply this average to the income statement items that have occurred during that period.

EXAMPLE 28.4

A simplified example of a corporate subsidiary's (located in Mexico) balance sheet is shown below. The peso exchange rate at the beginning of the year is assumed to be .08 to the dollar, while the rate at the end of the year is assumed to be .10 to the dollar. The primary difference in calculation from the current rate method shown in the last example is that the exchange rate for the inventory and fixed assets accounts have changed from the year-end rate to the rate at which they are assumed to have been originated at an earlier date. Also, there is no translation adjustment account in the equity section, as was the case under the current rate method.

A highly abbreviated income statement is also shown below. For the purposes of this exhibit, the blended full-year rate of exchange for the peso is assumed to be .09 to the dollar.

BALANCE SHEET CONVERSION

	Pesos	Exchange Rate	U.S. Dollars
Assets			
Cash	427	.08	34
Accounts Receivable	1,500	.08	120
Inventory	2,078	.10	208
Fixed Assets	3,790	.10	379
Total Assets	7,795		741
Liabilities & Equity			
Accounts Payable	1,003	.08	80
Notes Payable	4,250	.08	340
Common Stock	2,100	.10	210
Additional Paid-In Capital	428	.10	43
Retained Earnings	14	Note 1	68
Total Liabilities & Equity	7,795		741

Note 1: As noted in the income statement.

INCOME STATEMENT CONVERSION

	Pesos	Exchange Rate	U.S. Dollars
Revenue	6,750	.09	608
Goodwill Amortization	500	.08	40
Other Expenses	6,236	.09	561
Re-measurement Gain	—		**61**
Net Income	14		68
Beginning Retained Earnings	0		0
Add: Net Income	14		68
Ending Retained Earnings	14		68

What Exchange Rate Should I Use to Record Foreign Exchange Transactions?

There can be some confusion regarding the precise exchange rate to be used when conducting foreign currency translations. Here are some guidelines:

○ If there is no published foreign exchange rate available on the specific date when a transaction occurred that requires translation, use the rate for the date that most immediately follows the date of the transaction.

○ If the date of a financial statement that is to be converted from a foreign currency is different from the date of the financial statements into which they are to be converted into U.S. dollars, then use the date of the foreign currency financial statements as the date for which the proper exchange rate shall be used as the basis for translation.

○ If there is more than one published exchange rate available that can be used as the basis for a translation, use the rate that could have been used as the basis for the exchange of funds which could then be used to remit dividends to shareholders. Alternatively, use the rate at which a settlement of the entire related transaction could have been completed.

How Do I Account for the Foreign Exchange Effect of Intercompany Transactions?

When the results of a parent company and its subsidiaries are combined for financial statement reporting purposes, the gains or losses resulting from inter-company foreign exchange transactions must be reported in the consolidated statements. This happens when the parent has a receivable denominated in the currency of the subsidiary, or vice versa, and a change in the exchange rate results in a gain or loss. Thus, even though the inter-company transaction is purged from the consolidated financial statement, the associated gain or loss must still be reported.

EXAMPLE 28.5

The Seely Furniture Company owns a sawmill in Canada that supplies all of its wood raw materials. The subsidiary holds receivables from the corporate parent that are denominated in U.S. dollars. During the year, there has been a steady increase in the value of the dollar, resulting in a conversion into more Canadian dollars than was the case when each receivable was originally created. By the end of the year, the subsidiary has recorded a gain on currency transactions of $42,000 Canadian dollars. Accordingly, the Seely corporate parent records the gain on its books, denominated in U.S. dollars. Because the year-end exchange rate between the two currencies was $0.73 Canadian per U.S. dollar, the subsidiary's gain is recorded as a gain in U.S. dollars of $30,660 ($42,000 Canadian × 0.73 exchange rate) on the books of the parent.

What Foreign Exchange Information Should I Disclose?

You should disclose the following information in an entity's financial statements, or its accompanying notes:

- o The aggregate transaction foreign exchange gain or loss
- o A rate change that occurs after the date of the entity's financial statements, and its effects on

      unsettled balances pertaining to foreign currency transactions, if significant

○ An analysis of all translation adjustments reported in equity, including the beginning and ending amounts of accumulated translation adjustments, aggregate amounts of various adjustments during the period, income taxes allocated to translation adjustments, and any amounts transferred from cumulative translation adjustments and recognized in earnings

You are also encouraged to supplement these disclosures with an analysis and discussion of the effects of rate changes on the reported results of operations, with the intent of assisting users of the financial statements in understanding the implications of rate changes, as well as to compare recent results with those of prior periods.

EXAMPLE OF DISCLOSURES 28.6

About 40% of the company's revenue is earned from sales to Mexico. On January 14, subsequent to the date of these financial statements, the exchange rate of the Mexican peso dropped 12% from its value on the financial statement date. Since all of the company's sales to Mexico are denominated in pesos, this represents a potential loss of 12% when those revenues are eventually paid by customers in pesos. At this time, the drop in value would represent a foreign exchange loss to the company of approximately $412,000. As of the release date of these statements, no accounts receivable related to the sales had been paid by customers. All receivables related to the sales should be collected by the end of February, and so are subject to further fluctuations in the exchange rate until that time.

CHAPTER 29

INTEREST

 When Should I Capitalize Interest Cost?

You capitalize interest cost in order to obtain a more complete picture of the total acquisition cost associated with an asset, since an entity may incur a significant interest expense during the acquisition and start-up phases of an asset.

You should include interest expense in the cost of acquiring an asset during the period when an entity is carrying out those activities needed to bring the asset to its designated condition and location. The amount of interest capitalized should be the amount incurred during the period because of expenditures for the asset.

It is not always necessary to capitalize interest cost. The most optimum situation for doing so is when an asset requires substantial expenditures and a substantial period to construct, thereby accumulating a significant amount of interest cost. However, if there is a significant additional accounting and administrative cost associated with capitalizing interest cost, and the benefit of the additional information is minimal, you do not have to capitalize it.

You should capitalize the associated interest cost for the following assets:

○ Assets constructed for an entity's own use.
○ Assets constructed for an entity by a supplier, with deposits or progress payments having been made.
○ Assets intended for sale or lease that are constructed as discrete projects (such as a cruise ship).
○ Investments that the investor accounts for under the equity method, where the investee has activities in progress to start up its principal operations, and is using funds to acquire assets for those operations. In this case, the interest cost to be capitalized is based

on the investment in the investee, not the underlying assets of the investee.

You should *not* capitalize the associated interest cost for the following assets:

- Assets that are either in use already or ready for their intended use.
- Assets that are not being prepared for use.
- Assets that are not being used in an entity's earnings activities.
- Assets that are not included in the consolidated balance sheet of the parent entity.
- Investments that the investor accounts for under the equity method, when the principal activities of the investee have already begun.
- Investments in regulated investees that are capitalizing the cost of debt and equity capital.
- Assets acquired with gifts or grants from donors, where the gift or grant is restricted to the acquisition of those assets.
- Inventories that are routinely manufactured on a repetitive basis.

EXAMPLE 29.1

Aerial Devices is building a network of satellites for use in connecting remote locations to the Internet. Each satellite requires about one year to build, and involves a deposit and a series of progress payments to a contractor. Given the duration of construction and the cost of each satellite, it is appropriate for Aerial Devices to capitalize the related interest cost.

 ### Should I Capitalize the Interest Cost for Land?

You can only capitalize the interest cost associated with land if it is undergoing those activities necessary to prepare it for its intended use. If so, the expenditure to acquire the land qualifies for interest capitalization.

If an entity constructs a building on a newly-acquired land parcel, then the interest cost associated with the building should be capitalized as part of the building asset, rather than the land asset.

What Are the Components of an Interest Capitalization Calculation?

The primary inputs to an interest capitalization calculation are the capitalization rate and expenditures. The *capitalization rate* is the rate you should use to determine the amount of interest to be capitalized in an accounting period. *Expenditures* are those capitalized costs associated with an asset that were acquired either with a cash payment, the transfer of other assets or the incurrence of a liability on which interest is recognized (this does not include accounts payable or accruals).

How Do I Capitalize Interest Cost?

The capitalization of interest costs is a three-step process:

1. *Determine the capitalization period.* This period covers the duration of those activities required to bring an asset to the location and performance level needed for its intended use. You should continue to capitalize interest cost as long as these activities continue.
2. *Determine the capitalization rate.* The objective is to determine the interest cost that could otherwise have been avoided if an asset were not acquired. This rate is based on the rates applicable to the entity's borrowings outstanding during the period. If there is a specific incremental new borrowing associated with the asset in question, then you may use the rate on that borrowing as the capitalization rate. However, if the average accumulated expenditures on the asset exceed the amount of incremental new borrowings under the new borrowing arrangement, then the capitalization rate should be the weighted average of the rates applicable to the entity's other borrowings.
3. *Calculate the interest cost to be capitalized.* Apply the capitalization rate to the average amount of accumulated expenditures for the asset during the measurement period. You cannot capitalize more interest than the total amount of interest cost incurred by an entity in a specific period.

EXAMPLE 29.2

The Arabian Knights security company is building a new world headquarters in New York City. Arabian made payments of $25,000,000 on January 1 and
(Continued)

$40,000,000 on July 1; the building was completed on December 31.

For purposes of determining the basis upon which to calculate the interest cost to be capitalized, Arabian can include the full $25,000,000 of the first payment and half of the second payment, as noted in the following table:

Date	Payment	Capitalization Period*	Average Payment
1/1	$25,000,000	12/12	$25,000,000
7/1	40,000,000	6/12	20,000,000
			$45,000,000

*The number of months between the payment date and the date when interest capitalization ends.

During this time, Arabian has a loan outstanding on which it pays 7.5% interest. The amount of interest cost it can capitalize as part of the construction project is $3,375,000 ($45,000,000 × 7.5% interest).

If an entity suspends activities related to the preparation of an asset for its intended use, then stop capitalizing the related interest cost during that period.

EXAMPLE 29.3

Clay Pigeon Company is constructing a new corporate headquarters. It has acquired land in Newton, Massachusetts for this purpose, and is engaged in obtaining a variety of building permits. In the meantime, there is no activity to alter the land. Clay Pigeon cannot capitalize any interest cost until it begins to develop the property.

If an entity is constructing multiple parts of a project and it can use some parts while construction continues on other parts, then it should stop capitalization of borrowing costs on those parts that it completes. Conversely, if there are multiple parts of a project, but individual assets cannot function until the entire project has been completed, then you should continue to capitalize the interest cost until the entire project has been completed.

You can only capitalize interest cost if an entity is actually incurring interest cost at the time when an asset is being prepared for use.

EXAMPLE 29.4

Cape Cod Energy is constructing a wind farm off the coast of Provincetown, Massachusetts. It can begin using each of the wind turbines as they are completed, so it stops capitalizing the interest costs related to each one as soon as it becomes usable.

How Do I Account for Capitalized Interest Related to an Equity Method Investment?

If you have capitalized interest related to an equity method investment in an investee, you should associate the capitalized interest cost with the estimated useful lives of the investee's assets and amortize the cost over the same period as the lives of those assets.

How Do I Account for the Capitalized Interest Component of a Derecognized Asset?

Any interest cost that was originally capitalized as part of an asset is considered an integral part of that asset. Therefore, when you derecognize an asset by selling or otherwise disposing of it, the capitalized interest part of the asset must also be derecognized.

EXAMPLE 29.5

The Nocturnal Widget Company originally capitalized $150,000 of interest costs related to the construction of its widget warehouse. The total cost of the warehouse, including the capitalized interest, was $5,000,000. Five years later, Nocturnal has depreciated $1,000,000 of the building cost, leaving a carrying cost of $4,000,000. Nocturnal then sells the building for $3,900,000, resulting in a loss of $100,000 on the sale transaction, which it records with the following entry:

Cash	3,900,000	
Accumulated depreciation	1,000,000	
Loss on sale of building	100,000	
Building		5,000,000

(Continued)

> If Nocturnal had not capitalized the interest cost, the carrying amount of the building as of the sale date would have been $3,850,000, which would have resulted in a gain on the sale of $50,000.

 ## What Is an Imputed Interest Rate?

An imputed interest rate is an estimated interest rate used instead of the established interest rate associated with a note, because the established rate does not accurately reflect the market rate of interest, or there is no established rate at all. The imputed rate approximates the rate used for a note having an independent borrower and lender, and with comparable terms and conditions.

The intent of using an imputed interest rate is to more accurately reflect the components of an exchange transaction, so that the resulting face amount of a note reasonably represents the present value of the consideration paid.

Selecting a justifiable imputed interest rate is a matter of some importance, since an incorrect interest rate that is applied to a sufficiently large and long-term note can result in the inaccurate acceleration or deferral of earnings.

 ## When Should I Not Use an Imputed Interest Rate?

You should not derive an imputed interest rate in any of the following cases:

- ○ Accounts receivable and payable, arising in the normal course of business and that have trade terms not exceeding one year
- ○ Deposits, security deposits, advances, and progress payments
- ○ Cash lending activities by financial institutions
- ○ Transactions where interest rates are prescribed by a government entity (such as a tax-exempt obligation)
- ○ Transactions between a parent entity and its subsidiaries

 ## How Do I Impute Interest?

Follow these three steps to impute interest:

1. Establish the exchange price of the goods or services bought or sold, if there is trading on an open market from which this information can be obtained.

2. If there is no market from which to obtain this information, then estimate the interest rate that should apply to the transaction, and use this imputed interest rate to discount all future payments to arrive at the present value of the note. The interest rate you select may be influenced by the following factors:

- The note issuer's credit standing
- Restrictive covenants on the note
- Collateral attached to the note
- The prevailing interest rate for similar instruments by issuers having similar credit ratings
- The interest rate at which the debtor can obtain similar financing from other sources as of the transaction date (this is the overriding factor to consider)

3. Amortize the discount or premium on the note over the life of the note, charging the amortization to interest expense. The discount or premium is the difference between the present value and face amount of the note.

EXAMPLE 29.6

The Arabian Knights Security Company issues $1,000,000 of bonds at a stated rate of 8% in a market where similar issuances are being bought at 11%. The bonds pay interest once a year, and are to be paid off in 10 years. Investors purchase these bonds at a discount in order to earn an effective yield on their investment of 11%. The discount calculation requires one to determine the present value of 10 interest payments at 11% interest, as well as the present value of $1,000,000, discounted at 11% for ten years. The result is as follows:

Present value of 10 payments of $80,000	= $80,000 × 5.8892	= $471,136
Present value of $1,000,000	= $1,000,000 × .3522	= $352,200
		$823,336
	Less: stated bond price	1,000,000
	Discount on bond	($176,664)

In this example, the entry would be:

Cash	823,336	
Discount on bonds payable	176,664	
		1,000,000

(*Continued*)

The interest method holds that, in the first year of interest payments, the Arabian Knights Security Company's accountant would determine that the market interest expense for the first year would be $90,567 (bond stated price of $1,000,000 minus discount of $176,664, multiplied by the market interest rate of 11%). The resulting journal entry is:

Interest expense	90,567	
Discount on bonds payable		10,567
Cash		80,000

The reason why only $80,000 is listed as a reduction in cash is that the company only has an obligation to pay an 8% interest rate on the $1,000,000 face value of the bonds, which is $80,000. The difference is netted against the existing Discount on the Bonds Payable account. The following table shows the calculation of the discount to be charged to expense each year for the full 10-year period of the bond, where the annual amortization of the discount is added back to the bond present value, eventually resulting in a bond present value of $1,000,000 by the time principal payment is due, while the discount has dropped to zero.

Year	Beginning Bond Present Value (4)	Unamortized Discount	Interest Expense (1)	Cash Payment (2)	Credit to Discount (3)
1	$ 823,336	$176,664	$90,567	$80,000	$10,567
2	$ 833,903	$166,097	$91,729	$80,000	$11,729
3	845,632	154,368	93,020	80,000	13,020
4	858,652	141,348	94,452	80,000	14,452
5	873,104	126,896	96,041	80,000	16,041
6	889,145	110,855	97,806	80,000	17,806
7	906,951	93,049	99,765	80,000	19,765
8	926,716	73,284	101,939	80,000	21,939
9	948,655	51,346	104,352	80,000	24,352
10	973,007	26,994	107,031	80,000	26,994
	$1,000,000	$ 0			

(1) = Bond present value multiplied by the market rate of 11%
(2) = Required cash payment of 8% stated rate multiplied by face value of $1,000,000
(3) = Interest expense reduced by cash payment
(4) = Beginning present value of the bond plus annual reduction in the discount

What Information Should I Disclose about Interest Cost?

You should disclose the following information about interest cost in the notes accompanying the financial statements:

○ The amount of interest cost incurred, capitalized, and charged to expense during the period.
○ If there is an imputed interest rate on a note, disclose the imputed interest rate within a description of the note.

If there is a discount or premium associated with a note, list it in the balance sheet as a direct deduction from or addition to the face amount of the note, respectively.

CHAPTER 30

LEASES

What Is a Lease?

A lease is an agreement that conveys the right to use property, plant, or equipment (PP&E) for a stated period of time in return for a specified payment. The *lessor* is the party that owns the PP&E, and which conveys the right of use to the *lessee*, which is the party using the PP&E.

When Does an Arrangement Qualify as a Lease?

An arrangement is a lease if it conveys to the lessee the right to control the use of the underlying PP&E. The right of control is established under any of the following conditions:

- The lessee can operate the PP&E or direct others to do so in a manner it determines, while controlling more than a minor amount of its output or utility.
- The lessee can control physical access to the PP&E, while controlling more than a minor amount of its output or utility.
- There is a remote chance that other parties will take more than a minor amount of the output or other utility created by the PP&E during the term of the arrangement.

An arrangement is not a lease in any of the following contractual situations:

- There is no transfer of the right to use PP&E.
- The arrangement is not dependent upon the use of *specific* PP&E.
- The arrangement conveys the right to use inventory or natural resources.

Subsequent to the initiation of a lease, you should only reassess whether an arrangement contains a lease, or whether it should be treated as a different type of lease, in one of the following circumstances:

- ○ There is a change in the contractual terms.
- ○ There is a contract renewal or extension.
- ○ There is a change in the PP&E associated with the arrangement.
- ○ There is a substantial change in the physical location of the PP&E.

 ## How Do I Classify a Lease?

You can determine which type of lease you have by applying the following four criteria:

- ○ *Transfer of ownership.* The lease agreement shifts ownership of the property to the lessee by the end of the term of the lease.
- ○ *Bargain purchase option.* The lease includes a bargain purchase option. A bargain purchase option is a provision in a lease agreement, allowing the lessee to buy the leased property for a price so much lower than the expected fair value of the property on that date, that it is reasonably assured that the lessee will exercise the option.
- ○ *Lease term.* The lease term is 75% or more of the property's estimated economic life. If a lease agreement contains a fiscal funding clause, under which the lessee can cancel the agreement if the funding authority does not appropriate sufficient funds for a government unit to fulfill its lease obligations, then classify the lease as an operating lease, unless you consider the likelihood of exercising the clause to be remote. Do not use this criterion if the beginning of the lease is within the final 25% of the total estimated economic life of the property.
- ○ *Minimum lease payments.* At the beginning of the lease, the present value of the minimum lease payments equals or exceeds 90% of the excess of the property's fair value over any related investment tax credit retained by the lessor. You should exclude such costs as insurance, maintenance, and taxes from the lease payments when making this determination. Do not use this criterion if the beginning of the lease is within the final 25% of the total estimated economic life of the property.

From the perspective of the lessee, use the preceding criteria to determine if a lease is a capital lease or an operating lease. If a lease meets any one of the preceding criteria, designate it as a capital lease. Otherwise, designate it as an operating lease.

From the perspective of the lessor, if a lease meets any one of the preceding criteria, *and* the collection of minimum lease payments is reasonably assured, *and* there are no important uncertainties about the amount of unreimbursable costs yet to be incurred by the lessor under the lease, then you may classify it as one of the following types of leases:

○ *Sales-type lease.* It creates a manufacturer's or dealer's profit (or loss) to the lessor.
○ *Direct financing lease.* It does not create a manufacturer's or dealer's profit (or loss) and is not a leveraged lease (see next).
○ *Leveraged lease.* It meets the criteria for a direct financing lease, involves at least three parties (the lessor, lessee, and a long-term creditor). The long-term creditor's financing is non-recourse as to the lessor's general credit, and the lessor's net investment declines during the early years of the lease and rises during its later years.
○ *Operating lease.* It does not meet any of the four criteria used to determine a lease type.

 ## What Is an Operating Lease?

An operating lease is any lease other than a capital lease. The primary assumption behind an operating lease is that the asset being leased is owned by the lessor, who will retain it once the lease term has been completed.

How Does a Lessee Account for an Operating Lease?

The lessee accounts for an operating lease by charging lease payments directly to expense. There is no balance sheet recognition of the leased asset. If the schedule of lease payments varies in terms of either timing or amount, the lessee should consistently charge the same rental amount to expense in each period, which may result in some variation between the lease payment made and the recorded expense. However, if there is a demonstrable change in the asset being leased that justifies a change in the lease payment being made, there is no need to use straight-line recognition of the expense.

EXAMPLE 30.1

The Alabama Botox Clinics (ABC) Company has leased a group of operating room equipment under a 5-year operating lease arrangement. The monthly lease cost is $1,000 for the first 30 months and $1,500 for the second 30 months. There is no change in the equipment being leased at any time during the lease period. The correct accounting is to charge the average monthly lease rate of $1,250 to expense during every month of the lease. For the first 30 months, the monthly entry will be:

Equipment rent expense	1,250	
Accounts payable		1,000
Accrued lease liability		250

During the final 30 months, the monthly entry will be:

Equipment rent expense	1,250	
Accrued lease liability	250	
Accounts payable		1,500

If the lessee has guaranteed a residual value for a leased asset as part of the lease agreement, and it becomes probable that there will be a residual value deficiency, then the lessee should accrue the expected deficiency on a straight-line basis over the remaining term of the lease.

How Does a Lessor Account for an Operating Lease?

If the lessor treats a lease as an operating lease, it records any payments received from the lessee as rent revenue. As was the case for the lessee, if there is an unjustified change in the lease rate over the lease term, the average revenue amount should be recognized on a straight-line basis in each reporting period. Any assets being leased are recorded in a separate Investment in Leased Property account in the fixed assets portion of the balance sheet, and are depreciated in accordance with standard company policy for similar assets. If the lessor extends incentives (such as a month of no lease payments) or incurs costs associated with the lease (such as legal fees), they should be recognized over the lease term.

How Does a Lessee Account for a Capital Lease?

The lessee accounts for a capital lease by recording the lesser of the fair value of an asset or the present value of its minimum (i.e., excluding taxes and executory costs) lease payments (less the present value of any guaranteed residual asset value). When calculating the present value of minimum lease payments, use the lesser of the lessee's incremental borrowing rate or the implicit rate used by the lessor. The time period used for the present value calculation should include not only the initial lease term, but also additional periods where non-renewal will result in a penalty to the lessee, or where lease renewal is at the option of the lessor.

If the lessee treats a leased asset as a capital lease because the lease agreement results in an actual or likely transfer of ownership to the lessee by the end of the lease term, then depreciate it over the full expected life of the asset. However, if a leased asset is being treated as a capital lease when the lessor is still likely to retain ownership of the asset after the end of the lease term, then depreciate it only for the period of the lease.

EXAMPLE 30.2

The Arkansas Barrel Company (ABC) leases a woodworking machine under a five-year lease that has a one-year extension clause at the option of the lessor, as well as a guaranteed residual value of $15,000. ABC's incremental borrowing rate is 7%. The machine is estimated to have a life of seven years, a current fair value of $90,000, and a residual value (*not* the guaranteed residual value) of $5,000. Annual lease payments are $16,000.

The first step in accounting for this lease is to determine if it is a capital or operating lease. If it is a capital lease, Arkansas must calculate its present value, then use the effective interest method to determine the allocation of payments between interest expense and reduction of the lease obligation, and then determine the depreciation schedule for the asset. Later, there will be a closeout journal entry to record the lease termination. The five steps are as follows:

1. *Determine the lease type.* The woodworking machine is considered to have a life of seven years; since the lease period (including the extra year at the option
(*Continued*)

of the lessor) covers more than 75% of the machine's useful life, the lease is designated a capital lease.

2. *Calculate asset present value.* The machine's present value is a combination of the present value of the $15,000 residual payment due in six years and the present value of annual payments of $16,000 per year for six years. Using the company's incremental borrowing rate of 7%, the present value multiplier for $1 due in six years is 0.6663; when multiplied by the guaranteed residual value of $15,000, this results in a present value of $9,995. Using the same interest rate, the present value multiplier for an ordinary annuity of $1 for six years is 4.7665; when multiplied by the annual lease payments of $16,000, this results in a present value of $76,264. After combining the two present values, ABC's controller arrives at a total lease present value of $86,259. The initial journal entry to record the lease is as follows:

Leased equipment	86,259	
Lease liability		86,259

3. *Allocate payments between interest expense and reduction of lease liability.* ABC's controller then uses the effective interest method to allocate the annual lease payments between the lease's interest expense and reductions in the lease obligation. The interest calculation is based on the beginning balance of the lease obligation. The calculation for each year of the lease is as follows:

Year	Annual payment	Interest Expense	Reduction in Lease Obligation	Remaining Lease Obligation
0				$86,259
1	$16,000	$6,038	$9,962	76,297
2	16,000	5,341	10,659	65,638
3	16,000	4,595	11,405	54,233
4	16,000	3,796	12,204	42,029
5	16,000	2,942	13,058	28,991
6	16,000	2,009	13,991	15,000

4. *Create depreciation schedule.* Though the asset has an estimated life of seven years, the lease term is for only six years, after which the asset is expected to be returned to the lessor. Accordingly, the asset will be depreciated only over the lease term of six

years. Also, the amount of depreciation will only cover the asset's present value of $86,259 *minus* the residual value of $5,000. Therefore, the annual depreciation will be $\underline{13,543}$ (($86,259 present value − $5,000 residual value)/6 years lease term).

5. *Record lease termination.* Once the lease is completed, a journal entry must record the removal of the asset and its related depreciation from the fixed assets register, as well as the payment to the lessor of the difference between the $15,000 guaranteed residual value and the actual $5,000 residual value, or $10,000. That entry is as follows:

Lease liability	15,000	
Accumulated depreciation	81,259	
Cash		10,000
Leased equipment		86,259

How Does a Lessor Account for a Sales-Type Lease?

If the lessor treats a lease as a sales-type lease, the initial transaction bears some similarity to a standard sale transaction, except that there is an unearned interest component to the entry. A description of the required entry is contained in the following table, which shows all debits and credits.

Debit	Credit	Explanation
Lease receivable		The sum of all minimum lease payments, minus executory costs, plus the actual residual value
Cost of goods sold		The asset cost, plus initial direct costs, minus the present value* of the actual residual value
	Revenue	The present value* of all minimum lease payments
	Leased asset	The book value of the asset
	Accounts payable	Any initial direct costs associated with the lease
	Unearned interest	The lease receivable, minus the present value* of both the minimum lease payments and actual residual value

*The present value multiplier is based on the lease term and implicit interest rate.

Once payments are received, record an entry for the receipt of cash and corresponding reduction in the lease receivable, as well as a second entry to recognize a portion of the unearned interest as interest revenue, based on the effective interest method.

At least annually during the lease term, the lessor records any permanent reductions in the estimated residual value of the leased asset. It cannot record any increases in the estimated residual value.

When the asset is returned to the lessor at the end of the lease term, a closing entry eliminates the lease receivable associated with the actual residual value, with an offsetting debit to the fixed asset account.

EXAMPLE 30.3

The Albany Boat Company (ABC) has issued a seven-year lease to the Adventure Yachting Company (AYC) on a boat for its yacht rental business. The boat cost ABC $450,000 to build, and should have a residual value of $75,000 at the end of the lease. Annual lease payments are $77,000. ABC's implicit interest rate is 8%. The present value multiplier for an ordinary annuity of $1 for seven years at 8% interest is 5.2064. The present value multiplier for $1 due in seven years at 8% interest is 0.5835. ABC's controller constructs the initial journal entry with the following calculations:

○ *Lease receivable.* This is the sum of all minimum lease payments, which is $539,000 ($77,000/year × 7 years), plus the actual residual value of $75,000, for a total lease receivable of $614,000.

○ *Cost of goods sold.* This is the asset cost of $450,000, minus the present value of the residual value, which is $43,763 ($75,000 residual value × present value multiplier of 0.5835).

○ *Revenue.* This is the present value of all minimum lease payments, or $400,893 ($77,000/year × present value multiplier of 5.2064).

○ *Inventory.* ABC's book value for the yacht is $450,000, which is used to record a reduction in its inventory account.

○ *Unearned interest.* This is the lease receivable of $614,000, minus the present value of the minimum lease payments of $400,893, minus the present value of the residual value of $43,763, which yields $169,344.

Based on these calculations, the initial journal entry is as follows:

Lease receivable	614,000	
Cost of goods sold	406,237	
Revenue		400,893
Boat asset		450,000
Unearned interest		169,344

The next step is to determine the allocation of lease payments between interest income and reduction of the lease principle, which is accomplished through the following effective interest table:

Year	Annual Payment	Interest Revenue	Reduction in Lease Obligation	Remaining Lease Obligation
0				$444,656
1	$77,000	$35,572	$41,428	403,228
2	77,000	32,258	44,742	358,486
3	77,000	28,679	48,321	310,165
4	77,000	24,813	52,187	257,978
5	77,000	20,638	56,362	201,616
6	77,000	16,129	60,871	140,745
7	77,000	11,255	65,745	75,000

The interest expense shown in the effective interest table can then be used to record the allocation of each lease payment between interest revenue and principal reduction. For example, the entries recorded for Year 4 of the lease are as follows:

Cash	77,000	
Lease receivable		77,000
Unearned interest	24,813	
Interest revenue		24,813

Once the lease expires and the boat is returned to ABC, the final entry to close out the lease transaction is as follows:

Boat asset	75,000	
Lease receivable		75,000

How Does a Lessor Account for a Direct Financing Lease?

If the lessor treats a lease as a direct financing lease, it will only recognize interest income from the transaction; there will be no additional profit from the implicit sale of the underlying asset to the lessee. This treatment arises when the lessor purchases an asset specifically to lease it to the lessee. The other difference between a direct financing lease and a sales-type lease is that any direct costs incurred when a lease is originated must be amortized over the life of the lease, which reduces the implicit interest rate used to allocate lease payments between interest revenue and a reduction of the lease principal.

A description of the required entry is contained in the following table, which shows all debits and credits.

Debit	Credit	Explanation
Lease receivable		The sum of all minimum lease payments, plus the actual residual value
	Leased asset	The book value of the asset
	Unearned interest	The lease receivable minus the asset book value

At least annually during the lease term, the lessor should record any permanent reductions in the estimated residual value of the leased asset. It cannot record any increases in the estimated residual value.

What Is a Sale-Leaseback Transaction?

A situation where the owner of a property sells it to the eventual lessor, records the sale, removes all related assets and liabilities from its balance sheet, and then leases the property back from the lessor. The usual purpose of such a transaction is for the initial property owner to obtain immediate cash from sale of the property, in exchange for a long-term lease obligation.

How Do I Account for a Sale-Leaseback Transaction?

If the selling entity incurs a gain or loss on its sale of the property that it will lease back, you should generally defer

EXAMPLE 30.4

The Albany Leasing Company (ALC) purchases a boat from a third party for $700,000 and intends to lease it to the Adventure Yachting Company for six years at an annual lease rate of $140,093. The boat should have a residual value of $120,000 at the end of the lease term. Also, there is $18,000 of initial direct costs associated with the lease. ALC's implicit interest rate is 9%. The present value multiplier for an ordinary annuity of $1 for six years at 9% interest is 4.4859. The present value multiplier for $1 due in six years at 9% interest is 0.5963. We construct the initial journal entry with the following calculations:

○ *Lease receivable.* This is the sum of all minimum lease payments, which is $840,558 ($140,093/year × 6 years), plus the residual value of $120,000, for a total lease receivable of $960,558.

○ *Leased asset.* This is the asset cost of $700,000.

○ *Unearned interest.* This is the lease receivable of $960,558, minus the asset book value of $700,000, which yields $260,558.

Based on these calculations, the initial journal entry follows:

Lease receivable	960,558	
Initial direct costs	18,000	
Leased asset		700,000
Unearned interest		260,558
Cash		18,000

(Continued)

Next, ALC's controller must determine the implicit interest rate associated with the transaction. Though ALC intended the rate to be 9%, she must add to the lease receivable the initial direct costs of $18,000, resulting in a final gross investment of $978,558 and a net investment (net of unearned interest income of $260,558) of $718,000. The determination of the implicit interest rate with this additional information is most easily derived through an electronic spreadsheet. For example, the IRR function in Microsoft Excel will automatically create the new implicit interest rate, which is 8.2215%.

With the revised implicit interest rate completed, the next step is to determine the allocation of lease payments between interest income, a reduction of initial direct costs, and a reduction of the lease principal, which is accomplished through the following effective interest table:

Year	Annual Payment	Unearned Interest Reduction	Interest Revenue	Reduction of Initial Direct Costs	Reduction in Lease Obligation	Remaining Lease Obligation (1)	Remaining Lease Obligation (2)
0						$718,000	$700,000
1	$140,093	$63,000	$59,031	$3,969	$81,062	636,938	622,907
2	140,093	56,062	52,366	3,696	87,727	549,211	538,876
3	140,093	48,499	45,154	3,345	94,939	454,271	447,281
4	140,093	40,255	37,348	2,907	102,745	351,526	347,444
5	140,093	31,270	28,901	2,369	111,192	240,334	238,621
6	140,093	21,476	19,759	1,717	120,334	120,000	120,000*
	Totals	$260,558*		$18,000*			

The calculations used in the table are:

○ *Annual payment.* The annual cash payment due to the lessor.

○ *Unearned interest reduction.* The original implicit interest rate of 9% multiplied by the beginning balance in the Remaining Lease Obligation (2) column, which does not include the initial direct lease cost. The total at the bottom of the column equals the unearned interest liability that will be eliminated over the course of the lease.

○ *Interest revenue.* The revised implicit interest rate of 8.2215% multiplied by the beginning balance in the Remaining Lease Obligation (1) column, which includes the initial direct lease costs.

○ *Reduction of initial direct costs.* The amount in the Unearned Interest Reduction column minus the amount in the Interest Revenue column, which is used to reduce the balance of the initial direct costs incurred. The total at the bottom of the column equals the initial direct costs incurred at the beginning of the lease.

○ *Reduction in lease obligation.* The Annual Payment minus the Interest Revenue.

○ *Remaining lease obligation (1).* The beginning lease obligation (including initial direct costs) less the principal portion of the annual payment.

○ *Remaining lease obligation (2).* The beginning lease obligation, not including initial direct costs, less the principal portion of the annual payment.

(Continued)

Based on the calculations in the effective interest table, the journal entry at the end of the first year would show the receipt of cash and a reduction in the lease receivable. Another entry would reduce the unearned interest balance while offsetting the initial direct costs and recognizing interest revenue. The first year entries are as follows:

Cash	140,093	
Lease receivable		140,093
Unearned interest	63,000	
Interest revenue		59,031
Initial direct costs		3,969

recognition of the gain or loss, barring a few exceptions. You should recognize the gain or loss as follows:

- If the asset is land only, then amortize the gain or loss over the lease term.
- If the asset is not land only and is treated as a capital lease, then recognize the gain or loss in proportion to the amortization of the leased asset.
- If the asset is not land only and is treated as an operating lease, then recognize the gain or loss in proportion to the related gross rental charged to expense over the lease term.

If the fair value of the property at the time of the sale transaction is less than its undepreciated cost, you should recognize the full amount of any loss immediately.

If the selling entity subsequently retains all benefits and risks incident to the ownership of the property sold, then the sale-leaseback transaction is essentially a financing; in this case, the seller should treat the entire transaction as a capital lease, and retain the property in its records without recording a gain or loss.

 ## How Do I Account for a Lease Extension?

If a lessee extends an operating lease and the extension is also classified as an operating lease, then the lessee continues to treat the extension in the same manner it has used for the existing lease. If the lease extension requires payment amounts differing from those required under the initial agreement but the asset received does not change, then the lessee should consistently charge the same rental amount to expense in each period, which may result in some variation between the lease payment made and the recorded expense.

If a lessee extends an existing capital lease but the lease structure now requires the extension to be recorded as an operating lease, the lessee writes off the existing asset, as well as all associated accumulated depreciation, and recognizes either a gain or loss on the transaction. Payments made under the lease extension are handled in accordance with the rules of a standard operating lease.

If a lessee extends an existing capital lease and the structure of the extension agreement requires the lease to continue to be recorded as a capital lease, the lessee changes the asset valuation and related lease liability by the difference between the present value of the new series of future minimum lease payments and the existing balance. The present value calculation must use the interest rate used for the same calculation at the inception of the original lease.

When a lease extension occurs and the lessor classifies the extension as a direct financing lease, the lease receivable and estimated residual value (downward only) are adjusted to match the new lease terms, with any adjustment going to unearned income. When a lease extension occurs and the lessor classifies an existing direct financing or sales-type lease as an operating lease, the lessor writes off the remaining lease investment and instead records the asset at the lower of its current net book value, original cost, or present value. The change in value from the original net investment is recorded against income in the period when the lease extension date occurs.

How Do I Account for a Lease Termination?

On the date that a lessee notifies the lessor that it intends to terminate a lease, the lessee must recognize a liability for the fair value of the termination costs, which include any continuing lease payments, less prepaid rent, plus deferred rent, minus the amount of any sublease payments. The lessee records these changes immediately in its income statement.

If the lessor has recorded a lease as a sales-type or direct financing lease, it records the underlying leased asset at the lower of its current net book value, present value, or original cost, with any resulting adjustment being recorded in current earnings. At the time of termination notice, the lessor records a receivable in the amount of any termination payments yet to be made, with an offsetting credit to a deferred rent liability account. The lessor then recognizes any remaining rental payments on a straight-line basis over the revised period during which the payments are to be received.

How Do I Account for a Sub-Lease?

A sublease arises when leased property is leased by the original lessee to a third party. When this happens, the original lessee accounts for the sublease as though it were the original lessor. This means that it can account for the lease as an operating, direct sale, or sales-type lease. The original lessee continues to account for its ongoing lease payments to the original lessor as though the sublease did not exist.

What General Information Should I Disclose for a Lease?

You should disclose the following general information in the notes accompanying an entity's financial statements for all types of leases:

Lessees and Lessors

- The nature and extent of leasing transactions with related parties

Lessees

- The basis on which contingent rental payments are determined
- The terms of any renewal or purchase options, and escalation clauses
- Restrictions imposed by leasing agreements (such as restrictions on dividend payments)

Lessors

- A general description of the entity's leasing arrangements (but only if leasing is a significant part of the entity's business activities)
- The accounting policy for contingent rental income

EXAMPLE OF DISCLOSURES 30.5 (LESSEE)

The company's president owns a majority interest in Copier Leases International, from which the company has leased 11 copiers under operating leases. The total amount of payments due under these leases is $93,000, which continues until 2014. Company management is of the opinion that the lease rates obtained are highly competitive to those of other leasing companies.

EXAMPLE OF DISCLOSURES 30.6 (LESSEE)

Due to the downturn in the company's principal asparagus distribution market, it no longer requires its San Francisco trans-shipment warehouse, for which it has a lease obligation for another six years. The total lease obligation for this facility through the remainder of the lease is $3,025,000. The company is discussing lease termination options with the lessor, and is also searching for a sub-lessee. Given the market conditions, the
(Continued)

company does not feel that a sub-lease can be obtained, and so assumes that a lease termination fee will be required. Accordingly, it has recorded a lease termination charge in the current period of $2,405,000, which is the present value of the total lease obligation.

EXAMPLE OF DISCLOSURES 30.7 (LESSOR)

The company's leasing operations consist primarily of the leasing of various kinds of construction equipment and transportation equipment. The bulk of the company's leases are classified as direct financing leases. The leases related to the construction equipment expire over the next eight years, while the leases related to the transportation equipment expire over the next five years.

What Information Should I Disclose for an Operating Lease?

You should disclose the following information in the notes accompanying an entity's financial statements:

Lessees

- The rental expense, showing separate amounts for minimum rentals, contingent rentals, and sublease rentals.
- For leases with initial or remaining non-cancelable lease terms over one year, disclose the future minimum rental payments in aggregate and for each of the five succeeding fiscal years, and the total minimum rentals to be received under non-cancelable subleases.

Lessors

- The cost and carrying amount of property on lease or held for leasing, segregated by major property classes, as well as the total amount of accumulated depreciation.
- Minimum future rentals on non-cancelable leases, in the aggregate and for each of the five succeeding fiscal years.
- Total contingent rentals included in income for each period presented.

EXAMPLE OF DISCLOSURES 30.8 (LESSEE)

The company is leasing a number of copiers, which are all recorded as operating leases. There are no escalation or renewal options associated with these leases. All the leases require the company to pay personal property taxes, maintenance, and return shipping at the end of the leases. There are purchase options at the end of all lease terms that are based on the market price of the copiers at that time. The future minimum lease payments for these leases are as follows:

2011	$195,000
2012	173,000
2013	151,000
2014	145,000
2015	101,000
Total	$765,000

EXAMPLE OF DISCLOSURES 30.9 (LESSEE)

The company has sub-leased 25,000 square feet of its office building in Montgomery County under a three-year non-cancelable lease. The total minimum amount of payments to be received under this agreement is $425,000.

EXAMPLE OF DISCLOSURES 30.10 (LESSEE)

The company has entered into a new five-year rental agreement under which the first five months of rent are free. The company has chosen to charge to expense in each month the average monthly expense over the full lease term, rather than no expense at all for the first five months, since this more accurately reflects the periodic lease cost. The excess amount of lease expense recognized early in the lease period, totaling $85,000, has been recorded in the Other Current Liabilities account.

Example of Disclosures 30.11 (Lessor)

The company operates a leasing division that only issues leases accounted for as operating leases. The cost of assets leased as of the balance sheet date were $14,700,000 in the farm equipment category, $29,250,000 in the emergency services category, and $41,000,000 in the municipal government category. The company has recorded $21,750,000 in aggregate accumulated depreciation on the assets recorded in all of these categories. The minimum lease payments due under non-cancelable leases in each of the next five years are as follows:

2011	$20,000,000
2012	19,250,000
2013	14,750,000
2014	14,500,000
2015	10,000,000
Thereafter	16,500,000
Total	$95,000,000

What Information Should I Disclose for a Capital Lease?

You should disclose the following information about capital leases in the notes accompanying an entity's financial statements:

Lessees

- The gross amount of assets recorded as capital leases, segregated by major asset classes
- Future minimum lease payments, in aggregate and for each of the five succeeding fiscal years
- The total of minimum sublease rentals to be received in the future under non-cancelable subleases
- Total contingent rentals actually incurred for all periods presented

Lessors

- For sales-type leases and direct financing leases:

  - Future minimum lease payments to be received, with deductions for executory costs and an allowance for uncollectible minimum lease payments receivable

- Unguaranteed residual values accruing to the lessor's benefit
- Initial direct costs (only needed for direct financing leases)
- Unearned income
- Future minimum lease payments to be received in each of the five succeeding fiscal years
- Total contingent rentals included in income for all periods presented

---

EXAMPLE OF DISCLOSURES 30.12 (LESSEE)

The following is an analysis of the company's leased property under capital leases by major classes:

(000s) Classes of Property	Asset Balances at 12/31/13	
	2013	2012
Manufacturing facility	$14,700	$10,000
Office Equipment	2,500	2,100
Other	700	500
Less: Accumulated depreciation	(6,100)	(3,800)
	$11,800	$ 8,800

The following is a schedule by year of future minimum lease payments under capital leases, together with the present value of the net minimum lease payments as of December 31, 2013:

Year ending December 31:	
2014	$ 2,000
2015	1,800
2016	1,600
2017	1,400
2018	1,200
Later years	6,200
Total minimum lease payments	14,200
Less: Estimated executory costs included in total minimum lease payments	(500)
Net minimum lease payments	13,700
Less: Amount representing interest	(1,900)
Present value of net minimum lease payments	$11,800

What Information Should I Disclose for a Sale-Leaseback Transaction?

You should include a description of the terms of a sale-leaseback transaction, which includes the amount of future commitments, obligations, provisions, or circumstances resulting in the seller's continuing involvement in the arrangement.

EXAMPLE OF DISCLOSURES 30.13

(1) The company sold its headquarters building under a twenty-year sale and leaseback arrangement. Under the agreement, the company is obligated to make aggregate lease payments of $13.5 million over the term of the lease, which is net of $1.25 million in payments from certain non-cancelable sub-lease agreements. The future minimum lease payments for the next five years and thereafter for these leases are as follows:

2011	$595,000
2012	613,000
2013	621,000
2014	645,000
2015	701,000
Thereafter	10,325,000
	13,500,000

(2) The company sold its headquarters building under a twenty-year sale and leaseback arrangement. Under the agreement, the company is obligated to make aggregate lease payments of $13.5 million over the term of the lease. This is a financing arrangement under which the lessor's up-front payment of $12 million is recorded as a Long-Term Debt, future lease payments net of interest expense will reduce the balance of the debt, and the company continues to carry the property cost on its books and depreciate that cost.

CHAPTER 31

NONMONETARY TRANSACTIONS

 What Is a Nonmonetary Transaction?

A *nonmonetary transaction* is one in which there is an exchange with another entity that involves principally nonmonetary assets or liabilities, or where there is a transfer of nonmonetary assets for which no assets are received or paid in exchange. An example of a *nonreciprocal transfer* is the contribution of assets to a charitable organization, and an example of a *nonmonetary exchange* is an exchange of a real estate parcel for another real estate parcel.

 What Is the General Accounting for Nonmonetary Transactions?

In general, you should record a nonmonetary transaction at the fair value of the assets involved. Thus, you should record the cost of a nonmonetary asset acquired in such an exchange at the fair value of the asset surrendered to acquire it. You can recognize a gain or loss on this exchange.

If the fair value of the asset received is more evident than the fair value of the asset surrendered, then you can use this valuation instead to record the transaction.

If there is a nonreciprocal transfer, where one party issues an asset to another party for no exchange of value, then the receiving party recognizes the fair value of the asset received. In such a transaction, the party disposing of the asset should recognize the transfer at the fair value of the asset given up, and record a gain or loss on the transaction.

The preceding basic principles involving recording an exchange at its fair value do not apply in the following circumstances:

- ○ The fair value of neither asset being exchanged can be determined.
- ○ The transaction is a product exchange to facilitate sales to customers other than the parties taking part in the exchange.
- ○ The transaction lacks commercial substance. A transaction *has* commercial substance if the configuration of cash flows received differs significantly from the configuration of the future cash flows transferred, or there is a significant difference in the fair values of the assets exchanged.

In these exception situations, you should record the exchange at the recorded amount of the asset extinguished, rather than its fair value.

EXAMPLE 31.1

The Dakota Motor Company swaps a file server for an overhead crane. Its file server has a book value of $12,000 (net of accumulated depreciation of $4,000), while the overhead crane has a fair value of $9,500. The company has no information about the fair value of its file server, so Dakota uses its net book value instead to establish a value for the swap. Dakota recognizes a loss of $2,500 on the transaction, as noted in the following entry:

Factory equipment	9,500	
Accumulated depreciation	4,000	
Loss on asset exchange	2,500	
Factory equipment		16,000

 What Is Boot?

When a nonmonetary exchange involves a small amount of monetary consideration, the monetary consideration portion of the exchange is referred to as boot.

 How Do I Account for a Transaction Involving Boot?

A common transaction is for a company to trade in an existing asset for a new one, along with an additional payment that covers the incremental additional cost of the new asset over that of the old one being traded away. The additional payment portion of this transaction is the *boot*. When the boot comprises at least 25% of an exchange's fair value, both entities must record the transaction at the fair value of the assets involved. If the amount of boot is less than 25% of the transaction, the party receiving the boot can recognize a gain in proportion to the amount of the boot received.

EXAMPLE 31.2 (AT LEAST 25% BOOT)

The Dakota Motor Company trades in a copier for a new one from the Fair Copy Company, paying an additional $9,000 as part of the deal. The fair value of the copier traded away is $2,000, while the fair value of the new copier being acquired is $11,000 (with a book value of $12,000, net of $3,500 in accumulated depreciation). The book value of the copier being traded away is $2,500, net of $5,000 in accumulated depreciation. Because Dakota has paid a combination of $9,000 in cash and $2,500 in the net book value of its existing copier ($11,500 in total) to acquire a new copier with a fair value of $11,000, it must recognize a loss of $500 on the transaction, as noted in the following entry.

Office equipment (new asset)	11,000	
Accumulated depreciation	5,000	
Loss on asset exchange	500	
Office equipment (asset traded away)		7,500
Cash		9,000

On the other side of the transaction, Fair Copy is accepting a copier with a fair value of $2,000 and $9,000 in cash for a replacement copier with a fair value of $11,000, so its journal entry is as follows:

Cash	9,000	
Office equipment (asset acquired)	2,000	
Accumulated depreciation	3,500	
Loss on sale of asset	1,000	
Office equipment (asset traded away)		15,500

Example 31.3 (Less Than 25% Boot)

As was the case in the last example, the Dakota Motor Company trades in a copier for a new one, but now it pays $2,000 cash and trades in its old copier, with a fair value of $9,000 and a net book value of $9,500 after $5,000 of accumulated depreciation. Also, the fair value of the copier being traded away by Fair Copy remains at $11,000, but its net book value drops to $10,000 (still net of accumulated depreciation of $3,500). All other information remains the same. In this case, the proportion of boot paid is 18% ($2,000 cash, divided by total consideration paid of $2,000 cash plus the copier fair value of $9,000). As was the case before, Dakota has paid a total of $11,500 (from a different combination of $9,000 in cash and $2,500 in the net book value of its existing copier) to acquire a new copier with a fair value of $11,000, so it must recognize a loss of $500 on the transaction, as noted in the following entry.

Office equipment (new asset)	11,000	
Accumulated depreciation	5,000	
Loss on asset exchange	500	
Office equipment (asset traded away)		14,500
Cash		2,000

The main difference is on the other side of the transaction, where Fair Copy is now accepting a copier with a fair value of $9,000 and $2,000 in cash in exchange for a copier with a book value of $10,000, so there is a potential gain of $1,000 on the deal. However, because it receives boot that is less than 25% of the transaction fair value, it recognizes a pro rata gain of $180, which is calculated as the 18% of the deal attributable to the cash payment, multiplied by the $1,000 gain. Fair Copy's journal entry to record the transaction is as follows:

Cash	2,000	
Office equipment (asset acquired)	8,180	
Accumulated depreciation	3,500	
Office equipment (asset traded away)		13,500
Gain on asset transfer		180

In this entry, Fair Copy can only recognize a small portion of the gain on the asset transfer, with the remaining portion of the gain being netted against the recorded cost of the acquired asset.

How Do I Account for a Donation?

If an asset is donated to an entity (only common in the case of a not-for-profit entity), the receiving company can record the asset at its fair market value, which can be derived from market rates on similar assets, an appraisal, or the net present value of its estimated cash flows.

When an entity donates an asset to another entity, the transferring entity must recognize the fair value of the asset donated, which is netted against its net book value. The difference between the asset's fair value and its net book value is recognized as either a gain or loss.

EXAMPLE 31.4

The Nero Fiddle Company has donated to the local orchestra a portable violin repair workbench from its manufacturing department. The workbench was originally purchased for $15,000, and $6,000 of depreciation has since been charged against it. The workbench can be purchased on the eBay auction site for $8,500, which establishes its fair market value. The company uses the following journal entry to record the transaction:

Charitable donations	8,500	
Accumulated depreciation	6,000	
Loss on property donation	500	
Machinery asset account		15,000

How Do I Account for a Nonmonetary Inventory Exchange?

When two entities exchange inventory (such as finished goods inventory in exchange for raw materials inventory), you should recognize the exchange at the carrying amount of the inventory transferred.

EXAMPLE 31.5

Western Auto is experiencing a considerable demand for trucks, while Eastern Auto's demand for sedans is spiking. Western Auto agrees to send ten sedans to Eastern Auto in exchange for ten trucks, so that each dealership can meet its customers' requirements. Each dealership should record the cost of the incoming vehicles at the carrying amount of the inventory they sent to the other party.

What Are Barter Credits?

Barter credits are used as a medium of exchange in a barter network, where an entity exchanges a nonmonetary asset for barter credits, which the entity can then use to acquire goods or services from members of the barter exchange network. Barter credits may include a contractual expiration date, after which they have no exchange value.

 How Do I Account for Barter Credits?

You should report the fair value of barter credits at the fair value of the nonmonetary asset for which they were exchanged.

However, if it is possible to convert the barter credits into cash in the near term, then you can recognize the fair value of the barter credits received, rather than the fair value of the asset exchanged.

If the entity receiving barter credits is not likely to use all of its remaining credits, you should recognize an impairment loss. This is also the case if the fair value of any remaining barter credits declines below their carrying amount.

 How Do I Account for an Asset Purchased with an Entity's Stock?

If an asset is purchased with an entity's stock, you should assign a value to the assets acquired based on either the fair market value of the stock or the assets, whichever is more easily determinable.

EXAMPLE 31.6

The St. Louis Motor Car Company issues 500 shares of its stock to acquire a sheet metal bender. This is a publicly held company, and on the day of the acquisition its shares were trading for $13.25 each. Since this is an easily determinable value, the cost assigned to the equipment is $6,625 (500 shares times $13.25/share). A year later, the company has taken itself private, and chooses to issue another 750 shares of its stock to acquire a router. In this case, the value of the shares is no longer so easily determined, so the company asks an appraiser to determine the router's fair value, which she sets at $12,000. In the first transaction, the journal entry was a debit of $6,625 to the fixed asset equipment account and a credit of $6,625 to the common stock account, while the second transaction was to the same accounts, but for $12,000 instead.

What Information Do I Disclose about Nonmonetary Transactions?

You should disclose the following information about non-monetary transactions in the notes accompanying an entity's financial statements:

○ The nature of the transaction
○ The basis of accounting for those assets transferred
○ Any gains or losses recognized on transfers
○ The amount of revenue and costs, or gains and losses, associated with inventory exchanges recognized at fair value

CHAPTER 32

NOT-FOR-PROFIT ENTITIES

 What Is a Not-for-Profit Entity?

Not-for-profit organizations have several characteristics that distinguish them from business enterprises. A main one is that these organizations exist to provide goods and services without the objective of generating a profit. Rather than obtaining resources by conducting exchange transactions at a profit or from capital infusions from owners, a not-for-profit organization obtains most resources from others that share its desire to serve a chosen mission— an educational, scientific, charitable, or religious goal. Although not-for-profit organizations can be "owned" or controlled by another, the ownership interest is unlike that of business enterprises because the "owner" cannot remove resources from the entity for personal use or gain; the resources must be used for a mission-related purpose. Examples of not-for-profit organizations are: churches and religious organizations, colleges and universities, health care organizations, libraries, museums, performing arts organizations, civic or fraternal organizations, federated fund-raising organizations, professional and trade associations, social clubs, research organizations, cemeteries, arboretums, and zoos.

Entities that are not considered not-for-profit organizations are those that exist to provide dividends, lower costs, or other economic benefits directly and proportionately to their members, participants, or owners, such as mutual insurance companies, credit unions, farm or utility cooperatives, and employee benefit plans.

 What Is a Donor-Imposed Restriction?

A donor-imposed restriction is a donor stipulation that specifies a use for contributed resources that is narrower than the limitations that result from the nature and

purpose of the organization. A restriction may be temporary or permanent. A temporary restriction is a restriction
that will expire (be satisfied) either by an action of the organization (such as spending the resources for the purpose described by the donor) or by the passage of time. A
permanent restriction never expires. Instead, it requires
that the contributed resources be maintained permanently, although it allows the organization to spend the
income or to use the other economic benefits generated by
those resources.

 ## What Is a Donor-Imposed Condition?

A donor-imposed condition is a donor stipulation that
specifies a future and uncertain event whose occurrence
(or failure to occur) gives the donor the right of return of
resources it has transferred, or which releases the donor
from the obligation to transfer assets in the future. For
example, "I will contribute one dollar for each dollar
raised during the month of July in excess of $10,000" in-
cludes a donor-imposed condition. If only $9,000 is raised,
the donor has no obligation to transfer assets.

 ## What Is a Promise to Give?

A promise to give is a written or oral agreement to contribute resources to another entity at a future date. A
promise to give can be either conditional or unconditional. The obligation of the donor who makes a conditional promise to give is dependent on the occurrence
(or failure to occur) of a donor-imposed condition. An unconditional promise to give depends only on the passage
of time or demand by the donee for payment of the promised assets.

 ## How Do I Determine the Reporting Entity for Related Not-for-Profits?

If a not-for-profit has control of a related, but separate,
not-for-profit entity in which the reporting entity has an
economic interest, then consolidation is permitted but not
required. However, consolidation is encouraged if the situation meets *both* the following criteria:

1. The reporting entity controls a separate not-for-
   profit entity that it has an economic interest in, and

that control is not through either of the following means:

a. A controlling financial interest in the other not-for-profit through direct or indirect ownership of a majority voting interest
b. A majority voting interest in the board of the other not-for-profit

2. Consolidation would be meaningful

Different combinations of control and economic interest determine the appropriate accounting for relationships with other not-for-profit organizations, as shown in the following table. *Control* is the direct or indirect ability to determine the direction of management and policies through ownership, contract, or otherwise. *Economic interest* is an interest in another entity that exists if (1) the other entity holds or utilizes significant resources that must be used for the purposes of the reporting organization, either directly or indirectly by producing income or providing services or (2) the reporting organization is responsible for the liabilities of the other entity.

Control?	Economic interest?	Standards
Yes, via ownership of a majority voting interest	Yes	Consolidate
Yes, via ownership of a majority voting interest	No	Consolidate
Yes, via majority voting interest in the board of the other entity, as a majority owner	Yes	Consolidate
Yes, via majority voting interest in the board of the other entity, as a majority owner	No	Consolidation prohibited, and disclosure required
Yes, via a contract or an affiliation agreement	Yes	Consolidation permitted, but not required
Yes, via a contract or an affiliation agreement	No	Consolidation prohibited, and disclosure required
No	Yes	Consolidation prohibited, and disclosure required
No	No	Consolidation prohibited. No disclosure required

You should not consolidate financial results if control does not rest with the majority owner.

What Is Included in the Financial Statements of a Not-for-Profit?

Financial statements are intended to help donors, creditors, and others who provide resources to a not-for-profit organization assess the services provided by the not-for-profit organization and its ability to continue to provide those services. The statements should also help them assess whether management has properly discharged its stewardship responsibilities and whether it has performed satisfactorily in its other management duties.

A not-for-profit should present a statement of financial position, a statement of activities, a statement of cash flows, and notes to the financial statements. In addition, voluntary health and welfare organizations are required to present a statement of functional expenses as an additional basic financial statement. In most ways, the content and format of those financial statements are similar to the financial statements prepared by business enterprises.

However, three major differences between not-for-profit organizations and business enterprises cause differences in the content and format of financial statements of not-for-profit organizations. First, there is no profit motive in the nonprofit sector, and thus no single indicator of performance comparable to a business enterprise's net income or bottom line. In fact, the best indicators of the performance of a not-for-profit organization are generally not measurable in dollar amounts but rather in the reader's qualitative judgment about the effectiveness of the organization in achieving its mission. Information to help assess performance is provided in financial statements by classifying expenses based on the mission-related programs and supporting activities they sustain, rather than by their natural classifications.

Second, because the bottom line of a not-for-profit organization's statement of activities is not a performance measure, but simply a change in net assets for the reporting period, there is no need for not-for-profit organizations to distinguish between components of comprehensive income as business enterprises do. All revenues, expenses, gains, and losses are reported in a single statement rather than being divided between an income statement and a statement of other comprehensive income.

Third, not-for-profit organizations receive contributions, a type of transaction that is without counterpart in business enterprises. Those contributions often are subject to donor-imposed restrictions, which can affect the types and levels of service that a not-for-profit organization can offer. Because donor-imposed restrictions are prevalent, recurring, and, in some cases, permanent, financial reporting by not-for-profit organizations needs to reflect the nature and extent of donor-imposed restrictions and changes in them that occur during the reporting period.

 How Do I Report Asset Restrictions?

You should report the nature and extent of donor-imposed restrictions in the statement of financial position by distinguishing between the portions of net assets that are permanently restricted, temporarily restricted, and unrestricted.

You should report changes in donor-imposed restrictions in the statement of activities. The organization's revenues, expenses, gains, and losses for the period are classified into the three classes of net assets so that the statement of activities reports amounts for the change in permanently restricted net assets, the change in temporarily restricted net assets, and the change in unrestricted net assets, as well as the change in net assets in total. You should separately report any transactions and events that do not change the net assets of the organization as a whole, but only their classification. Reclassifications are events that simultaneously increase one class of net assets and decrease another. For example, unrestricted net assets increase and temporarily restricted net assets decrease when the purchase of a long-lived asset fulfills a donor-imposed restriction to acquire long-lived assets with the gift.

 What Is a Performance Indicator?

If a reporting entity is a not-for-profit health care organization, it should include within its statement of activities an intermediate subtotal called a performance indicator. The performance indicator is analogous to income from continuing operations of a business enterprise, and thus excludes items that are required to be reported in or reclassified from other comprehensive income, extraordinary items, the effect of discontinued operations, the cumulative effect of accounting changes, transactions with owners, and equity transfers from entities that control the reporting entity, are controlled by the reporting entity, or are under common control with the reporting entity. The performance indicator also excludes restricted contributions, contributions of and reclassifications related to gifts of long-lived assets, unrealized gains and losses on investments not restricted by donors or law (except for investments classified as trading), and investment returns restricted by donors.

 ## How Do I Report Not-for-Profit Revenues?

Report revenues in the statement of activities as increases in unrestricted net assets, unless a donor-imposed restriction controls the not-for-profit's use of the resources. Thus, contribution revenues increase unrestricted net assets, temporarily restricted net assets, or permanently restricted net assets, depending on the existence and nature of donors' restrictions. You should classify revenues from most exchange transactions (such as sales of goods or services) as unrestricted.

Revenues from exchange transactions only increase restricted net asset classes if a preexisting donor-imposed restriction limits the use of the resources received.

EXAMPLE 32.1

A donor contributes a car to the local library and requires that the proceeds from the sale of the car be used to purchase children's books. The proceeds from the sale of the car (an exchange transaction) increase temporarily restricted net assets.

Investment income and gains (which are also exchange transactions) increase unrestricted net assets unless the donor required that the gift be invested and the investment return used for a restricted purpose.

EXAMPLE 32.2

A donor contributes securities worth $85,000 to a zoo, and requires that all dividends and gains be retained and reinvested until the accumulated value is $100,000, and states that the $100,000 must be maintained as a permanent endowment fund, the income of which is to be used for the purchase of animals. In the early years of the endowment, before the accumulated value reaches $100,000, investment income and gains increase permanently restricted net assets. Investment income and gains earned after the accumulated value of the fund reaches $100,000 increase temporarily restricted net assets with the restriction expiring upon use of those funds to purchase animals.

How Do Restrictions and Conditions Impact Revenue Recognition?

If there is a contribution to a not-for-profit, you should recognize it as revenue at the time of the gift and measure it at the fair value of the contributed assets. Donor-imposed *restrictions* do not change the timing of recognition of a contribution. Such restrictions, or the absence of them, affect only a contribution's classification as an increase in permanently restricted net assets, temporarily restricted net assets, or unrestricted net assets. Donor-imposed *conditions*, however, affect the timing of recognition. Because a contribution is an unconditional transfer, a transfer of assets subject to donor-imposed conditions is not a contribution yet, although it may become one at a future date. Conditional transfers are not recognized as contribution revenues until the conditions are substantially met. Thus, the distinction between donor-imposed restrictions and donor-imposed conditions is very important to the timing of recognition. If a donor's stipulations do not clearly state whether a gift depends on meeting a stated stipulation and the ambiguity cannot be resolved by communicating with the donor or by examining the circumstances surrounding the gift, you should consider the transfer to be conditional.

When Do I Recognize Promises to Give?

You should recognize unconditional promises to give cash or other assets in a not-for-profit's financial statements when the promise is made and received, provided that there is sufficient evidence in the form of verifiable documentation (written, audio, or video). If payments of the promises are due in future periods, the promise has an implied time restriction that expires on the date the payment is due. Thus, unless circumstances surrounding the receipt of the promise indicate that the donor intended the gift to support the current period's activities, unconditional promises increase temporarily restricted net assets. You should use a present value technique to measure unconditional promises to give, although you may report short-term promises (due in less than one year) at their net realizable value. Conditional promises are not recognized as revenue until the conditions are substantially met; however, you should disclose them in notes to the financial statements.

 ## When Do I Recognize Contributions Held by a Trustee?

In a manner similar to recognizing promises to give, you should recognize contributions held on a not-for-profit's behalf by an agent, trustee, or intermediary. For example, if the assets held by an agent were transferred subject to a condition that is not yet met, the beneficiary does not recognize its potential rights to the assets held by the agent. If a beneficiary has an unconditional right to receive cash flows from a charitable trust or other pool of assets, the beneficiary recognizes its rights when the beneficial interest is created and measures the rights using the present value of the estimated expected cash flows. However, if the beneficiary and the agent, trustee, or intermediary are financially interrelated organizations, the beneficiary reports its rights to the assets held using a method similar to the equity method of accounting for investments.

 ## How Do I Account for the Value of Volunteer Services?

You can recognize the value of volunteer services received by a not-for-profit in certain circumstances. You can recognize contributed services that create or improve a nonfinancial asset (such as building a shed or replacing a roof) as revenue either by valuing the hours of service received or by measuring the change in the fair value of the nonfinancial asset created or improved.

You can recognize other contributed services only if they meet all three of the following criteria:

1. They require specialized skills.
2. They are provided by persons possessing those skills.
3. They would typically need to be purchased if not provided by donation.

If volunteer services neither meet those three criteria nor create or improve nonfinancial assets, you cannot recognize them in the organization's financial statements. However, organizations are required to describe the programs or activities for which contributed services are used, the nature and extent of services received for the period (regardless of whether those services are recognized), and disclose the amount of volunteer services recognized as revenues.

An organization that maintains works of art, historical treasures, and similar assets in collections does not recognize gifts of items that are added to its collections unless it also capitalizes its collections. However, gifts that are not added to collections or items given to organizations that do not maintain collections are recognized as revenues and measured at the fair value of the assets received.

How Do I Classify Not-for-Profit Expenses?

You should recognize expenses in the statement of activities as decreases in unrestricted net assets. Financing an expense with donor-restricted resources does not make the expense restricted; instead, it releases the restriction on the restricted resources, causing a reclassification to be reported in the statement of activities.

You must report expenses by functional classifications either on the face of the statement of activities or in the accompanying notes. The functional classifications describe the major classes of program services and supporting activities of an organization. Program services are the mission-related activities of the organization that result in goods and services being distributed to clients, customers, or members. For example, a not-for-profit organization with the mission of enhancing the lives of the community's senior citizens might have senior center, home visits, transportation services, and home maintenance as its program expense classifications. Supporting activities are all activities of a not-for-profit organization other than program services. Fund-raising expenses as well as management and general are two common supporting activity classifications.

You are encouraged, but not required, to provide an analysis of expenses by natural classification. Information about expenses by natural classifications (salaries, benefits, rent, depreciation, and so forth) can help readers of the financial statements understand the mix of fixed and discretionary costs incurred by the organization. Only voluntary health and welfare organizations are required to report information about expenses by both functional and natural classification. Those organizations must provide that information in a matrix format in a statement of functional expenses.

 ## Does a Not-or-Profit Depreciate Its Assets?

You must depreciate the land, buildings, and equipment used by not-for-profit organizations, though there is an exception for certain works of art, historical treasures, and similar assets. If a not-for-profit organization can demonstrate both (1) that an asset individually has cultural, historical, or aesthetic value worth maintaining in perpetuity and (2) that the organization has the ability to protect and preserve that value essentially undiminished and is doing so, then you do not need to recognize depreciation. Depreciation expense is a natural expense classification that must be allocated to programs and supporting activities in reporting expenses by functional classification.

 ## How Do I Record Joint Costs?

Joint costs are the costs of conducting joint activities that are not directly identifiable with a particular component of an activity. Joint costs might include the costs of salaries, professional fees, paper, printing, postage, event advertising, telephones, broadcast airtime, and facility rentals.

There is a presumption that the costs of a joint activity are reportable as fund-raising expenses. To overcome that presumption, a not-for-profit must meet three criteria: purpose, audience, and content. If it meets all three of the criteria, you can charge the costs of the joint activity as follows:

○ Charge costs identifiable with a particular function to that function.
○ Allocate joint costs between fund-raising and the appropriate program or management and general function.

Determining whether all three criteria are met is complicated because the purpose and audience criteria have additional tests within them. The purpose test includes a call to action test, a compensation or fees test, a similar scale and same medium test, and another evidence test. The audience criterion includes a prior donor test, an ability and likelihood to contribute test, and a need to use or reasonable potential for use test. Failure of one of the additional tests often causes the activity to fail the criterion.

If any of the three criteria is not met, you must report all costs of the joint activity as fund-raising expense. "All costs" include the costs that would have been considered program or management and general if they had been incurred in a different activity. There is an exception to the rule that all costs are charged to fund-raising expense if one or more of the criteria is not met. The costs of goods or services provided in an exchange transaction (sometimes referred to as a quid pro quo contribution) that are part of the joint activity are charged to cost of goods sold rather than fund-raising expense. For example, the costs of direct donor benefits, such as the value of items sold at a fund-raising auction or meals served at a fund-raising dinner, are not charged to fund-raising expenses.

How Do I Account for Investments and Endowment Funds?

If a not-for-profit invests in equity securities with readily determinable values, and any debt securities, you should recognize them at their fair value. If there are gains or losses on the recognition of these investments, you should report them in the not-for-profit's statement of activities.

If a not-for-profit has other types of investments, you have the option of reporting them at either their cost or the lower of cost or market.

Many of the investments held by not-for-profit organizations are held as the investments of endowment funds. Endowment funds generally are established by gifts from donors who are providing permanent support for the organization (a permanently restricted endowment fund) or support for a specified period of time (a term endowment fund). In addition, a governing board may determine that certain resources be invested and that only the return generated be spent by the not-for-profit. The net assets of an endowment fund are classified in accordance with the restrictions placed on the resources by donors, if any.

Each source is unrestricted unless its use is temporarily or permanently restricted by the donor or by law. Thus, you would classify the net assets of an endowment fund created by the governing board from a large unrestricted bequest (or from unrestricted net assets) as unrestricted, because all amounts transferred to that fund are free of donor-imposed restrictions.

EXAMPLE 32.3

Mr. Higgins contributes $50,000 to the Industrial Art Museum and stipulates that the gift be invested in perpetuity and the investment income be used to purchase works of art. Mr. Higgins further stipulates that any gains on the investment be added to the original gift and invested in perpetuity. Mr. Higgins' original gift of $50,000 increases permanently restricted net assets because of the stipulation that the gift be invested in perpetuity. The income earned by the investment of the gift increases temporarily restricted net assets.

When works of art are purchased, the restriction on net assets resulting from the income is fulfilled and the net assets are reclassified to unrestricted net assets. The realized and unrealized gains from investment of the gift increase permanently restricted net assets because the donor required that those gains also be reinvested in perpetuity.

 ## What if a Donor Does Not Specify Restrictions on Investment Gains?

In the absence of explicit donor restrictions, the law in most states provides some direction about the restrictions on investment gains of donor-restricted endowment funds. The Uniform Management of Institutional Funds Act (UMIFA) extends certain donor restrictions to the net appreciation (accumulated net gains) of donor-restricted endowment funds. In states that have adopted UMIFA, net appreciation is expendable unless the donor states otherwise. UMIFA provides that the net appreciation can be spent for the uses and purposes for which the endowment fund was established. Thus, unless the donor specifies otherwise, gains increase unrestricted net assets if the endowment's income is not restricted by the donor, and gains increase temporarily restricted net assets if the endowment's income is temporarily restricted by the donor.

EXAMPLE 32.4

Assume in the preceding example of the $50,000 gift to the Industrial Art Museum that Mr. Higgins was silent about the use of gains earned by investing the original gift. In a state that has adopted UMIFA, the accumulated gains on the endowment fund would be restricted to the purchase of artwork because the law requires that the donor's restriction be extended to those gains. The restrictions on those temporarily restricted net assets expire when the museum purchases works of art, even if the money to purchase the work of art is not withdrawn from the fund. Thus, this single endowment fund can be composed of permanently restricted net assets (the original $50,000 gift), temporarily restricted net assets (the gains on which restrictions have not yet been met), and unrestricted net assets (the gains on which restrictions have been met).

How Do I Account for Perpetual Restricted Donations?

Not-for-profits that are subject to an enacted version of the Uniform Prudent Management of Institutional Funds Act of 2006 are required to classify a portion of a donor-restricted endowment fund that are of a perpetual duration as being permanently restricted net assets. The amount that is to be classified as permanently restricted should be the amount of the fund (1) that is required to be permanently retained due to an explicit stipulation by the donor, or (2) that in the absence of such donor stipulations, the organization's governing board determines must be permanently restricted to comply with applicable laws.

Losses incurred on the investments of the funds should not reduce the portion of the donor-restricted endowment fund that is to be classified as permanently restricted net assets, unless this is a requirement of the donor. Furthermore, the amount of permanently restricted net assets is not to be reduced by an organization's appropriations from the fund.

A not-for-profit organization should classify the portion of the funds that are not classified as permanently restricted net assets as temporarily restricted net assets until they are appropriated for expenditure by the organization, unless the gift instrument states otherwise.

Losses on the investments of an endowment fund reduce temporarily restricted net assets to the extent that temporary restrictions on net appreciation have not yet been met before the loss occurs. The remainder of the loss, if any, reduces unrestricted net assets. If the losses reduce the value of the fund below the level required by the donor or by law, future gains that restore the value to the required level are classified as unrestricted net assets.

EXAMPLE 32.5

Expanding on the earlier example, assume that several years after the fund was established, the assets of the fund have increased in value to $65,000. Assume also that the classification of the net assets in the fund is $50,000 permanently restricted (the original gift), $10,000 temporarily restricted (accumulated gains on which the restrictions have not been met), and $5,000 unrestricted (gains on which the restriction was met by purchasing a work of art with unrestricted funds in years after the inception of the fund). A market correction causes the value of the investments to fall to $58,000. The $7,000 loss decreases temporarily restricted net assets from $10,000 to $3,000. Assume that a further market correction reduces the value of the investments another $9,000 from $58,000 to $49,000. The $9,000 loss reduces temporarily restricted net assets by $3,000 (the amount remaining after the $7,000 loss decreased the original $10,000) and reduces unrestricted net assets by $6,000. After recording the loss, the classification of the $49,000 value of the endowment fund would be $50,000 permanently restricted (the original gift) and ($1,000) deficit in unrestricted net assets.

Continuing the example, assume that the next year the value of the investments increases from $49,000 to $53,000. The $4,000 gain increases unrestricted net assets by $1,000 (the restoration of the deficit) and increases temporarily restricted net assets by $3,000. After the gain, the net assets of the endowment fund are $50,000 permanently restricted (the original gift) and $3,000 temporarily restricted for the purchase of works of art.

How Do I Account for a Collection?

If a not-for-profit maintains collections of works of art, historical treasures, or similar assets, it can choose whether it will capitalize and report those collections in its statement of financial position. To qualify for the exception, an organization must:

○ Hold the items for public exhibition, education, or research in service to the public rather than for financial gain
○ Protect the items, keep them unencumbered, care for them, and preserve them
○ Use the proceeds from the sale of any items to acquire other items for the collection

If a not-for-profit meets those criteria, it can choose to either capitalize or not capitalize its collections. It is not permissible to selectively choose to capitalize only certain collections.

If a not-for-profit does not capitalize its collections, you must report transactions involving collection items separately in its statement of activities.

If a not-for-profit does not capitalize its collections, you should include descriptions of the collections, as well as stewardship policies and items removed from the collections, in the notes to its financial statements.

If a not-for-profit does not designate an item as being part of a collection, then you must capitalize it. This may occur when a contributed item is a duplicate of an item already in a collection. In this case, you should recognize the contribution and report the asset in the not-for-profit's statement of financial position, as a work of art held for sale.

What Is a Split-Interest Agreement?

A split-interest agreement is an arrangement in which a donor transfers assets to a not-for-profit organization or a charitable trust, and requires the benefits of ownership of those assets be split among multiple beneficiaries.

You should report a not-for-profit organization's interest in irrevocable split-interest agreements. If another party, such as a bank, holds the assets, you should recognize the not-for-profit's interest as a contribution and measure its interest at fair value, usually based on the present value of the cash flows to be received. If the not-for-profit holds the assets and is also a beneficiary of the agreement, you should report the fair value of the assets received from the donor as its assets and report the actuarially computed present value of the payments to be made to other beneficiaries as its liability. The difference between the two amounts is the contribution received by the not-for-profit organization. Each year thereafter, re-compute the liability to the beneficiaries based on revaluations of the amounts to be paid, the expected lives of the beneficiaries, and other actuarial assumptions.

You normally classify the net assets resulting from a split-interest agreement as temporarily restricted because they are subject to time restrictions and purpose restrictions. The net assets are time-restricted either because the distributions are not yet due or because the contribution amount cannot be used by the not-for-profit organization until the death of the beneficiary or some other specified date. However, the net assets are classified as permanently restricted if the donor has permanently restricted the organization's use of the assets. Similarly, if the organization can immediately spend the contribution portion without restriction, then classify the net assets as unrestricted.

How Does a Trustee Handle a Contribution?

A donor may make a contribution by using an agent, trustee, or other intermediary, all of which are known as recipient organizations. The donor transfers assets to the recipient organization, which accepts the assets from the donor and agrees to use the assets on behalf of or transfer the assets, their investment return, or both to another entity — the beneficiary — named by the donor.

A recipient organization reports a liability if it accepts assets from a donor and agrees to use those assets on behalf of or transfer those assets to another organization or individual specified by the donor. When it subsequently spends the assets on behalf of the beneficiary or transfers the assets, the recipient organization reduces the liability it recorded earlier.

If the recipient organization and the beneficiary are financially interrelated organizations, the recipient organization reports contribution revenue and the beneficiary recognizes its interest in the net assets of the recipient organization, using a method similar to the equity method of accounting for investments in common stock. Organizations are financially inter-related if the relationship between them has *both* of the following characteristics:

1. One organization has the ability to influence the operating and financial decisions of the other, as evidenced by any of the following:

   a. The organizations are affiliates
   b. One organization has considerable representation on the governing board of the other entity
   c. The charter or bylaws of one organization limits its activities to those beneficial to the other entity
   d. The organizations have an agreement that allows one entity to participate in the policymaking processes of the other entity

2. One organization has an ongoing economic interest in the net assets of the other. This can be a residual right to the other organization's net assets.

A common example of financially interrelated organizations is a foundation that exists to raise, hold, and invest assets for a specific beneficiary that it supports.

 ## What Is Variance Power?

If the donor explicitly grants the recipient organization variance power, the recipient organization, rather than the beneficiary, recognizes contribution revenue. *Variance power* is the unilateral power to direct the transferred assets to an entity other than the specified beneficiary. Unilateral power means that the recipient organization does not have to contact the donor, the beneficiary, or any other interested party in order to substitute a different beneficiary. Variance power must be granted by the instrument transferring the assets.

 ## What Information Should I Disclose about a Not-for-Profit Organization?

You should disclose information that will enable users of a not-for-profit's financial statements to understand the net asset classification, net asset composition, changes in net asset composition, spending policies, and related investment policies of its endowment funds. Therefore, at a minimum, make these eight disclosures:

1. The governing board's interpretation of the law that supports the organization's net asset classification of donor-restricted endowment funds.
2. The organization's endowment spending policies.
3. The organization's endowment investment policies.
4. The make-up of the organization's endowment by net asset class. Present these amounts in total, as well as by endowment fund, and separately show donor-restricted endowment funds from board-designated endowment funds.
5. Reconcile the beginning and ending balance of the organization's endowment, in total and by net asset class.
6. Information about the net assets of its endowment funds, such as:

   a. The nature and types of any permanent restrictions or temporary restrictions.
   b. The aggregate amount of the deficiencies for all donor-restricted endowment funds where the fair value of the assets at the reporting date is less than the level required in the donor stipulations or by law.

7. If the not-for-profit allocates joint costs, then disclose the types of activities in which these costs have been incurred, state that the costs have been allocated, note the total amount of joint costs allocated, and the portion of joint costs allocated to each functional expense category.
8. If you do not present consolidated statements when consolidation is permitted, but not required, then disclose the identity of the other organization, the nature of the relationship, and summarized financial data.

INDEX

Accounting change
  Definition, 291
  Interim period treatment
    of, 53–54
Accounting policies,
  see Policies
Accounting estimate,
  294–295
Accounting principle
  Changes in, 291–294
  Retrospective, 292
Accounts receivable,
  see Receivables
Accrual basis of
  accounting, 23
Acquisition
  Asset, 304
  Costs, 310
  Disclosures, 312–313
  Inclusion date for
    income statement,
    24–25
  Measurement period,
    310–311
  Reverse, 305–310
  Step, 304–305
Additional paid-in capital,
  183
Advertising costs
  Accounting for, 261–262
  Amortization of,
    114–116
  Capitalization of,
    113–114
  Disclosure of, 116–117,
    262
Alternative minimum tax,
  277–278
Anti-dilution, 38
Assembled workforce
  asset, 304

Asset acquisition,
  accounting for, 304
Asset group, 119–120, 129
Asset retirement
  Conditional obligation,
    155
  Definition, 151
  Disclosure, 156
  Obligation, 151–155, 156
Available-for-sale
  securities
  Accounting for, 83–84, 87
  Definition, 325
  Disclosure of, 88

Balance sheet
  Line items included in,
    6–7
  Offsetting, 9
Bargain purchase, 301
Barter credits, 390
Basic earnings per share,
  see Earnings per share
Benefits
  Accounting for, 217–222,
    224–232
  Pension plan,
    curtailment of,
    231–232
Boot, 386–388
Business combination
  Accounting for, 300–303,
    312
  Definition, 299
  Disclosures, 312–313

Cash flow hedge, 321–323,
  328
Cash flows statement,
  see Statement of cash
  flows

Change order accounting, 209–210

Claim accounting, 210

Claims-made insurance, 258–260

Common stock, definition of, 37

Compensated absence, 218–219

Completed contract method, 208–209

Consolidated financial statements
Changes upon loss of control, 25
Definition, 23
Disclosures, 25
Procedure, 24

Construction revenue recognition, 205–211

Contingencies
Accounting for, 163–165
Definition, 163
Disclosure, 166
Expropriation, 165
Gain, 165
Litigation, 165–166

Contingent consideration, 302–303

Contingent issuance, definition of, 37

Contributions, 260

Convertible securities
Accounting for, 173–174
Definition, 173

Cost approach, 332

Cost method of accounting
Definition, 97–98
Disclosure of, 98

Cost recovery method, 200

Cost to cost method, 207–208

Current assets, 8

Current liabilities, 8–9

Current rate method, 344–347

Customers, disclosure of, 35

Debt
Acceleration clauses, 170
Contingently adjustable, 175
Conversions, 175
Covenants, 169–170
Disclosures, 172
Due on demand, 170
Inducement offers, 175–177
Issuance costs, 174–175
Refinanced, 170–171

Debt security, definition of, 79

Defensive intangible asset, 138

Deferred compensation, 221

Defined benefit pension plan
Accounting for, 222–231
Disclosure of, 232–233

Defined contribution plan, 233–234

Depreciation
Duration of, 124–125
Methods, 125–126

Derivative
Accounting for, 325–326
Definition, 315–316
Disclosure of, 326–327
Embedded, 316

Diluted earnings per share, see Earnings per Share

Dilution, 38

Diminishing balance method, 126

Direct method, 15–16

Discontinued operations
Earnings per share representation of, 45
Disclosures about, 19–20
Reporting of, 19–20

Dividends, accounting for, 66, 87

Donations, accounting for, 389

Donor-imposed
    Condition, 394
    Restriction, 393–394

Early debt extinguishment,
    178–179
Earnings per share
    Basic, 38–40
    Diluted, 40–45
    Disclosure of, 46–47
    Presentation of, 46
    Reporting requirements,
        37–38
    Retrospective
        adjustments, 45
Effective interest method,
    167–169, 320–321
Employee, definition of,
    235
Employee stock purchase
    plan, 251–252
Endowment funds,
    accounting for,
    403–404
Environmental
    remediation obligation
    Accounting for, 156–157,
        158–161
    Benchmarks, 157–158
    Disclosure of, 161–162
Equity
    Definition, 183
    Disclosure of, 190–191
Equity method of
    accounting
    Accounting for,
        92–96
    Definition, 91–92
    Disclosure of, 96–97
    Evaluation of, 92
Equity security
    Definition, 79
    Marketable, 87
    Measurement of,
        82
Error correction, 295–298
Exchange rate, definition
    of, 341

Expenses
    Interim period treatment
        of, 54
    Reimbursement of, 203
Expropriation
    contingencies, 165
Extraordinary items
    Accounting for, 12–13
    Earnings per share
        representation of, 45
    Interim period treatment
        of, 55

Factoring arrangements,
    72–73
Fair value
    Definition, 329
    Disclosures, 334–335,
        337–339
    Measurements, 330–334
    Option, 335–337,
        338–339
Fair value hedge, 319–320,
    328
FIFO inventory,
    measurement of,
    100–105
Financial statements
    Aggregation of
        information, 22
    Available to be issued,
        63
    Consistency of
        presentation, 22
    Consolidated, 23
    Contents of, 5–6
    Frequency of issuance,
        22
Fiscal year-end differences
    between parent and
    subsidiary, 25
Fixed assets, see Property,
    Plant, and Equipment
Foreign currency
    Current rate method,
        344–347
    Definition, 341
    Disclosures, 350–351

Foreign currency
  (*Continued*)
  Remeasurement method,
    347–349
  Transaction accounting,
    342–343
Functional currency,
  341–342

Geographical areas,
  disclosure of, 34–35
Goodwill
  Assignment to reporting
    units, 133–134
  Definition of, 133,
    299–300
  Disclosures, 137
  Impairment testing,
    134–136
Grant date, 235–236

Hazardous substance, 156
Hedging
  Accounting, 318
  Cash flow, 321–323, 328
  Definition, 317–318
  Effectiveness, 318–319
  Fair value, 319–320,
    328
  Instrument, 317
  Net investment, 323–324
Held for sale asset,
  accounting for, 130
Held-to-maturity
  investment
  Accounting for, 84
  Designation as, 80–81,
    325
  Disclosure of, 88
  Reclassification of, 81

Immediate family,
  definition of, 59
Impairment testing, 135,
  142
Imputed interest rate,
  358–360
Income approach, 332

Income statement, line
  items included in,
  9–11
Income tax, 275–276,
  282–283, 286–288
Indirect method, 15–16
Initiation fees, 212–213
Installment method,
  197–200
Insurance, claims-made,
  258–260
Intangible assets
  Class, 138
  Defensive intangible
    asset, 138
  Definition, 137–138
  Disclosure, 143–145
  Examples of, 303–304
  Impairment testing,
    141–142
  Internally developed,
    138
  Measurement of,
    138–140
  Research and
    development, 142–143
  Residual value, 140–141
Interest expense
  Capitalization of,
    121–123, 353–358
  Disclosure, 361
Interest income, accounting
  for, 74, 87
Interest rate, imputed,
  358–360
Internal-use software,
  145–147
Interim financial reporting
  Accounting errors
    impacting, 296
  Accounting principle
    changes impacting,
    292–294
  Definition, 49
  Disclosures, 49–50,
    285–
  Reporting requirements,
    49–51

Retrospective
adjustments to, 53
Tax rate, 284–285
Use of estimates for, 57
Inventory
Costs included in, 99–100
Definition of, 99
Disclosures, 109
Measurement methods,
100–105
Valuation above cost,
108
Write down, 105–108
Inventory losses, interim
period treatment of,
55–56
Investments
Accounting for, 87
Classification of, 79,
81–82
Disclosure of, 88–90
Cost method, 97–98
Equity method, 91–97
Impairment of, 84–86, 89

Joint costs, 402–403

Lease
Capital, 367–369,
382–383
Classifications, 364–365
Definition, 363–364
Direct financing, 372
Disclosures, 379
Extension, 377–378
Operating, 365–366,
380–382
Sales-type, 369–371
Sub-, 378
Termination, 378
LIFO Inventory
Interim period treatment
of, 55
Measurement, 100–105
Line of credit charges,
179
Litigation contingencies,
165–166

Loan
Impairment of, 75–76
Loss allowance, 76
Disclosures, 76–77

Management, definition of,
59–60
Market approach, 332
Materiality
Accounting error
assessment of, 296
Interim period
assessment of, 51
Multiple element
arrangements, 211–212

Net investment hedge,
323–324
Net realizable value, 105
Non-monetary
transactions, 385–389,
391
Not-for-profit entity
Art collection, 407
Asset depreciation,
402
Asset restrictions, 397
Definition, 393
Disclosures, 409–410
Endowment funds,
403–404
Expenses classification,
401–402
Financial statements,
396–397
Joint costs, 402–403
Performance indicators,
397–398
Perpetual restricted
donations, 405–406
Promises to give,
399–400
Revenues, 398–399
Split-interest agreement,
407–408
Variance power, 409
Volunteer services
valuation, 400–401

Operating segment
  Aggregation of, 27
  Definition, 27
  Disclosures, 31–33,
    33–35
  Quantitative thresholds,
    28–30
  Reporting requirements,
    27
Option, definition of, 37
Ordinary income, 284
Other comprehensive
  income, definition of,
  3–5

Percentage of completion
  method, 206–207
Policies
  Application of in interim
    periods, 51–53
  Disclosure of, 21
Perpetual restricted
  donations, 405–406
Preferred stock, definition
  of, 37
Preliminary project stage,
  145
Prepaid expense, 111
Preproduction cost,
  111–113
Principal owner, definition
  of, 60
Prior service costs, 226–228
Product financing
  arrangement, 177–178
Profit or loss, definition of,
  3
Promise to give, 394,
  399–400
Property, plant, and
  equipment
  Abandonment
    accounting, 130
  Borrowing costs to
    include in, 121–123
  Costs to include in,
    120–121, 123
  Definition, 119

  Depreciation, *see*
    Depreciation
  Derecognition, 130
  Disclosures, 131
  Impairment losses,
    127–129
  Property taxes, 260–261
  Purchase commitments,
    losses on, 107–108
Pushdown accounting, 312

Rabbi trust, 220–221
Receivables
  Classified as current
    assets, 69–70
  Delinquency fees,
    accounting for, 72
  Disclosure of, 76–77
  Factoring, 72–73
  Uncollectible, accounting
    for, 70–71, 73
  Valuation of, 74–75
Related party
  Definition, 59
  Disclosures, 59–61
  Transaction, 60
Remeasurement method,
  347–349
Reporting unit, definition
  of, 133
Research and development
  Accounting for, 266–267
  Acquired, 142–143
  Arrangements, 267–268
  Definition, 265–266
  Disclosure of, 267,268
Restricted stock,
  measurement of, 82
Retail method, 105
Reload feature, 247
Retained earnings
  Appropriation of, 184
  Definition, 184
Revenue
  Advertising barter,
    213–214
  Construction project,
    205–211

Cost recovery method, 200
Definition, 195
Disclosure of, 214–215
Gross or net, 200–203
Initiation fees, 212–213
Installment method, 197–200
Interim period treatment of, 54
Multiple element arrangements, 210–211
Recognition, 195–197
Right of return, 212
Service, 196–197
Third party, 214
Warranty, 213
Right of return, 212
Risks, disclosure of, 21–22

Sabbatical leave, 219
Sale-leaseback transaction, 372–377, 384
Share-based payment
Accounting for, 237–252
Definition, 189–190
Disclosure, 252–255
Shipping and handling costs
Recordation of, 204
Sick pay benefits, 219–220
Software, internal-use, 145–147
Specific identification method, 105
Split-interest agreement, 407–408
Standard cost
Method, 105
Variance treatment in interim periods, 56–57
Start-up costs, 257
Statement of cash flows
Direct method, 15–16
Indirect method, 15–16
Line items included in, 16–19

Main components of, 13–15
Statement of changes in equity, line items included in, 13
Statement of financial position, see Balance sheet
Step acquisition, 304–305
Stock
Buyback accounting, 188
Definition, 183–184
Dividend, 185–186
Split, 184–185
Subscription, 188–189
Treasury, see Treasury stock
Straight-line method, 126
Subsequent events
Definition, 63
Disclosure of, 66
Recognition of, 63–66

Tax
Alternative minimum, 277–278
Basis, 269–270
Carryback and carryforward, 270
Deferred, 270
Disclosures, 282, 286–288
Income, 275–276
Liability, 270
Penalties, 281
Planning, 278
Position, 279–280
Property, 260–261
Rates, 277
Valuation allowance, 276–277
Taxable profit, 269
Temporary difference, 270–275
Termination benefits, 221–222
Trading securities
Accounting for, 82–83
Sale of, 87

Treasury stock
   Constructive retirement
      method, 187–188
   Cost method, 186–187
   Definition, 186
Troubled debt
   restructuring
   Accounting for, 77–78,
      180–181
   Definition, 180
   Disclosure of, 78,
      181–182

Uncertainties, disclosure
   of, 21–22
Units of production
   method, 126

Valuation allowance,
   276–277
Variance power, 409
Vested benefits,
   217
Vesting, 236
Volunteer services
   valuation, 400–401

Warrants
   Definition, 37
   Detachable, 172–173
Warranty revenue
   recognition,
   213
Website development
   costs, 148–149